Law and Liberation

Law and Liberation

ROBERT E. RODES, JR.

UNIVERSITY OF NOTRE DAME PRESS
NOTRE DAME, INDIANA 46556

Library of Congress Cataloging in Publication Data

Rodes, Robert E.
  Law and liberation.

  Includes index.
  1. Sociological jurisprudence. 2. Liberation
theology. I. Title.
K370.R63 1986   340'.115   85-41011
ISBN 0-268-01279-2

To Oscar Romero

from every shires ende . . .

Contents

Preface   ix

1. Toward a Jurisprudence of Liberation   1

2. Poverty   22

3. Trivialization   56

4. Powerlessness   90

5. Rootlessness   128

6. Sex   153

7. Violence   186

8. Conclusion   211

Notes   219

Index   249

Preface

I owe to the teaching of Gustavo Gutierrez the basic structure and approach that I have used in this book. I was fortunate enough to read his *A Theology of Liberation* when I was becoming aware of serious weaknesses in the social and historical components of my legal thinking. He spoke powerfully to my concerns, and I set out to incorporate his insights into my work. This is a preliminary result. It is devoted mainly to constructing legal agendas for liberating American society from some of its particular burdens. I have not attempted a systematic presentation of theory. It is good liberationist doctrine (good common law doctrine as well) that theory should grow out of a critical reflection on practice. I have allowed it to do so: I hope to try a more systematic approach another time.

If what I have done here seems somewhat afield from what generally passes for liberation theology, it is because I am building on Gutierrez's doctrines, not expounding them. The work remains one of jurisprudence, not one of theology.

Nor is it a political work. By and large, I have disregarded the obstacles to getting my proposals enacted into law. By and large also, I have limited myself to agendas within the general framework of the Anglo-American legal system. I have not addressed the possibility that more radical agendas are required.

The orthodoxy of some liberationist writers has been questioned, apparently because of their emphasis on class struggle. Granted, the advocacy of class struggle seems inconsistent with a Christian understanding of universal love. But mainstream liberationists as I understand them do not advocate class struggle any more than people with umbrellas advocate rain. Nor do they perceive class struggle in Marxist terms as something that one class must inevitably win and the other inevitably lose. It is the unjust institution that creates the class distinction between oppressor and oppressed, and when that institution is reformed or dismantled, everybody wins. A Christian should be no more content with being an oppressor than with being oppressed.

The class analysis that I have used in this book is basically *ad hoc*, but it owes a considerable debt to Milovan Djilas and William H. Whyte. Djilas's book *The New Class* shows how a managerial elite displaces the proletarian leadership envisaged by Marx and Engels. Whyte's *The Organization Man* shows how the same class comes to the fore in societies nearer home than Yugoslavia or the Soviet Union. The books, one published in 1956, the other in 1957, seem remarkably complementary today.

Because of my concern with unjust structures and with class, I have given only peripheral attention to current agendas for the liberation of women and minorities in our society. Certainly, both are overrepresented among the victims and underrepresented among the beneficiaries of the structures we have now in place, and it is important to redress the balance. But I believe we will do more justice to more people if we reform our structures across the board.

It will be apparent that many of the "Christian" principles to which I appeal here are Jewish principles as well and that many are the common property of the human race. I call them Christian because I am trying to develop a Christian approach to my subject, and because I feel that working respectfully with a tradition not one's own entails dues in the form of study and reflection that I have not paid. But I know there is much common ground.

> The joys and the hopes, the griefs and the anxieties of the men of this age . . . these too are the joys and hopes, the griefs and anxieties of the followers of Christ.

I am grateful to my friends and colleagues Thomas L. Shaffer, John T. Noonan, Jr., and Donald P. Kommers, who have read the manuscript and made valuable suggestions, to Karen Werme of our 1984 law school class who helped with the notes, and to Aniela Berreth and Wanda Cortier who did most of the typing. I have also to thank Stanley Hauerwas and John Yoder for reading the first chapter before I decided to make a book of it, the Christian Legal Society for listening to it at one of their meetings, and

Ann and Peter Walshe for beginning my education in these matters through the conversations of many years.

Finally, to my wife, beyond her stringent reading of my text, beyond the enrichment of my thought by decades of exposure to her wisdom, scholarship, and critical acuity, I am grateful for the support of a shared life in the faith, for multiple liberations.

Notre Dame, Indiana
Feast of St. Teresa of Avila, 1985

1

Toward a Jurisprudence of Liberation

The theology of liberation has grown up in a social context of unjust structures supported by law, and in an intellectual context influenced by a Marxist perception of law as an instrument of the dominant class for perpetuating its dominance. Also, it has been drawn on in support of revolutionary positions that seem far removed from the rule of law. As a result, people who try to use the law in pursuit of the higher ends of justice and human fulfillment have found in the theology of liberation scant contribution to their enterprise.

They ought to find more. Particularly in this country, liberty has long been considered high on the list of purposes served by law. The Harvard Law School at every Commencement proclaims its graduates fit for the shaping and applying of "those wise restraints that make men free." And as long as we include Patrick Henry, Thomas Jefferson, and Samuel Adams among our Founding Fathers, we cannot deny a possible connection between lawyers and revolutionaries.

Furthermore, reflection, especially Christian reflection, on the actual experience of making and applying law will show us that liberation is what we are most often concerned with. The higher reaches of human fulfillment are in large part imponderable and in even larger part inaccessible to the processes and techniques of law. Law is ineffective and often oppressive when it sets out directly to make people happy, whereas it has had some real successes in trying to liberate people from destructive forces in their lives.

1

Since liberation is so important in the work and rhetoric of law, it stands to reason that a systematic theological treatment of it will have important consequences for legal theory. I will try to develop and apply some of these consequences in this book. In this first chapter I will describe the main tenets and concerns of liberation theology as I understand them, then sketch a theoretical and conceptual structure that I hope will serve in applying these tenets and concerns to the legal problems dealt with in the remaining chapters.

I. LIBERATION THEOLOGY

The primary liberationist insight, as I see it, is eschatological. God calls all mankind to work with Him toward the consummation of history in His kingdom, a state of enhanced union of all people with Him and with each other. All history is working toward that end, and a person's work in the world takes value from contributing to it. Thus, there is no fundamental distinction between secular history and salvation history, or between temporal and spiritual "orders." The Enlightenment vision of a privatized faith in a secularized world is unacceptable; so is the modified version of the same doctrine that accepts a spiritual motive for secular action but not a spiritual content.

Human beings are able by God's gift to cooperate with Him in the carrying forward of His kingdom. This carrying forward has the Exodus as its paradigm. It involves following the promptings of God's Spirit toward an unknown destination. A growing openness to these promptings, a growing ability to respond to them, is what the liberationists mean by liberation.

The second major liberationist insight is that our cooperation in God's purposes is powerfully impeded by unjust economic and social structures. This is not to say that sinfulness plays no part or that we are unable, with God's help, to respond lovingly to God and neighbor in spite of oppressive economic or social conditions. But we cannot work in cooperation with God's purposes, cannot work for the coming of God's kingdom, if our work is appropriated and trivialized by the economic and social order. Nor can we love as largely as God means us to if our love cannot be given effective expression in our work. This understanding of the effect of unjust structures seems related to the idea expressed in Marx's early writings that the economic system alienates the worker from his work.

It follows that liberation — the freeing of the worker from this alienation through reforming or dismantling the economic and social structures that bring it about — is itself a major work of cooperation in the coming of God's kingdom. While the work of liberation will not be complete until the final coming of the kingdom, no liberating act or event is without its eschatological significance.

Concern for the reform or dismantling of unjust structures is a source of class conflict, since the classes of people who benefit from the structures in question are generally unwilling to have them reformed or dismantled. Liberationists insist that Christians must accept the reality of class conflict, and must identify themselves with the oppressed classes. Christians, as such, did not create the class struggle, and are not responsible for it, but if they ignore its existence or profess neutrality in it they are in effect siding with the oppressor class.

The problem of reconciling participation in the class stuggle with the Christian commitment to peace and brotherhood is one which liberationists take seriously. They have no pat solution to offer, but they point out that the oppressor, like the oppressed, needs to be liberated from oppressive social structures. To the extent that he clings to these structures, the only way to love him may be to confront him. Christ tells us to love our enemies: He does not say we are not to have any. In any event, Christians have no choice but to participate in the class struggle; therefore, there must be a Christian way of doing so.

This stress on class struggle naturally invites comparison with Marxist theory. There are important differences. The debt of liberation theology to Marxism is real, but it has been consistently overstated — generally by people who have no love for either. For the mainstream liberationists, those who do not fall within the recent strictures out of the Vatican, the class struggle is an empirical fact, not a philosophical principle as the hard-line Marxists make it. With the recognition that the oppressor too needs to be liberated, the classes are philosophically reconciled, even though they are empirically in conflict. Marxists are right to scorn the conservative reconciliation of classes that proceeds on the supposition that if the poor understood their true interests they would love the institutions that make them poor. Liberationists achieve a more realistic reconciliation by insisting that if the rich understood their true interests they would hate the institutions that make them rich.

A final liberationist insight concerns the church. As all mankind is working toward a single eschatological consummation, the church cannot be seen as a community of people moving in a different direction from other people. The church is meant to be for all mankind a sign and a celebration of God's salvific and liberating purpose. It is not meant to be an exclusive carrier of salvation or an exclusive location of liberating events. This view of the church follows both from the eschatological doctrine I have been describing and from recent theological statements concerning the status of non-Christians before God. The legal structures and manifestations of the church should reflect this view if they are to play a liberating part in the whole law.

II. LIBERATION AND THE ENDS OF LAW

In the ultimate scheme of things, the end of law is the same as that of humankind, so that if law serves liberation it will serve its own end by serving humanity. But there are in the literature a number of subordinate ends offered for law, and it will pay us to see how the service of liberation will fit in with these. The ones I take up here are all familiar enough; I have put them in no particular order:

A. PEACE

Peace, personal security, "law and order," is one of the oldest and most basic of the claims people make on their legal systems. Peace is itself a form of liberation, for without it every person would be at the mercy of those who are more powerful or more aggressive. But to the victims of injustice peace can also be burdensome: it deprives them of their most obvious means of redress. It is important, therefore, for people who support peace to support justice also—to work to see that those on whom peace is bestowed deserve peace. If peace is an end of law, the reform or dismantling of unjust structures must necessarily be another end.

B. MORALITY

The promotion of virtue is less accepted than it used to be as an end for law, but there is still a good deal to be said for it. In any event, it seems that liberation and the promotion of virtue go hand in hand. Christians generally place their vices high on the list of things from which they would like to be liberated—although they may be skeptical of the law's capacity to do the liberating. More to the point, a good deal of vice can be laid at the door of the economic and social structures under which people live. The reform or dismantling of these structures may do more for the promotion of virtue than any mere commandment or prohibition.

C. JUSTICE

That legal dispositions are intended to serve justice is a commonplace, and that justice will be served by reforming or dismantling unjust structures would seem to be a tautology. Still, the whole notion needs some elaboration. In the first place, justice is a moral virtue, the virtue that moves us to render to everyone his due. In what sense, then, can an economic or social structure be said to be unjust, i.e., to lack that virtue? To be sure, such a structure can fail to render to someone what is due him, but the structure as such is not a morally responsible agent and therefore its failure cannot without further analysis be called a lack of virtue. For instance, a natural disaster would not be characterized as "unjust" even if it bore on people as heavily as any unjust structure did.

The crucial distinction to my mind, is the human responsibility for the structure. People made it, and people can get rid of it if they set their minds to doing so. Therefore, if it deprives anyone of what is his due, the people who let it continue to operate are being unjust. They are failing in social justice. Their injustice can be attributed to the structure they maintain.

Because it is due to every person that he be permitted to respond to the promptings of God's Spirit in his life, structures that place obstacles to his responding are unjust. To pursue liberation through the reform or dismantling of such structures is, therefore, to pursue justice.

D. THE COMMON GOOD

Traditional scholastic learning calls for law to pursue the "common good," meaning that good which must be enjoyed by everyone in the community if it is to be enjoyed by anyone. For instance, keeping a boat afloat is part of the common good of the passengers, because it cannot float for some of them and sink for the others.

In this regard, reforming or dismantling unjust economic and social structures is a good deal like keeping the boat afloat. To be sure, a structure can be reformed or dismantled for some people and left intact for others in the sense that some people can be removed from its field of operation and others left inside. But within its field of operation it still affects everyone it touches. That is, it may be possible to abolish capitalism in Cuba and leave it going in Puerto Rico, but it is not possible to abolish it as far as the workers are concerned and leave it going for the capitalists. Or, in the early nineteenth century it was possible to abolish slavery in the British Empire and leave it intact in the United States, but it was not possible to abolish it for the slaves and leave it intact for the masters.

But even if a structure affects everyone in the society, its reform or dismantling cannot be said to be for the common good if it is good for some people and bad for others. For those who pursue the class struggle without any transcendent values against which class interests can be measured, the dismantling of oppressive structures cannot be for any common good. All they can say is that reforming or doing away with an oppressive structure is in the interest of the oppressed, although it is counter to the interest of the oppressor.

The liberationist, however, adhering to a Christian understanding of human solidarity, can go beyond class interests and say that the abolition of an oppressive structure is liberating to the oppressor as well as to the oppressed. It follows from this understanding that the liberation of one class through the reform or dismantling of unjust structures is the liberation of all classes in the society. Liberation, therefore, is an aspect of the common good.

E. SPECIFICATION OF NATURAL LAW

Scholastic doctrine sees "human" law as implementing the principles of "natural" law—the principles, that is, that govern how people should deal with one another in the light of their common humanity. These principles of natural law are for the most part so general that they can be implemented in many different ways. Accordingly, it is a function of the lawgivers in a particular time and place to say which way of implementing a given principle will be adopted in that time and place. For instance, from a rudimentary principle of common living that you should not conduct your affairs in such a way as to endanger other people comes a corollary principle that you should not drive your car dangerously. From that principle in turn, it is left to human lawgivers to derive a complex of speed limits, traffic lights, one-way streets and the like.

Liberation, like safe driving, can be seen as a requirement of human nature, and therefore as a principle of natural law. God has created us so that we may respond freely to Him, and cooperate with Him in the completion of the world. What we are created for is by definition what our nature requires. Hence, we are implementing natural law when we reform or dismantle unjust structures that stand in the way of our accomplishing what we are created for.

But how to go about reforming or dismantling unjust structures without establishing others equally unjust is a problem—the same kind of problem as how to provide for traffic safety without bringing transportation to a standstill. If we abolish slavery, we will have to find some way for the newly freed slaves to earn a living. If we redistribute land, we will have to make sure the new owners are able to raise enough food to support the population. Emancipation-plus-unemployment or land-ownership-plus-starvation might not be experienced as liberating.

Note that the problem thus stated is as much a problem for the oppressor as for the oppressed. The plantation owner who chooses to free his slaves or redistribute his land has no more idea how to keep the workers working and the land growing crops than the slaves or peasants would have if they were to take power on their own behalf. The reason the oppressor stands in need of liberation as much as does the oppressed is not merely that every sinner needs to be liberated from his sin. A person may wish to stop being an oppressor and not know how. With all the good will in the world, there is a certain intractability in any social or economic situation. To effect significant change takes more than power; it takes thought.

In serving as a vehicle for this kind of thought, law specifies, makes explicit, how the demand for liberation is to be implemented in the particular time and place. This is just what it does with the other demands of natural law.

This kind of specification is especially important in a context of class conflict. It makes it possible for the classes to address specific proposals to one another, and so perhaps achieve reconciliation or at least a *modus vivendi*. If reconciliation is impossible, the specification will at least let the parties to the struggle know what they are fighting about. Note that in classical just war doctrine one of the conditions for fighting a just war is to have a definite set of goals so that your adversary may understand clearly what needs to be done to make peace with you. This condition seems as important to a just revolution as to a just international war. It can be met by the couching of demands and proposals in legal terms.

III. LIBERATION AND HISTORY

Liberation theology shares its orientation toward the future with those schools of jurisprudence that see law as an instrument of social change. Like those schools, it has problems with the intractability and perverseness of history. The philosophy of history teaches that the process of change is dialectical and its results ambivalent. Historiography teaches that the process is also convoluted and unpredictable. It follows that we can never be sure that a projected social change will turn out to be, on balance, for the better; nor can we be sure that whatever means we choose will be efficacious to bring it about. Similarly, we cannot be sure that a chain of events that we set in motion for the sake of liberation will prove to be truly liberating in the end.

This does not mean that the quest for liberation or the quest for social change is illusory; nor does it mean that we have no way of telling good laws from bad ones. It only means that our interventions, legal or otherwise, must be made with circumspection and (a virtue that liberationists stress) hope. While we cannot be sure what the effect of our interventions will be in the long run, we are not primarily responsible for the long run. The effect of a new infusion of justice or freedom into history at some particular point may be incalculable, but Christians may hope that in God's providence their good purposes will not be wholly frustrated. In any event, justice is an imperative, not an expedient. The traditional legal maxim on the point is *fiat justitia, ruat coelum*: let justice be done though the skies fall. If, as I have suggested, the pursuit of liberation is something justice requires of us, we must pursue liberation though the skies fall. Certainly we must pursue it even though we cannot foresee that the pursuit will be unambiguously successful.

The circumspection imposed on us by the ambivalence and unpredictability of history is a matter of not conceiving our ends in utopian terms, and not conceiving our means in technological ones. Utopia, i.e., an unambiguously desirable overall state of affairs, may exist within the mind of God, but no human mind can encompass it. Our work in the world cannot be one of making over society in conformity to a model; indeed, we are called on to resist the imposition of any such model. This brings us back to the fundamental liberationist insight: our work is one of clearing the way for the operation of forces we cannot fully comprehend.

As for technology, it seems to have been Roscoe Pound who popularized the idea that lawyers are in the business of "social engineering," using legal "tools" and "machinery"to accomplish results. Obviously, these technological terms are metaphorical, but even as metaphor they are dangerous. They lead us to suppose that social structures operate by mechanical necessity, and that laws move people the way a backhoe moves earth. This is far from a realistic view of what happens when people make laws and try to enforce them. Legal dispositions are made up of words, and before they have any power someone must listen and respond to them. They do not control people and they certainly do not control history. They make claims on people, and, through people, on history.

To the extent that law purports to be final and certain in its effects, it cannot be either just or liberating, because liberty and justice are not to be accomplished with finality or certainty this side of the eschaton. But once free from utopian or technological hubris, law can give a clear and accurate voice to the demand for liberty and justice as that demand is experienced in a concrete situation.

By doing so, it can assure liberty and justice of a continuing presence within history.

IV. LAW AS LIBERATING EVENT

I have tried so far to show the place of liberation in the work of making and applying law. Let me now turn to the place of law in the work of liberation. We have seen that for the liberationist there are liberating events which have an eschatological significance even though they may be ambiguous in their results. They further the coming of God's kingdom even though they are not capable, in themselves, of bringing it about. What we must do at this point is examine how the characteristic operations of law may take their places among events of this kind.

A. LAW AS SYMBOL

We hear so often that actions speak louder than words that we are sometimes tempted to think that words do not speak at all. So we are apt to think that laws are useless except to the extent that they trigger the immediate application of incentives that effectively modify behavior along desirable lines. This thinking goes with the technological metaphors to which I have just objected. Actually, laws often play a very important part as expressions of community aspirations. If they are genuine aspirations, expressing them is not in vain even if we fall far short of achieving them.

This is particularly true of an aspiration to feedom. The radical freedom of human beings—i.e., their ability to respond to God— is in a certain sense indestructible. It can be curtailed, hidden, belied or otherwise lost from recognition, but it cannot be finally abolished. It follows that in a certain sense freedom is not lost but lost sight of, and it can be restored by being restored to view. To believe in your freedom, to claim it resolutely, is in this very important sense to possess it already. Hence the insistence on "consciousness-raising" in the political movements of oppressed groups. Hence also Gutierrez's argument that the work of evangelization must be "to conscienticize, to politicize, to make the oppressed person become aware that he is a person . . . ." This theme has been heavily drawn on by "black" theology, with its stress on the Gospel as teaching black people to accept and value their blackness. But the point is not a new one. The stratification of medieval society was tempered in many subtle ways by the universal acceptance of a religion in which all were of equal ultimate worth.

The decision of the United States Supreme Court in *Brown* v. *Board of Education* has become a commonplace example of how legal dispositions can liberate through consciousness-raising. The court, after determining that segregation of the races in public schools was illegal, set up so gentle a pattern for the enforcement of its decision that for rather more than a decade only a handful of school systems were actually desegregated. But the same period of negligible desegregation was one of tremendous growth in the militancy of black people — in their willingness to confront segregated structures and claim equality. Ultimate desegregation (to the extent that it has come about) probably owes more to this militancy than it does to the *Brown* case. But it is generally felt that the *Brown* case did more than any other single event to call the militancy into being.

The proposed Equal Rights Amendment to the United States Constitution suggests similar considerations. It is possible with some ingenuity to think of a concrete legal case that would be decided differently were the amendment in force from the way it would be decided now, but such cases are of peripheral importance to the position of women in our society. It is the effect, or the supposed effect, of the amendment on people's attitudes that gives it an important place on political agendas. And its effect on the attitude of women toward themselves seems to be as important for its proponents as any effect it might have on the attitude of men toward women.

The criminal law offers other examples of liberating symbols. The exercise of power over the criminal is a symbolic vindication of the victim for whom it tends to restore a sense of security and self-worth. The solemn denunciation of the crime is a symbolic support to those citizens who are resisting the temptation to commit it. These functions are no less important than the more utilitarian ones of rehabilitating past offenders and deterring future ones.

B. LAW AS CONFRONTATION WITH POWER

That law is a source of liberation from unrestrained government is a tradition that goes at least as far back as Bracton's statement that the king is under God and the law. The history of the Anglo-American legal system abounds in episodes in which the law has successfully confronted the power of the government in the name of freedom. We have not been as consistently successful in confronting economic power. But we have done it often enough to know that it can be done. Contaminated meat, substandard wages, and harassment by debt collectors are examples of things from which our laws have liberated a good many of our people and challenged powerful economic forces in the process.

More basic than these confrontations is the law's confrontation with physical power. Samuel Johnson, in his famous response to James Macpherson's threat to thrash him said, "Any violence offered me I shall do my best to repel; and what I cannot do for myself the law shall do for me. I hope I shall not be deterred from detecting what I think a cheat by menaces of a ruffian." We may suppose that the menaces would have deterred him more had the law not been available to do for him what he could not do for himself. Thus the law may be said to have supported his freedom as a literary critic by confronting the power of Mr. Macpherson. In the same way, when the law confronted the power of medieval kings and barons, it supported the peasant's freedom to plow his field, and when it confronts the power of purse snatchers and muggers, it supports the freedom of the modern city dweller to walk the streets.

C. LAW AS CONFRONTATION WITH HISTORY

We have seen that history, although it may be liberating in the long run, is convoluted and ambivalent in its immediate effects. A particular historical force or turn of events may therefore be quite the opposite of liberating, or it may be liberating in certain of its aspects and the opposite in others. It follows that the course of liberation may on occasion involve a confrontation with some or all of the forces of history as they are working at the moment.

It is to make law a vehicle for confrontations of this kind that we embody our most cherished freedoms in constitutional documents. These are the freedoms that we feel should be immune to historical change: anyone who finds historical forces weighing too heavily on him tends, rightly or wrongly, to invoke them. We should not allow the misuse of these freedoms to blind us to their real importance. Granted, they retarded the liberation of working people for a time by affording a shelter to the yellow-dog contract and a check to minimum wage regulation, and granted that they are less than liberating today to the religiously committed, to the would-be chaste, and, God knows, to the unborn. But without them, all the children in the country could be forced into public schools (except for black children who would often be in no schools at all), policemen could beat confessions out of suspicious looking characters, and legitimate union organizers might spend much of their time in jail.

Indeed, the freedoms in question, long before they obtained constitutional status, were raised in England in the seventeenth-century confrontations between medieval legalism and Renaissance kingship. Absolute monarchy, though it would be a reactionary institution today, was a new, authentic, and in some ways liberating historical development in the time of the Tudor and Stuart kings. To limit it with a string of medieval precedents, as the common lawyers did under James and Charles, was to confront history. A comparison of developments in England with those in France, where absolute monarchy prevailed without legal restraint, suggests that history turned out better for the confrontation. It is unfortunate that the Industrial Revolution did not undergo any similar confrontation in the late eighteenth or early nineteenth century: most of the medieval laws that might have restrained the excesses of industrial capitalism were repealed at the outset.

History cannot be normative because it is convoluted and ambivalent. It follows that not every authentic historical development is authentically liberating. Liberation is furthered in history through the evaluation of what is going on in the light of higher principles. In the light of these principles, some developments are to be supported, others confronted. In any encounter with history, there are choices to be made, and law is an important vehicle for making them.

D. LAW AS MEDIATION

It is not until a major historical change results in new laws that individuals can adequately gauge how they will be affected by the new situation. Until new laws are made, the change, although liberating in conception, and perhaps liberating in the long run, will not be experienced as liberating. People cannot feel free if they do not know how to stay out of trouble, or if they lack the information they need to make reasonable decisions about their own affairs. One does not have to be an apologist for the Ancien Régime in France to believe that the Reign of Terror was not liberating.

In addition, the liberation actually brought about by a particular historical change may be precarious until it is consummated by law. For instance, it seems likely that the downfall of the Allende administration in Chile was due in part to its own failure to embody its reforms in specific and effective legislative enactments instead of encouraging workers and peasants to take matters into their own hands.

The point is that the law, by specifying what liberation requires in a given situation, consummates a liberating historical change by mediating between the forces behind the change and the individuals who will have to live with it. The law itself is a liberating event in that, without it, the liberating force of other events would be frustrated or incomplete.

The same specifying role enables the law to mediate between classes. Here, it is liberating because it enables the oppressed to state their claims effectively and enables the oppressors to see what is required of them, whether for a clear conscience or for peace. Mediating legal dispositions take various forms. They can be demands upon legislators, such as the famous People's Charter presented to the British Parliament in 1839, and the various Civil Rights Acts presented to Congress and the state legislatures during the 1960s. Or they can be concessions on the part of those in power, such as the legislation enacted in England in the 1830s and '40s to defuse the Chartist agitation, or the land reform measures taken in Latin America to defuse modern revolutionary movements.

They can also serve as a bone of contention and a focus for dispute, as is the case with our welfare legislation. At the outset, this legislation was probably a concession by the middle class to the poor. But with the advent of welfare rights organizations and legal services agencies it has become also a vehicle for demands made by the poor upon the middle class. The poor see this legislation as quantitatively inadequate and qualitatively demeaning: they try to undermine it by vigorous and litigious enforcement. The middle class, on the other hand, consider it overly lenient: they often vent their discontent by harassment of would-be recipients. The two sides carry on the struggle in legislatures, newspapers, administrative agencies, and courts—which is better (and probably more liberating) than carrying it on in the streets.

Finally, legal dispositions can serve to institutionalize the confrontation between classes and so turn it into peaceful negotiation. This seems to be what is accomplished by our laws in favor of collective bargaining. To see what our labor relations might be without these laws, look at the situation in agriculture where for the most part they do not apply.

Through mediation, then, the law structures and consummates both liberating events and the quest for further liberation. In doing so, it becomes a liberating event in its own right.

E. LAW AS ADVOCACY BEFORE HISTORY

In criticizing the use of technological metaphors in law, I offered some verbal metaphors to take their place. Law makes "claims" on people, and "gives voice" to the demand for freedom and justice. It is through verbal metaphors of this kind that we can describe how appropriate legal dispositions can be liberating events.

Man proposes and God disposes. Making laws is, so to speak, a way of proposing. We do not know what the results of a law will be. All we know is that some of them will probably be desirable and others undesirable. It is quite possible that among the desirable results will be a solution to the problem we had in mind when we made the law, a liberation from the particular form of oppression we experienced most insistently at the time. But until the final coming of God's Kingdom, we must expect the solution to give rise to new problems.

It is important for us to recognize that today's problems are due in great part to the success, not the failure, of yesterday's solutions. If one were to list the problems facing our country when Franklin

D. Roosevelt became president—underpaid industrial workers lacking job security, credit squeeze wiping out debtors at the downswing of the business cycle, etc.—one could make a fairly good case for saying that they were largely solved by now. Important and generally successful measures (minimum wages, unemployment compensation, legal enforcement of collective bargaining) have been taken to support wages and job security and to keep money coming in despite economic downswings. In fact, we have protected workers so well that the cost of hiring them is becoming prohibitive, and we are more and more worried about technological unemployment. And we are maintaining income so well that we are able to experience inflation and economic stagnation at the same time.

The laws that embody these problematic solutions are liberating events not because they necessarily leave people freer than before, but because they represent a human and hopeful response to the particular forms of bondage experienced in a particular time and place.

V. THE CHURCH AS A LIBERATING JURIDICAL PRESENCE

For the liberationist, the church is a sign and celebration of the coming liberation and of the events by which it is even now being brought to pass. It is not easy to connect this vision of the church with the church as the maker of canon law, but the connection must be made. Whether for sign or for celebration, the church acts most effectively when it acts officially—that is, through the legal forms that make the acts of individuals attributable to the body to which they belong. This is why a pastoral letter gets more attention than would the private opinions of a group of clerics, however eminent. It is also why a priest who habitually wears sport shirts to parish functions will wear a Roman collar to a political demonstration. Christians all have their own witness to bear and their own celebrating to do, but only a legal form can make their witness or their celebration that of the church. Whatever the church's divine origin or mission, its presence in society is that of a corporate body like any other and the question of how or when the acts of natural persons are attributable to a corporate body is one of law.

Once past the threshold of incredulity evoked by the thought,

we find that church law has an important place in the work of liberation, partly similar to the place of civil law, partly complementary
to it.

In the first place, church law helps to define church teaching.
It can give official status to a liberating witness, and it can officially repudiate the witness of Christians who would in some way
sanctify oppression. Church law also governs deployment of the
ministry and access to the sacraments. It can provide sacramental
and liturgical support to the work of liberation, and, if need be, withdraw such support from those who work for oppression. Against
criteria of this kind we can measure such questions as whether the
church in Namibia should appoint chaplains to minister to members
of black guerrilla forces, or whether slum landlords in American
cities should be denied the sacraments.

The church has command of powerful symbols, many of which
are deployed under legal forms. Whatever the shortcomings of the
medieval church, it was able through such institutions as public
penance, celibacy, sanctuary, clerical immunity, and certain forms
of the religious life to witness that the human condition was not
circumscribed by the disordered sexuality, the self-glorification, the
venality, and the meaningless warfare that infected so much of the
society of the time. This witness to the freedom of the Christian
from some of the more baneful concerns of the wider society has
been attenuated in recent times, but it could be revived. Small groups,
notably the Amish, have kept it up, and it has begun to appear again
in the mainstream churches with causes such as the civil rights movement, the right to life movement, the anti-war movement, and the
sanctuary movement.

The church has always been able to confront power by de-
nouncing it. Besides the pulpit and the pastoral letter, the church
had at one time some extremely colorful legal forms such as inter-
dict and formal excommunication through which its denunciations
could be brought home to particular malefactors. Fasts, demonstrations, boycotts, and picket lines are modern equivalents. These
are not usually carried out under official church auspices, but they
could be, and might be more effective if they were.

The nonconfrontive functions of the church in supporting liberation tend to complement those of the state. They are based on
a conception of the church as one social institution among others.

The church conceived in this way offers, among other things, a corporate moral witness that reinforces and expands the moral commitments of the state, a range of social services that the state may wish to encourage but not to support with tax money, and a more complete set of marriage regulations than the state can justify in a pluralist society. Many of these church operations have a juridical dimension, and many of them can liberate through mediation of the kind I described as one of the functions of law. The desire of human beings to do right by one another is by no means as all-embracing or as careless of adverse consequences as a dedicated Christian might wish. Still, it is not negligible, and it is not necessarily limited to those aspects of right-doing that the state finds it expedient to enforce. Within an established social order, there is room for churches to set standards for their members to live by in dealing with other individuals, and in dealing with other classes as well. For instance, a church, or a consortium of churches, could establish guidelines for the treatment of agricultural workers without going through the tradeoffs between rural and urban legislators that have impeded the state in setting such guidelines.

In calling Christians to a community life different from that imposed by secular law, church law becomes advocacy before history. Consider for example the enduring effort of Christian bodies to maintain a higher level of social services than the community at large provides. This effort is juridical in that it is organized, official, and in some cases coercive—as in a church where no one can be a member who does not tithe. The effort is liberating because it proposes to the wider society a state of affairs in which the resources of the rich are freely available for the necessities of the poor. That state of affairs has not yet come to pass. But the church, by organizing for it with compassion, resourcefulness, and humility, is calling on history to bring it about, and is providing a sign and a celebration of the hope that history will one day respond.

VI. CONCLUSION

To accept liberation as an end of law does not rule out such other purposes as peace, virtue, or justice between individuals. But it does rule out any global agenda derived from first principles ("blueprint for society" the social engineering people would call it), any attempt to discern and implement upcoming historical changes, and any a priori limitation on the function of law (e.g., Mill's version of liberty). Liberation is the opening of individuals and peoples toward an unknown future.

Therefore, a liberationist approach to law will call for dispositions based not on abstractions or blueprints, but on what is experienced as oppressive, here and now, by the actual people that we see around us. Such an approach would be broader than any agenda that anyone is currently offering. We will all have different lists of oppressive conditions from which people ought to be liberated. But a humble and compassionate reflection on our society in the light of the Gospel might enable us to compile a master list. It would include, I suggest, at least the following items:

1. Poverty, exploitation, unemployment, lack of access to essential social services, and the rest of the problems that go with not having the means to live even modestly in an affluent society.
2. The general trivialization of life, through commercialism, consumerism, mindless technology, the constant quantification of standards of value (Nielsen ratings, gross national product, Scholastic Aptitude Tests, etc.), destruction of the environment and establishment of plastic substitutes.
3. Powerlessness—that of the poor who find themselves dependent on caseworkers, doctors, lawyers, policemen, landlords, employers, teachers and other middle-class people who often do not understand their lives and their needs; and that of the middle class, whose health, education, work, credit standing, and access to other amenities of life are subject to control by institutions, some public and some private, that become more and more bureaucratized and unresponsive as their workload increases.
4. Rootlessness, a product of mass culture, nationwide job markets, urbanization, centralization of functions in business and government, destruction of neighborhoods through urban renewal and consolidated schools, alteration of rural living patterns through the establishment of shopping centers and condominiums, and other more complicated causes.
5. Sexual license, which becomes more and more intrusive, more and more coercive under the repeated promptings of the followers

of Sigmund Freud and John Stuart Mill, supplemented by the forces of Madison Avenue and the publishing industry as loosed by the Supreme Court.

6. Violence—What the unemployed teenager suffers from the police and inflicts on the elderly apartment dweller; what the union organizer suffers from the employer and inflicts on the strike-breaker; what the poor Southern white suffers from the mining company and inflicts on his black neighbor; what the working-man suffers from his foreman and inflicts on his wife.

In the following chapters, I will deal with these items one by one. I will try to show how each has been perceived in the past and what legal dispositions have been framed to address it. I will then propose my own legal agenda for a liberating approach to the problem as it presently appears. In each case, I will try to discern the "class enemy" whom the present situation casts in an oppressive role—the person who will have to give up some form of comfort or privilege in order to be liberated from being an oppressor. Finally, I will take up the institutional role of the church as sign and celebration of liberation from each of the items being considered.

In presenting this material, I have tried to steer a middle course between, on the one hand, an overly coercive imposition of what is after all only a tentative theoretical structure, and, on the other hand, a merely conversational or polemical treatment with no theoretical framework at all. I find that the categories of symbol, mediation, and confrontation, as I have described them, are useful in describing a variety of actual or proposed legal dispositions, and I have drawn on them freely for the purpose as the occasion has served. But I have not found any inherent symmetry of symbols, confrontations, and mediations in any given body of material, and I have not tried to impose any.

Pursuant to the liberationist insight that the institution creates the class conflict, I have tried to maintain a pragmatic, non-theoretical class analysis, based mainly on the traditional question *cui bono*—who are the beneficiaries of the institution under scrutiny. As we shall see, the answers tend to keep pointing to the same group of people—an organizational and professional elite whose power comes from having skills that other people lack.

These people have little resemblance to either the capitalists or the proletarians of conventional Marxist analysis. On the other hand, they are pretty similar to the New Class discerned by the Marxist continuator Milovan Djilas in his book of that name. Djilas carries the class dialectic of Marx and Engels a step farther, arguing that the proletariat as a class is too unwieldy, too ill-organized to exercise power. It therefore creates a class of surrogates to exercise power on its behalf. These surrogates then form a new class distinct from the proletarians in whose name they act.

The cogency of Djilas's analysis is not limited to the Communist societies to which he applies it. The various economic and political constituencies of a modern Western industrial society — voters, stockholders, union members, consumers — are also too ill-organized and too unwieldy to exercise power without the intervention of a class of surrogates with special interests and special skills that give them more in common with each other than with the groups in whose name they act. I do not intend to pursue a Marxist analysis in this work, but I believe that such an analysis, as corrected by Djilas, would point to pretty much the same people as my pragmatic approach does.

I have not tried in my analysis to do ultimate justice between liberation and some of the more pedestrian or utilitarian purposes that can be assigned to a legal disposition. While any good law is in a sense liberating, there are some laws (e.g., those against drunk driving), which it seems a work of supererogation to take beyond their obvious and immediate utilitarian ends. Liberation, by holding before the law an object of removing obstacles to an unknown future, does not so much displace utility as relativize it. While there is nothing wrong with doing something materially useful when the occasion arises, material usefulness cannot be made a general criterion for law. I have tried here to deal with both the immediate and the transcendent as the need for one or the other has arisen.

2

Poverty

I. PERCEPTIONS OF THE PROBLEM

When we try to contribute to the liberation of the poor in our society, we have a great weight of history to contend with. Poverty has haunted the consciences of Christians, evoked the pity and benevolence of good people, and challenged the ingenuity of social reformers in every generation. People of many different times and many different ideologies have had a hand in constructing our present program—if it can be called a program—for taking care of the poor. Their successive perceptions of the causes and cure of poverty have left their marks on our institutions rather like successive waves on a beach.

When the English began to colonize the New World, they had in place a program of poor relief developed over the period between the Black Death (1348) and the Reformation (roughly, 1530-1600). The program was based on a recognition that some people were poor because of misfortune, others because of indolence. Measures were taken to separate the two types and deal with each as it deserved. Social disruption as a source of poverty was dealt with by a tenacious and naïve insistence on the local community as the source of all relief. Poor persons were to be cared for in their home parishes. Those found wandering were to be sent back where they came from. Parish officials ("overseers of the poor") were to make anyone work who was able to do so, and to relieve anyone who was not. Established charities were meshed into this system—that is, they were used to relieve the local taxpayers rather than to give additional benefits to the poor. Measures were taken to discourage indiscriminate alms, and channel new benefactions into the overall program.

Ancillary to this program was a certain tendency to institutionalize the poor, a tendency that set in in the eighteenth century, and grew apace with the development of utilitarianism and social Darwinism in the nineteenth. In a proper institution or poorhouse, those able to work could be more effectively made to do so, and those unable to work could be relieved at minimum cost. Moreover, conditions could be made so unattractive that the screening process was almost automatic: the authorities could be confident that no one would apply for relief who could possibly maintain himself in some other way.

Even today, this ancient and tough-minded system and the perceptions behind it play a substantial part in our provisions for relieving the poor. Institutionalization, to be sure, has become fairly rare, although there is still some legislative provision for it. In other respects, though, the old arrangements for keeping the poor on short commons and making them work if they can are still in effect. Anyone who cannot bring himself under any of our more modern programs must be subjected to them. Also, the underlying perception that many if not most of the poor are merely lazy and will find jobs if the relief option is made unattractive enough is still very much with us; it enters into the politics and the administration of all programs.

Our next layer of legal materials corresponds to a perception that began to make its way into the statute books toward the end of the last century, began to get past the Supreme Court in the second decade of this one, and culminated in the New Deal legislation under Franklin Roosevelt. That perception is that some people are poor because of working in jobs that do not provide enough compensation to meet their needs. Minimum wage legislation, compulsory fringe benefits (Workmen's Compensation, Unemployment Compensation, Social Security), and legal supports for collective bargaining all come out of this perception. The laborer is worthy of his hire. An employer who does not give his employees enough to live on, support their families, and provide against contingencies does them an injustice.

Along with their moral doctrines of just compensation for the worker, the New Deal theorists tended to follow Keynesian economic doctrines. They believed that if working people got more money they would buy more things and so put more people to work. They expected, therefore, that the same measures that provided just compensation to the worker would eventually provide jobs for the unemployed.

Accordingly, their program for relieving the poor made no permanent provision for people who could be expected to work. Such people, if they did not have jobs, were the victims of temporary economic displacement, and could be provided for through stopgap measures like the W.P.A. Once the government's other programs had restored prosperity (in the event, it was World War II that did that, rather than the programs), any further victims of temporary economic displacement could be provided for under the traditional system of locally administered and financed poor relief.

For poor people who could not be expected to work, however, a permanent program of assistance was set up in 1935 as a combined project of state and federal government. Provision was made for financial assistance out of the federal treasury to any state program that complied with federal guidelines. Four categories of people were covered: the "aged" (i.e., those sixty-five and over — the retirement age established by Bismarck and generally accepted since), the blind, the disabled, and children in families deprived of a breadwinner through illness, death, or desertion. The program is generally called "categorical" assistance, because one has to fall into one of these categories to be eligible, whereas for the traditional "general" assistance one has only to be poor.

Federal provision for the poor continues to be dominated by the four categories established in 1935. Aid to Families with Dependent Children (AFDC), our largest and most intractable program, is the original New Deal arrangement for one category virtually intact. For the other three categories, the federal-state programs were replaced in 1974 by a fully federal program called Supplemental Security Income (SSI), but there was only a minor change in the categories themselves. The Medical Assistance program (Medicaid), adopted in 1965, requires the states to cover the same four categories in order to be eligible for federal funding. Many states cover no more. Only in the case of food stamps is there a general federal relief program that reaches substantially beyond the four New Deal categories of poor people.

More recent initiatives have clustered around a perception that there is something more than temporary economic displacement standing in the way of people getting jobs. The most prevalent version puts the blame on inadequate skills. This understanding of the problem supports programs like CETA, WIN, and the Job Corps aimed at giving poor people marketable skills, and programs like Head Start and Upward Bound aimed at giving them a mainstream social orientation.

A more radical response to the same perception is the "negative income tax." This term embraces a number of different proposals. The common element is that they would make the dispenser of relief as indifferent to why people are poor as the tax collector is (or should be) to why they are rich. They would do away with the age-old distinction between the indolent and the unfortunate, and treat the person who is poor because he will not work the same as the one who is poor because he cannot work. That is, they would restore the situation as it was before the Statute of Laborers of 1349. Their theory is that since the poor have the same motivations as other people, no significant numbers of them will be content with the modicum of sustenance afforded under the relief program if they can earn more by working. All the proposals are so arranged that only a part of a recipient's earnings goes to reduce his benefits: he is always better off if he works.

No full-fledged negative income tax proposal has gained significant political backing, though some proposals that made a substantial showing (without, to be sure, getting enacted) have been influenced in some part by the idea. Also, a plan was tried on an experimental basis in a couple of places. The disincentives to work seem to have been greater than expected.

One other perception that must be taken into account is that poverty is an inherent part of the capitalist system—that as long as we have that system some people will be poor. Those who see the matter in this way have never gathered enough votes to abolish the system democratically. But they have made their views felt in some measure in the agenda of the British Labor Party, and in some of the Great Society programs of the sixties in this country. In Britain, they have had a hand in measures for nationalizing industry, redistributing wealth through selective and sometimes confiscatory taxes, and making social services like education and medical care available at public expense to the whole population regardless of need. In this country, they have been involved in efforts (largely unsuccessful) to turn the legal provisions for participation by the poor in the governance of anti-poverty programs into a means of politicizing the poor and giving them a power base in opposition to the existing institutions of local government.

So much, then, for the perceptions that have affected our various attempts to relieve the poor. Let us now look at the burdens of poverty in our society, and see how far we have succeeded in alleviating them.

II. THE BURDENS OF POVERTY – A LIBERATIONIST INVENTORY AND PROGRESS REPORT

Poverty is not so much a burden as a matrix of burdens. What you have to put up with if you are poor depends on what, in your particular economic and social context, people have to have money to avoid. A migrant tomato picker in California does not lack for fresh air and sunshine, and a teenager in the South Bronx does not lack for leisure. Some burdens, though, are fairly general. It is to these that most of our legal measures have been addressed, with varying degrees of success.

A. DESTRUCTIVE WORK AND UNEMPLOYMENT

An obvious burden of the poor is the kind of work that they are forced to do. Especially is this the case in a society where the conditions of employment are generally bargained for. The poor have no bargaining power because they have no resources to fall back on. They must take whatever job they are offered, even if it is hard, long, underpaid, dangerous, and without any prospect of advancement. They cannot afford the alternative of no job at all. A poor person in this condition is deprived of more than material comfort. His human dignity is affronted in that someone else is appropriating the satisfaction he ought to have in doing a good job and enjoying its fruits.

The remedies of choice for this situation have been to enhance the bargaining power of workers by supporting unions, and to supersede the bargaining process at crucial points through legislation prescribing wages, hours, and working conditions. There has also been legislation to eliminate artificial barriers to advancement by forbidding discrimination against women and minorities, and by subsidizing training and apprenticeship programs. In very great part these remedies have done their work. They have upgraded mainstream jobs in our society to the point that people with such jobs, unless they have unusually large families to support, or have unusual medical problems, cannot really be included among the poor.

But not all jobs are mainstream. There are people who have to work outside the reach of our protective legislation, and they are no better off than poor workers were before that legislation was enacted. Indeed, their condition is all the more bitter in that there are fewer to share it.

The most noticeable victims of marginal jobs are agricultural workers. For political reasons, they were left out of most of the basic legislation that protects the rest of the work force. In recent years, some measures have been adopted for their protection, but in most places their condition is still grim.

Illegal aliens form another large class of victims. Many of these are engaged in agricultural employment. Others are in jobs theoretically protected by law, but they have no access to the law's protection, because they will be deported if the authorities find out about them, and their employers will report them to the authorities if they make trouble.

Finally, there are odd jobs, casual jobs, jobs with employers too small to fall within the coverage of the major federal laws or to engage the attention of the major unions, and jobs with marginal businesses that can survive only by exploiting their workers. In all these cases, the poor are still exposed in some degree to the burden of harsh and unrewarding work.

At the same time, there are more and more of the poor who can find no work at all. Upgrading wages, hours, and working conditions naturally costs money, so that employers often find that they are better off cutting down their work force and spending their money on capital intensive labor saving technologies. Accordingly, as the burden of work is alleviated for the poor, the burden of unemployment becomes more severe. Today, it is the most characteristic burden of young people in the great urban ghettos.

Efforts are being made through programs like the Job Corps to educate these victims of technological unemployment and give them new marketable skills. The programs are far from reaching all the people who need them. Even if they had a much greater reach, they would not solve the problem. There may be some jobs in our economy vacant for lack of people with the skills to fill them, but there are not enough such jobs to begin taking care of all the unemployed.

B. UNMET NEEDS

The poor people of traditional literature lacked the standard amenities of food, shelter, and clothing. Their food was mostly carbohydrate, and not enough of that. They lived in damp, dark, overcrowded hovels with no sanitary facilities. Their clothes were thin, dirty, and ragged; when the wind blew, they shivered. They also lacked provision for medical care. If they took sick, they either died or got well without the intervention of a doctor. Or else they were hospitalized in facilities especially provided for their kind— perfunctory, impersonal, and not always clean. Finally, they did not have the education they needed to reflect usefully on their situation or to move among their fellows as equals.

This level of privation has long been considered unacceptable. We have tried to eliminate it in its educational aspect through our public school system, and in its other aspects through regulating the economy and the employment relation. But there are still many cases where direct intervention is required to meet people's needs, and the programs for that intervention have serious gaps.

The most important of these programs is the old New Deal Aid to Families with Dependent Children (AFDC), which affords a measure of assistance (inadequate in some states, barely adequate in most, better than adequate in a few) to one-parent families with children. The original idea was to provide for families lacking a breadwinner; that is why it does not cover two-parent families unless one of the parents is disabled. About half the states have adopted a supplementary program, AFDC-U, which covers a family with a second parent who cannot get a job.

There is now one other program of categorical assistance, Supplemental Security Income (SSI), a fixed payment to poor people who are aged, blind, or disabled. The states may, and sometimes do, provide additional benefits to people on SSI, but the basic payment is directly administered by the federal government. Benefit levels are good as welfare benefits go.

For poor people who do not fall within any of the categories covered by AFDC or SSI, there is general assistance, derived with varying amounts of updating from the Elizabethan poor law. In some states, this program has been meshed with the others, and pays comparable benefits. In other states, though, both administration and benefits are extremely haphazard. New legislation and lawsuits are gradually ameliorating the old program, but there is a long way to go. In much of the country, it must still be assumed that a person eligible for no program but general assistance will be inadequately provided for.

The food stamp program is an important additional source of support not only for people who receive other forms of assistance but also for low income households not eligible for other programs. Food stamps are coupons in different dollar amounts, redeemable in grocery stores for goods at the stores' regular prices. The federal government issues them through state agencies. A household is entitled to enough stamps to make up the difference between thirty percent of the members' combined incomes and a dollar amount set by the Secretary of Agriculture as enough to feed them all. Since the Secretary has no mandate to consider either the economics of grocery shopping in the slums or the cultural obstacles to using some of the cheaper sources of protein, his figures are never adequate. The stamps help, but not as much as they are supposed to.

Taken together, these programs insure that most Americans have enough (or almost enough) to eat, have clothes on their backs, have a roof over their heads. There are exceptions, however. There are young adults who cannot find work. There are members of intact families who cannot get AFDC and cannot live on general assistance as it operates in their particular localities. There are manual workers in their late fifties or early sixties, who are no longer at-

tractive on the job market, but who are neither disabled enough
nor old enough to be eligible for SSI. There are migrant workers
who do not stay put long enough for their applications to be pro-
cessed. There are other people who are eligible for one program
or another, but do not find out that they are—often officials are
in no hurry to let them know.

For many of those who have a roof over their heads, it is not
much of a roof. In our society, comfortable housing eludes low income families, whether or not they are on welfare. While conditions are not as overcrowded and unsanitary as the ones in the nineteenth century, they are still unacceptable for many people. To
remedy the situation, measures have been tried both for upgrading
existing units and for building new ones. Neither approach has
worked very well.

Upgrading existing units tends to put them beyond the reach
of the poor. If a landlord spends his own money on upgrading a
building, he will have to raise the rent to recover his investment.
If the upgrading is subsidized, he will still have to raise the rent,
because he cannot upgrade without eliminating overcrowding: he
will have to raise the same money from fewer people. If the rent
too is subsidized, there is still the problem of where to put the people who have been displaced by the elimination of overcrowding.
Usually they go and increase the overcrowding somewhere else.

As for building new units, concentrating the poor in high rise
projects, as was done in the fifties, has turned out to be socially
destructive, whereas scattering them among the rest of the population is apt to be politically unacceptable. Another possibility is to
subsidize low income families so they can seek housing on the same
market as other people. Theoretically, normal market forces would
then take care of the building of additional units. An experimental
program along these lines has been tried in a couple of places with
inconclusive results.

Medical treatment for the poor is a particularly complicated
problem under our existing laws. The basic program, Medical Assistance (Medicaid), is another state program supervised and partly
funded by the federal government. It pays full doctor and hospital
bills, along with most other health care expenses, for those who
are eligible. But eligibility is severely limited. A state program, to
comply with federal law, need cover only persons actually receiv-

ing AFDC or SSI. Some states are content to cover only those persons. The results are sometimes bizarre. A sixty-five year old man whose income is one dollar less than the monthly SSI payment gets one dollar plus all his medical expenses; if his income goes up by a dollar a month, he gets nothing. A runaway husband by coming home can make it impossible for his child to have a necessary operation because he makes his family ineligible for AFDC, and therefore for Medicaid.

Some states have undertaken a gingerly extension of Medicaid to the "medically indigent," that is, to those who can meet other expenses but cannot pay for the medical treatment they need. But federal law sets very strict limits to such extensions. It permits coverage only where family income, exclusive of amounts spent for medical care, is no more than 150% of what a state's maximum AFDC payment would be for a similar family. The literature is full of horror stories produced by the stern mathematics of this program. A man making $7,000 a year is told to quit his job because there is no other way he can get Factor VIII for his hemophiliac son. Another man divorces his wife because she has multiple sclerosis. Under his state's Medicaid program, he can keep only $4,000 a year for himself and his four children if he wants assistance in paying her medical bills—but as a single person unable to work she will get both full medical coverage and a fixed monthly payment under SSI.

For poor people not eligible for Medicaid, health care is generally inadequate. There are a few programs that pick up hospital expenses for some of them. The most important is the Hill-Burton Act, whereby hospitals built with federal money must offer a certain amount of free care. Otherwise these people are dependent on general assistance or on occasional free clinics. If general assistance is haphazard in providing food, shelter, and clothing, it is still more so in providing medical care. Free clinics differ widely in quality; in any event, there are not enough of them. The fact that so many people are eligible for Medicaid has tended to dry up other sources of free health care.

Also, the programs other than Medicaid, even if they give effective coverage for serious illness, do not pay for the routine checkups, elective dental procedures, investigation of warning symptoms and the like that most Americans rely on to keep healthy. A person who has to cut into a marginal food budget to pay for such items is apt to omit them.

In many places, poor children get a much worse education than middle-class children, even when both attend the public schools. It is not entirely clear why this should be the case. There are of course many things wrong with our public school system, but most of them are as baneful to the rich as to the poor. Various reasons have been offered as to why the poor fare worse under the system than the rest of us do. One is that the inner city, where many of the poor live, has a lower tax base than the suburbs, where many of the middle class live. Others are the difference in home environment, the middle-class orientation of the curriculum, and the demoralization and apathy that affect both teachers and students in schools where there is a large concentration of the poor. The federal government has tried to remedy deficiencies in home environment with programs such as Head Start and Upward Bound. The other problems have not been dealt with directly, but measures aimed at racial integration tend to spread the poor around and place a certain number of them in some of the better run and better supported schools. Of course, whether poor children learn better in a student body dominated by middle-class children is a debatable point.

Some private schools, mostly church-related, have had notable success in educating students drawn entirely from the inner-city poor. Perhaps they are successful because they can be more flexible than the topheavy city systems in meeting the needs of their particular constituencies. Perhaps it is because they are freer than the public schools from enervating educational philosophies. Or perhaps it is because they can screen would-be students and keep only those who are well motivated. The number and impact of these schools would be greater if most of them were not barred from government support by the Supreme Court's current (and in my opinion erroneous) understanding of the constitutional separation of church and state.

C. PERSONAL INDIGNITIES

There is always a temptation to look down on the poor, belittle them, and order them about. The apostle James had to rebuke the early Christians for doing it. The situation is, if anything, worse in a nominally egalitarian society such as ours, where the tendency is to see poor people as losers rather than as one of the constituent elements of the community. Worse still, by not having a defined position with definite, if meager, perquisites, poor people are constantly being thrust into positions of dependency for things that they need or would like to have. A welfare caseworker can decide whether to give them extra money for blankets. An employer can decide whether to give them work, a landlord whether to put them out on the street, a creditor whether to take away their television set or their bed, a policeman whether to search them, run them in, or even beat them up.

Our most systematic degradation of the poor is probably in the administration of our welfare programs. The very eligibility requirements tend to frustrate any aspiration to self-respect. The limitation of AFDC to one-parent families makes the unemployed father a financial burden in his own home, enhancing his negative feelings about not having a job, and sometimes even forcing him to leave home. Indeed, it is often not enough for him to leave home. Any effort at parenting on his part, any serious involvement in the lives of his children, may be sufficient to make his family ineligible for AFDC and for Medicaid.

Often too, eligibility requirements discourage work. It is logical enough to say that anything recipients earn reduces their need, and justifies a corresponding reduction in benefits. But if every dollar of earnings results in a dollar less in benefits, it is hard for recipients to keep up enthusiasm for sporadic, low paying, or grubby work of the kind that is apt to be available. The situation is made worse if benefits are reduced with alacrity when income goes up, and restored only after delay and paperwork when income goes down. The better programs try to counter this discouragement of work by providing that certain dollar amounts and certain sources of income shall be disregarded in computing need. But on the whole the disregards are not generous enough to give real support to recipients during the crucial period when they are trying to get back on their feet. The lack of generosity in this regard seems endemic. Concern that the poor not get a bit more out of the taxpayers than they need to keep body and soul together seems to go far deeper than concern for bringing them back into the mainstream.

Legislators and administrators tend to make up for the discouragement of work by the harassment of idleness. In some rural counties, they have tried to turn off whole programs during the harvest season, or to go from house to house rousting out recipients and driving them into the fields. Expedients like these are generally stopped by the courts, as are attempts to put recipients in jail for fraud if they fail to show up for work. But it is still routine in some places to have them work off their general assistance by chopping weeds along the highway or polishing administrators' cars. These tasks are conceived rather like convict labor, as the performance of a duty owed the state. They are not allowed to carry either the fringe benefits or the self-respect of a regular job.

We are ambivalent about making AFDC mothers work. The original idea of the program was that they ought to be home taking care of their children. Today, though, mothers in all walks of life work, leaving their children with babysitters or in day care. It is not clear why AFDC mothers should be always and everywhere an exception. Accordingly, caseworkers are usually given a good deal of discretion to decide which individual mothers shall be made to work and which ones shall not. Like other exercises of caseworker discretion, the decision is backed by a threat of termination of benefits if the recipient does not comply.

This is one of several points at which the discretion of the caseworker creates dependency on the part of the recipient. In many programs, benefit levels are based entirely or in part on a caseworker's determination of need. Thus, the recipient's standard of living will rise or fall with the ability to convince the caseworker that the family needs new shoes or another bed or a bigger apartment. Recipients can appeal the caseworker's determinations, but they are apt to lose. Besides, they often feel, rightly or wrongly, that they can lose more money by antagonizing the caseworker than they can gain by winning appeals.

There are various forms of investigation required that also pit the caseworker against the recipient and tend to demean the recipient. On applying for assistance, a person is generally required to satisfy a caseworker of his or her eligibility, usually with appropriate documentary evidence. The caseworker has considerable latitude in deciding what documents have to be brought in, and a person who fails to bring all the necessary documents the first time has no alternative but to come back. Keeping appointments in an office is not easy for the poor—especially for those of the poor who are applying for AFDC, because they have to take care of children at home. Also, applicants are apt to be many, caseworkers few, and offices stark due to cuts in funding. Showing up for appointments and waiting to be seen can be long and intimidating, and the whole intake process can have a Kafkaesque air about it.

In addition to the examination of documents in the office, some laws require field investigation before eligibility is determined. This will involve visiting the applicant at home, and sometimes even asking questions of the neighbors. Periodic investigations of the same kind may be required to make sure the recipient continues to be eligible.

At least some of the degradation of welfare recipients is due to the ambiguous position of the caseworkers. These people are trained in social work, that is, in intervening in people's affairs for the purpose of helping. They refer to their welfare recipients as "clients," and try to show them things like how to buy nutritious food, what contraceptives to use, or how to keep up an apartment. At the same time, they have almost complete control over the money supply. Despite both good will and professional competence, there is a coercive element in their efforts to help, and an intrusive element in their dispensation of funds.

Outside the realm of welfare, the main indignities suffered by the poor in our society are at the hands of employers, landlords, merchants, and the police. The poor are not alone in suffering from arbitrary firings, vindictive job assignments, bedbugs, malfunctioning toilets, shoddy merchandise, onerous credit terms, or police brutality. But they are less able than other people to defend themselves. They have little power to change jobs, move out, take their business to another store, or call the police to account. To be sure, they are beginning to get somewhat better legal protection than they have had in the past, partly thanks to new developments in the law, partly thanks to the expansion of legal services organizations to give the poor the benefit of whatever legal protections there are.

D. DOWNWARD MOBILITY

The prospect of falling on account of some likely contingency from a condition of modest comfort into one of total abjection is a burden of poverty that affects many who would not otherwise be poor. Most of the mainstream amenities in our society are severely dependent on some member of the family having a mainstream job, and are inadequately protected against the qualifying job being lost.

The first line of protection in such a case is the unemployment compensation system. It pays a weekly benefit for half a year (plus another quarter if certain economic indicators are present). The weekly benefits are not as high as the lost wage, but they will generally be sufficient to put food on the table and keep up the house, car, and furniture payments until the family wage earner goes back to work. The program is an important protection against fortuitous layoffs, and an income supplement in certain industries where periodic layoffs are a way of life.

But it is not a guarantee against extrusion from the economic mainstream. For one thing, it runs out. In the case of a person on the margins of the work force—an unskilled laborer, a person weak in English or in reading, a middle-aged man with less physical stamina than he used to have, or a victim of technological displacement—it can very well run out before he finds another job.

Also, a worker will not get unemployment compensation if he quits voluntarily or is fired for just cause. Courts differ widely in the application of these concepts. In some jurisdictions, an employee must put up with a good deal of mistreatment, unpleasant working conditions, and disruption of his personal life before quitting, or he will be held to have quit voluntarily, and he must display considerable humility if he is to avoid giving his employer just cause for firing him.

Further, unemployment compensation is not available if a person is unable to work. Those out of work through sickness or injury are not covered. There is often a gap between conditions invoking the various disability payment programs and conditions making a person actually unable to work. If the sickness or injury results from the job, there will be workmen's compensation payments plus medical expenses. These will continue indefinitely, but are apt to be scant replacement for the wages the recipient was earning. The disability programs, if they are available, are apt to be scanter still.

One way or another, then, when the job goes, the amenities of mainstream American life begin drifting off in its wake. The first thing to go is health insurance. The typical mainstream job offers a comprehensive package of benefits for doctor and hospital bills for the worker and his family. The plan may include an option to convert to an individual policy when the employee ceases to be covered; but the coverage is apt to be limited and the premium is apt to be prohibitive. A major increase in expenditure at the very moment of a major reduction in income is apt to be foregone. As a consequence, a serious illness, if it hits while no one in the family is working can wipe out even a fairly well-off family.

The next thing that happens is that the installment payments begin to be missed. The normal American family is heavily in debt. Often the house, car, kitchen appliances, television set, and furniture are all only partially paid for. Even a moderate reduction in income can result in payments being missed, collection agencies dunning, and, before long, in the repossession of the amenities one by one, and finally, in the foreclosure of the mortgage on the house.

Meanwhile, the family will be reorienting its attitude toward welfare. Before long they will be eligible for food stamps. Often deep-seated inhibitions have to be overcome before they take advantage of their eligibility. Generally, the need is urgent enough for the inhibitions to give way — sometimes at considerable psychological cost.

The food stamp application is the family's first introduction to the welfare agencies and their application procedures. As the slide into indigence continues, other programs will become involved, often with different agencies or different people within the same agency. If the family is to stay together in a state where intact families are ineligible for AFDC, it may tax the collective ingenuity of a whole battery of agencies and caseworkers to keep them clothed and housed (the food stamps will presumably keep them fed). They will be spared some of the more objectionable kinds of treatment as long as agency people are able to recognize them as members of their own social class. But maintaining the social carriage of a middle class person while living off a congeries of welfare programs is a considerable feat.

The loss of social carriage is the final step in the descent into dependency. It is one that few can avoid taking. Theoretically, an unemployed factory worker could accept welfare benefits with the same insouciance as an oil baron accepting a depletion allowance or a brain surgeon a tax shelter. But society does not encourage such an attitude. Philosophy and theology may teach that the welfare recipient has a right to what he gets and the capitalist has not, but the prevailing wisdom is the opposite. Because we like to think our society is one in which people can make it if they try, we like to think no one is poor but freeloaders and social misfits. We expect the poor to be freeloaders or social misfits and to act accordingly. In the end, they will probably live up to the expectation, partly because it is their own as well as other people's.

III. LIBERATING THE POOR—A LEGAL AGENDA

A. REVISING THE SYMBOLS

The beginning of a legal agenda for the liberation of the poor is a set of symbols that recognize their place in society as equal and responsible citizens. The point at which these symbols have most urgently to be introduced is in the field of welfare administration, which, as we have seen, is now dominated by very different symbols.

Much of the grief to which we have long put recipients and would-be recipients of welfare stems from a feeling that we are conferring on them a gratuitous benefaction for which they should be humbly grateful, or a feeling that they are losers in the game of life through their own ineptitude, and should undergo whatever course of remedial exercises we competent players prescribe for them. We have tended to be disconcerted or even outraged if they stand on their dignity or claim the same rights as other citizens to control their own affairs.

The classic case embodying this attitude toward welfare is *Wilkie* v. *O'Connor*, in which an old man who lived under a barn was denied an old age pension because of an administrative regulation that required the recipient of such a pension to live in a "suitable home." He contended that this was an impermissible invasion of his freedom. The court said:

> Appellant . . . argues that he has a right to live as he pleases while being supported by public charity. One would admire his independence if he were not so dependent, but he has no right to defy the standards and conventions of civilized society while being supported at public expense.

This case and the thinking behind it are countered by a good deal of literature insisting that the welfare recipient has a "right" to the benefits conferred upon him—the same rights, say, that a veteran has to his education benefits. The state can no more attach onerous and intrusive conditions to the one right than to the other.

In practice, the only welfare recipients who are treated as having a right of this kind are the ones whose condition can be attributed to old age or misfortune. That is why the SSI program, which is limited to such persons, is relatively free from the demeaning incidents attached to other programs. To extend the same respect to the rest of the poor, we will have to see them as victims also—not of specific misfortunes, but of the economic system itself.

The perception is not a new one. Here is a presentation of it from an English novel of 1851, *Yeast*, by Charles Kingsley. The protagonist, Lancelot Smith, is listening to the rural sage Paul Tregarva, who tells him that the poor law has made people

> "slaves and beggars at heart. It taught them not to be ashamed of parish pay—to demand it as a right."

> "And so it is their right," said Lancelot. "In God's name, if a country is so ill-constituted that it cannot find its own citizens in work, it is bound to find them in food."

It appears that our country today, like England in 1851, is so ill contituted that it cannot find its own citizens in work, and is therefore bound to find them in food. In principle, all welfare recipients are entitled to the same respect that we give to the aged and the disabled. Establishing this respect is the beginning of a legal agenda for liberating the poor. We can and should make it possible for a person to claim and receive the welfare benefits the law provides in his case just as matter-of-factly as a person claims and receives a driver's license or a tax refund.

A few simple reforms would do a great deal to enhance the dignity of welfare recipients. The ones most often talked about, and already embodied in some programs, are these: (1) Disregarding a sufficient amount of earned income to encourage recipients to try their hand at working, and offering a trial work period so recipients who take full-time jobs will not be terminated from the program until they are firmly established in their jobs. (2) Fixing benefits at a definite number of dollars rather than basing them on a flexible standard of need as applied by a caseworker. In this way, recipients would be in the same situation as the rest of us—having a predictable income and making intelligent decisions about how to spend it. (3) Accepting the word of applicants as to their circumstances, subject to prosecution if information or spot checking discloses a fraud. This is the way we collect income tax. If it would put more undeserving people on the welfare rolls (as arguably it would not), the cost would be more than outweighed by the saving of intake costs. (4) Separating such social casework services as the government chooses to provide from the function of determining eligibility for welfare and distributing the benefits. (5) Making the same benefits available to intact families as to one-parent families.

All these proposals have been adopted in one place or another; most of them have been included in the SSI program, and all of them were included in the "Better Jobs and Incomes Act" which the Carter administration presented unsuccessfully to Congress in 1978.

B. Confronting the Industrial Revolution

The symbolic value of reforming our patchwork system of welfare and social insurance is not to be scorned; still, reforms of this kind will not by themselves be any great help in liberating the poor in our society. They will increase the cost of poverty for those who are not yet poor—who have to pay for more generous programs with higher taxes, and are showing less and less willingness to do so—without doing anything to halt the process of impoverishment, a process that is gradually reducing the number of taxpayers while increasing the number of people they have to support.

Even symbolically, reforms in the existing programs are no final answer. They do nothing to acknowledge the solidarity of rich and poor in our society, the moral and economic interdependence between the prosperity of those of us who prosper and the poverty of those of us who are poor.

That interdependence as we experience it today is a product of the Industrial Revolution. The essence of industrialization is the replacement of human effort by other ways of accomplishing results. The process has relieved people of a great deal of drudgery and has brought about a far wider distribution of social amenities than would otherwise have been possible. At the same time it has tended to drive workers into a state of economic superfluity.

One way or another, the burdens of poverty as I have described them here can be traced back to this endemic superfluity. The acceptance of harsh and unrewarding work is naturally dictated by the ever-present possibility of no work at all. Similarly, people put up with compensation insufficient to provide against contingencies, or even to meet all their present needs, because they are subject to the law of supply and demand in the job market. The degradation and belittlement, as well as the short rations, that welfare recipients experience are inherent in an economic situation in which they have nothing to offer, and so must depend on the benevolence of others for what they need.

The law's approach to the process of industrialization has been mediative rather than confrontive. The laws we have been considering here, along with most other laws affecting our economy, are based on the assumption that we are to go on indefinitely using our ingenuity and our resources to accomplish more with less human effort, and, concomitantly, to go on making parts of our work force superfluous. Given the assumption that this process is to continue, our laws have made a very good effort to mediate its impact upon individual persons with the maximum possible fairness and good will.

In the first place, we have an arsenal of measures calculated to maintain economic growth—that is, to retard the spread of superfluity by producing more with the same work force instead of producing the same with a smaller work force. Then, we have laws calculated to help people upgrade their skills to keep pace with developing technology. Such laws have provided the Jobs Corps, CETA, and on the job training at one level, subsidized college or graduate school at another.

We also have measures aimed at a fair distribution of the benefits flowing from the process. As between capital and labor, we provide standards for the treatment of working people so that all the avails will not go to the investors. As between investors and managers, we have the Securities Act, the Blue Sky Laws, and other provisions that keep or try to keep managers honest and investors happy. As between producers and consumers, we have laws against monopolies, laws against false advertising, and laws against harmful products. All these mediate the process of economic and technological growth for the benefit of the individuals affected by it. The welfare laws we have considered here are a last line of mediation to provide a minimum standard of support for those on whom the effect of the process has been most severe.

For all these mediative efforts, it is becoming more and more difficult to find our citizens in work, and more and more burdensome to find them in food. As long as the process of industrialization continues, we will have to consume more goods, invest more capital, and use more energy every year than we did the year before for every human being we keep at work. As capital and energy are finite, and even the ability to consume is not totally unlimited, the struggle is one that we will eventually have to lose; indeed, it is one that we are already in the process of losing, a little bit at a time.

Our losses go to increase the ranks of the hopelessly unemployed, whom we keep on welfare, as far out of sight and as far out of mind as we can (a cartoon that I saw on a bulletin board a few years ago has one penthouse dweller telling another that "the ghetto isn't a problem; the ghetto is a solution"). Between these people and the rest of the community, there is a growing cultural gulf as well as an economic one. Work is a vital element in our culture, and the hard-core unemployed are isolated from the mainstream of society in more ways than it would be possible to enumerate.

I believe, therefore, that we cannot liberate the poor in our society without liberating the hard-core unemployed, and that we cannot liberate the hard-core unemployed without directly confronting and limiting, rather than simply mediating, the long historical process that is making them superfluous as workers. The process is not something inevitable like the winds and the tides. Human beings set it in motion, and when it ceases to serve human purposes, human beings can put a stop to it.

As I see it, the elements of a confrontive program would be some check to the accumulation of capital in large units—the so-called economies of scale seem always to involve getting rid of workers—and a corresponding encouragement of small units; direct support for more labor-intensive forms of production and distribution, and the imposition of new criteria of "efficiency" to support a change in outlook.

The tendency of corporations to accumulate capital through expanding their operations or through big corporations gobbling up little ones has been regulated in the interest of preserving competition (the Clayton Act) and in the interest of protecting investors (tender offer laws). But the accumulations of capital themselves have not been regarded as inherently objectionable. Thus, nothing has been done about the complicated tax provisions that make it profitable to buy more companies or to expand one's own operation instead of paying dividends or cutting prices. Nor have the antitrust laws that keep competitors from joining together been applied to "conglomerate" combinations, such as the acquisition of a brewery by a shoe manufacturer.

The effect of corporate expansion and consolidation on the work force has not been as much studied as have some of the other effects of the process. It has been noted that when one brewery buys up another, there is a tendency for one of the two plants to be shut down, but it is not apparent why the purchase of the brewery by a shoe company should lead to fewer workers making either shoes or beer. Still, it stands to reason that a unit with a large accumulation of capital will tend to invest it in more capital-intensive operations, whether its activities extend over many businesses or are limited to one. The oversize corporation has capital to invest and will not forego the opportunity to invest it. Furthermore, it will have access to the money market, where it can borrow more capital at relatively low rates and invest it at relatively high ones (a phenomenon referred to by corporate finance people as "leverage").

Also, a large corporation, again even if its operations are spread over many different businesses, has far more ability than a small one to create "structural" unemployment by shifting its capital and operations around the country faster than its work force can catch up—to say nothing of its greater ability to move operations to foreign countries, where it can take advantage of cheap labor. In doing so, it displaces not only its own American work force, but also other American laborers whose employers cannot afford to compete. These contributions to structural unemployment are enhanced by the fact that the decisions for large corporations tend to be made in the great financial centers of the country, both physically and psychologically removed from the communities where their effects are felt.

So the liberation of the poor through confronting the Industrial Revolution and its tendency toward the displacement of labor seems to call for a serious check to the further concentration of capital. Less than a century ago there was such a check built into many of our state corporation laws. There were limits on the amount of capital any one corporation could assemble and in some cases on the amount of property it could acquire. These limitations dropped out during the latter part of the nineteenth century not because of a policy decision that they were undesirable but because of competition between states for the business of supplying corporate status to entrepreneurs. The state of incorporation reaped a number of financial benefits, and other states had but little constitutional power to exclude the corporation once formed.

It is probably too late for us to revive flat limits on the amount of capital a corporation can have. But we could certainly adopt legal measures to discourage further accumulations or at least to stop actively encouraging them. We could tax large units more heavily than small ones; the constitutional objections to doing so are probably obsolete. We could require large corporations to pay out their profits in dividends rather than accumulate them for further investment. Then they would have to compete with other enterprises if they wanted new capital for expansion. We could also extend the antitrust laws to cover combinations on the basis of size, even if the combining units are not competing with each other.

For the government to exempt small units from some of its regulations, or at least to pick up part of the cost of complying, would also do a good deal to improve the position of small units vis-à-vis large ones. Costs of this kind are often only slightly less for the small unit than for the large one, and the large one has much more volume to spread them over. A filing system or a computer program to supply all the data required by various government agencies will cost an employer of a thousand people about the same as an employer of five thousand, but it will cost him five times as much per employee. Similarly, altering a large building to comply with regulations as to access for the handicapped may not cost much more than altering a small building for the same purpose. Hence, it will cost far less per square foot of floor space. These cost differences will of course be reflected in cost per unit of production, and will give the large business a heavy competitive advantage if nothing is done to offset them.

In addition to limiting capital accumulations, we could by appropriate legal measures directly encourage a more labor-intensive or a less capital-intensive pattern of production and distribution. Some laws having that effect are already on the books, adopted in the interest of safety (e.g., full train crew laws) or energy conservation (e.g., the fifty-five m.p.h. speed limit). Certainly some of these laws, whatever their ostensible purpose, were helped along by the fact that they meant more jobs.

Some of our drift toward capital-intensive patterns is attributable to the law itself. While minimum wages and compulsory fringe benefits have made it more expensive to employ labor, fast tax writeoffs and investment tax credits have made it less expensive to invest capital. Changes could easily be made in both respects. Not that the hard-won benefits of working people should be abolished as a way to expand the labor force, but subsidies could be offered for employers who keep more people working for the amount of capital they invest. Since 1976, the Internal Revenue Code has contained a tax credit for increasing one's payroll over the previous year. This credit could be expanded to cover more than the first year of the increase. Also, its effect could be enhanced by repealing the countervailing encouragements to new capital. Better still, the whole set of incentives could be reworked to depend on a favorable or an improving ratio between capital invested and persons employed.

If all else fails, it may become necessary to make someone hire people who want to work and are able to work, but who cannot get jobs. There has been talk of making the government the "employer of last resort," hiring such people and putting them to work on public projects. Programs like the WPA and the CCC worked in this way during the New Deal period. There would probably be enough work in conservation, restoring sub-standard housing, rebuilding railroads, and other such projects to maintain such a program indefinitely.

A more radical, and perhaps a better plan would be to have all the employers of the country absorb all the workers and would-be workers. Each employer could be assigned a quota based on invested capital, and could be required to accept that many people for full-time employment. Presumably, if he had to pay them, normal business considerations would lead him to find something useful for them to do. I gather that something similar is done in Japan, though not under legal compulsion. The major employers of the country collaborate informally to make sure that all workers and would-be workers are offered jobs.

It is possible that these measures for moving toward a more labor-intensive economy will tend to reduce our "standard of living." For reasons that I shall develop shortly, I believe we must take the risk; still, it is worth noting that a certain amount of the anticipated reduction will be illusory. The statistics we use to determine our standard of living and the cost-effectiveness of our various industrial processes are compiled on presuppositions that go with our existing economic system. They presuppose that labor is a cost with no benefit except what the laborer produces, that the depletion of resources costs no more than the dollars necessary to acquire them and deplete them, and that everyone in a society derives some kind of benefit when more goods and services are exchanged.

I am no statistician, but I can envisage some indicators of national prosperity that might be dramatically improved by the measures I have been proposing. On the spur of the moment, I have invented the following:

The Gross National Budget Deficiency—The amount of money that would have to be distributed to the poor in order to bring everyone in the country up to the "poverty line," that is, to the level of consumption that passes for common decency in the prevailing culture. I suspect that this figure would be larger per capita for the United States than for many other countries.

The Net National Budget Deficiency—The same figure reduced by the money that is in fact being distributed to the poor under welfare programs; the amount by which these programs fall short of bringing everyone up to the poverty line.

The Labor Displacement Index—The Gross National Product divided by the total number of persons employed full time, adjusted for inflation and compared with a base year, say, 1959. This will tell us to what extent we are enhancing or reducing the opportunities of our people to contribute to the economic achievements of our society.

In addition to these global statistics, we could do a great deal more to determine the social costs of particular operations. Many such operations would look less cost-effective under this kind of scrutiny than they do under the kind of scrutiny we now give them. There has already been discussion among cost accountants of how to account for such environmental costs as the replacement of land surfaces after strip mining. There should be similar discussion of labor displacement costs—how to take into account the wage loss to persons put out of work by a new capital investment. Here too, a more imaginative compiling of figures might indicate that the measures I have been proposing are less costly than they look.

IV. THE CLASS ENEMY

The people in our society with the most intractable stake in other people's poverty are the managerial and professional elite, who derive generous compensation, intellectual stimulation, and job satisfaction from running the high technology and complex organizations that go with a capital intensive economy. It is not clear that their skills could all be transferred to comparable positions in a labor intensive economy. Nor can we expect to have an easy time getting them to reconsider their ideological commitment to the economic system that gives them such handsome material and psychic rewards.

Still, there are signs that they are not altogether comfortable with their role as beneficiaries and ministers of our ill-distributed affluence. The phenomena referred to as radical chic and middle-class guilt are not effective political or social movements, but they bear witness to the discomfort I have in mind. They are beginning to spread beyond academic and literary circles into the main body of the elite.

Another sign, perhaps more important, is the changing conception of "corporate social responsibility." A generation or two ago, corporate managers thought of social responsibility in terms of enhancing the impact of their corporations on society. Today, they think of it in terms of mitigating that impact. Henry Ford was very much concerned with social responsibility—so much so that his minority stockholders took him to court—but what he understood by social responsibility was providing the American people with more, better, and cheaper cars. Today, corporate managers understand social responsibility in terms of protecting the environment, contributing to educational and charitable causes, maintaining honesty in advertising claims, being compassionate in debt collection, hiring and training minority workers, and in general doing as little harm as is compatible with continued solvency and a reasonable return to the investors. People whose consciences are engaged by matters of this kind may resist the shift to new forms of production, but they may well find it liberating in the end.

There is one group of managerial and professional people with an especially poignant need for liberation. These are the welfare administrators and their counterparts in the private sector. They have limited resources to distribute, and they often have to apply eligibility standards that are complicated, discretionary, or both. Their concern with helping the poor is constantly being overshadowed by their responsibility for safeguarding the interest of the wider society in the proper allocation of funds. Their terms of reference keep forcing them into an oppressive role from which neither good will nor professional ability (and many of them have both) can extricate them. The high turnover in their jobs bespeaks the enervation and frustration that they experience. It would be vastly liberating to them, as well as to the rest of society, if their dedication and training could be used in some more constructive way.

A more problematic stake in poverty is that of the mainstream work force. Our economic system pits them against the poor by making their jobs dependent on the constant expansion of the capital intensive technology that is driving unskilled or marginal workers out of their ranks. At the same time, they are the ones who bear the brunt of any mitigations of poverty that we attempt. If we try to upgrade job skills, we will jeopardize their opportunities by increasing the applicant pool. If we raise taxes to the point necessary to fund an adequate relief program, they are the ones who will have trouble paying. If we try to fund an adequate relief program without raising taxes, they are the ones whose savings will be wiped out by inflation. They are the ones who cannot meet the increased food prices if agricultural workers are to be adequately paid. Theirs are the neighborhoods that must adjust to new economic and social conditions if the poor are to be adequately housed.

They tend, therefore, to appear as enemies of the poor. They or their spokesmen are responsible for much of the self-serving politics and insensitive rhetoric that stands in the way of reform. But their real stake in the status quo may not be as great as it looks. They have less to lose from the more radical measures that I have been proposing than they do from the palliatives that they resist. For instance, while their hold on the job market is threatened by programs that create new applicants without creating new jobs, a program that created jobs faster than applicants would do them good. Similarly, all the proposals that increase welfare benefits without cutting down the number of people who receive them will necessarily place new burdens on everyone who makes enough money to pay taxes, whereas a plan that turned people from welfare recipients into taxpayers could reduce individual tax burdens and still support adequate benefits for those remaining on welfare.

It is probably true in the short run that the prosperity of the mainstream work force depends on the continued mistreatment of the poor. But in the long run, that prosperity is so precarious as to be illusory. For workers cannot hope to prosper unless the work that they are doing keeps on needing to be done. The prospect of our economy going on forever investing more capital and expending more energy to create fewer jobs is as threatening to the work force as it is discouraging to the poor. The change of direction that I have been suggesting can be as liberating to the one group as to the other.

V. THE CLAIM ON HISTORY

It may be objected that all this is a program for economic disaster. Certainly, up to now our standard of living has depended on a continuous infusion of new capital and new technology. We can have very little idea of what will happen if we turn the infusion off. Nor have I offered any plan for countering the deleterious consequences of what I propose.

I might answer that the end of the era of new technology and new capital is in sight whatever we do. We are rapidly discovering that our material resources are finite, and we are beginning to suspect

that our intellectual resources are equally so. Furthermore, even if
we were able to continue our present pattern of growth indefinitely,
we could not go on indefinitely providing for the people displaced
from the work force by the process.

But these economic forebodings, like other lines of economic
analysis, can be carried only so far. The real answer to the objection I have stated is not economic but historiographical. History,
as I tried to show in the last chapter, is ambivalent in its various
effects, and is only marginally subject to prediction or control. It
is not surprising, therefore, that under our historic free enterprise
system we have paid a price for our standard of living. By the same
token, we will have a new price to pay if we make a change. Furthermore, the question of whether to make the change and pay the price
is one that we must answer with no more than a dim notion of what
the new price will be. The choice of liberation is therefore a matter
of faith. It involves breaking out of a known bondage at an unknown
cost — the paradigm of the Exodus.

The alternative bases for decision making are cost benefit
analysis and total planning. Both are profoundly illusory. Because
history cannot be accurately predicted, neither the costs nor the
benefits of any proposed course of action can be accurately assessed.
Because history cannot be effectively controlled, no plan can be
adopted with any real confidence that events will go as planned.
It is this uncooperativeness of history, I suppose, that makes so much
cost-benefit analysis turn callous and so much planning turn tyrannical. The person who has put his trust in predicting events will
tend to close off reality when benefits he has predicted do not ma-
terialize, and costs he has not predicted do. The person who has
put his trust in controlling events will tend to strive all the more
insistently to control them as they demonstrate more and more
clearly that they are not subject to control.

This understanding of history provides the background for the
legal agenda that I am putting forward here. What I am offering
is not a set of measures whose benefits will outweigh their costs;
still less is it a plan for a new and better economic system. As I said
in the last chapter, the making and application of laws is advocacy,
not technology. The object of the measures proposed here is to claim
the liberation of the poor in our society through confronting what

seem to be at this particular moment the causes of their poverty.

This is how it has always been with great social changes. The French Revolution started as nothing more than a claim to be rid of the oppression experienced at a particular time and place. What kind of cost-benefit analysis could have helped the members of the États-Généraux in deciding whether to begin? The cotton gin started as nothing more than an easier way to get the seeds out of cotton. What kind of economic planning could have controlled the consequences of inventing it?

My point is simply that people can — must if they love justice — launch new forces in history without knowing exactly what will come of them. This is what we will be doing if we take new legal measures for the liberation of the poor. We will be voicing expectations, not controlling events. It is perhaps fanciful to speak of this enterprise as advocacy before the tribunal of history — but a good deal less fanciful than is the current talk of social engineering. In any event, it is the faith of a Christian that the tribunal of history is presided over by One before Whom the cause of the poor is not advocated in vain.

VI. THE CHURCH AND THE VISION OF JUSTICE

The church, in serving as a sign and a celebration of our hoped-for liberation from poverty, can draw on both mediative and confrontive legal forms. Through mediative forms, the corporate hope of the church can be presented to individuals in the form of truths to be believed and actions to be performed. Through confrontive forms, the forces and institutions that maintain poverty can be met with a proclamation of the judgment of God.

The central place among the mediating forms should be given to a steadfast official witness that the condition of the poor in contemporary American society is unacceptable to God. It is theoretically possible for there to be a society like that adumbrated in Gray's *Elegy in a Country Churchyard* where rich and poor have their respective and respected places, and each can be content with the state of life to which God has been pleased to call him, but the United States of America in the last quarter of the twentieth century is not that society. Here, no reconciliation between rich and poor can be founded on either of them being content with the status quo. The church's message of reconciliation must be a message of shared discontent.

With this message of discontent, the church need not—and probably should not—officially embrace any particular political or economic agenda. There is nothing wrong with the church pressing traditional concerns like the right to a family wage and the right of collective bargaining, or more recent concerns like fair housing and welfare rights. But it is more important to tell the poor as a general matter that they have a right to serious changes in the system and a right, perhaps a duty, to organize politically to bring such changes about. Most important of all is to offer the poor a clear witness to their own dignity and worth. We have seen how the self-esteem of the poor is undermined by the attitudes with which we administer the welfare system, and by our continuing insistence that our economic system offers such opportunities that no one need be poor unless there is something wrong with him. Groups like the Black Muslims have shown that religious teaching can counter these negative attitudes that we have given the poor about themselves. It seems a reproach to Christians that an esoteric version of Islam should teach a fundamental truth of the Gospel more effectively than most churches do.

The witness that the church offers to the rich, the elite, the middle class, the generality of prosperous people, should be complementary to the witness it offers to the poor. The first thing all these people must be told is that their prosperity is founded on the sufferings of the poor—that the poor are suffering vicariously on their behalf. Not only does this follow from general principles of human solidarity as Christians understand them; it follows from the specific character of our economic system, where the same technology that spells prosperity for the prosperous spells uselessness and poverty for the poor. The object of the church's witness on this point should not be to make people feel guilty about not being poor—not poor is what God wants everyone to be—but to make them understand that poverty is everyone's burden, not just a burden for the poor.

I have some trouble here with the "difference principle" advocated by Professor John Rawls. Rawls argues that inequalities in society are justified if they result in advantage to everyone, including those at the short end of the inequalities in question. In other words, if the standard of living of the poor in a capitalist economy is higher than in a socialist economy, then capitalism is justified despite the discrepancies it introduces between rich and poor. There is a certain practical wisdom in this formula, but I find it disconcertingly reminiscent of the "trickle down" theory that keeps cropping up in Republican politics. Also, it makes the prosperous in our society more comfortable than I think they ought to be. My own feeling is that when inequality is justified it is not through an increase of social amenities at the bottom, but through some kind of moral and spiritual identification running through the whole community, so that those at the bottom of the social scale can take pride in the status of those at the top, as, for instance, disciples do with a leader or fans with a star.

So if a lower standard of living for the rich in our own society will involve a lower standard of living for the poor as well, that may be a reason for going slowly in the dismantling of particular institutions, but it will not be a reason for being comfortable with things as they are. We who are prosperous in this society should believe, and the church should teach us, that incremental amenities cannot justify keeping some of our people in what our culture regards as poverty, and that we must work and pray for a better ordering of our affairs even if it is not clear what form such an ordering would take.

It follows that we do wrong if we move to defend our privileges simply because we enjoy them. For instance, there are many reasons for opposing any given program of public housing, but to oppose such a program because we are more comfortable without poor people living too near us is immoral. Similarly, there are many reasons for opposing any given welfare reform project, but to oppose such a project because we are unwilling to pay higher taxes is immoral. The distinction may not be apparent except within individual consciences; hence, it is important that the applicable principles be mediated to individual consciences through the witness of the church.

We should also be learning from the church to be sensitive to the causes of the poor when those causes come before us for support. We are frequently asked to participate in boycotts, to sign petitions, to walk on picket lines and the like. It is not our Christian duty to respond uncritically to such appeals, but the church should be teaching us to respond generously.

Finally, the official witness of the church should be encouraging a simpler lifestyle. In our society, consumerism and poverty go hand-in-hand. We keep trying to step up consumption because Keynesian economics teaches that there is no other way to keep people working; then we invest in labor-saving technologies because that is the only way to meet the increased demand. So the forces that produce a plethora of superfluous goods and services for those who can afford them are the same forces that are responsible for the condition of the poor. To be sure, if we accept Keynesian premises, frenetic consumption by the better-off members of society is the only thing that keeps the poor from being even poorer and more numerous than they are. I have already indicated that I think Christians should claim from history a better set of options than that. And I believe that the church through its official witness should be teaching them to do so.

Confrontations with power in the form of demonstrations, boycotts, and the like often take place under the leadership of particular churchpeople, although not usually under official church auspices. Neighborhood associations, welfare rights organizations, and other groups that move more or less confrontively in the jungle of organizations that grow up around the poor also have heavy clerical involvement but no official status in any church. I would like to see church law giving recognition, support, and guidance to initiatives of this kind, without taking control of them.

There is great confrontive potential in the status of many church bodies as owners of corporate stock. A stockholder has power under state and federal law to examine corporate books, call management to account, and put proposed measures before the rest of the stockholders through mailings at company expense. The SEC resisted for some time the use of these powers to press views of social justice, but the courts overruled the SEC in a case involving the manufacture of napalm by the Dow Chemical Company. Some religious orders, notably the Sisters of the Precious Blood, have used their status as stockholders to agitate for, and to some extent to gain, major concessions to social justice on the part of corporate management. Recently also, there has been developed a consortium of ecclesiastical and institutional investors to investigate issues of corporate policy and take a common stand on them. Such a consortium could potentially wield enormous power. It probably requires some kind of institutional safeguards, as other powerful agencies do.

Church agencies such as shelters and soup kitchens that directly relieve the material wants of the poor are not generally confrontive, but I suspect that they should be. They are making up for the failures of our welfare system. As long as the welfare system is in fact failing, they will have to go on making up, but they should make it clear that they are doing so under protest. If, say, the St. Vincent de Paul Society gives clothes to a family because their AFDC payments are insufficient to clothe them, it is making up out of charity for what the state has failed to do out of justice. The public stance of the Society should be clear on the point; otherwise, the alms of Christians will lead people to believe that there is no need for welfare reform.

The capstone of the church's signifying and celebrating our liberation from poverty should be the institutions of evangelical poverty, those of the religious life. Unfortunately, they have not filled that role very well. On the whole, in our society, religious enjoy a higher standard of living than do many of the middle class or any of the poor. The original significance of evangelical poverty seems to have been not so much acceptance of privation as reliance on God to furnish whatever is necessary. I would like to see a revision of the conception to reflect the actual condition of the poor in today's society. It is hard to formulate exactly what I have in mind, but somehow those who live the life of evangelical poverty should be visibly reflecting the solidarity of Christ, and of all Christians, with those who suffer want and injustice.

3

Trivialization

It is not altogether easy to pin down what it is about contemporary American life that strikes us as trivial; indeed, not all of us would hit on the same things. Some of those most often mentioned are that the quest for efficiency has eroded job satisfaction in many walks of life; that quality goods and services, or even honestly functional ones, are beyond the reach of most people; that major cultural achievements are little recognized or rewarded; that our entertainment is packaged in such a way as to appeal to our crasser tastes; that nature and natural beauty are being ravaged in the name of development; that individuality is discouraged; and that concern with many of the serious questions of life and death tends to be regarded as eccentric.

All these trivializing tendencies seem to arise more from things we have been doing right than from things we have been doing wrong. They illustrate the resourcefulness of the destructive forces in history. They seem to grow out of our commitment to a version of the good life, and to making that version available to as many as possible of our people. I will try in this chapter to show what we have understood by the good life, how it has led to trivialization, and what kind of legal dispositions may help to free us from the situation as it has developed.

I. THE GOOD LIFE

Our perception of the good life seems to be compounded of elements that were in a way characteristic of European civilization, but which our forebears, under the circumstances they encountered in that civilization, were not able to enjoy as fully or distribute as largely as they desired. These we established first by freeing the individual to pursue them up to his or her capacity, and, later, by developing legal and institutional forms to give them active support.

A. ABUNDANCE

The first of these elements is abundance, a high standard of living, a broadly distributed material prosperity. Much of our institutional creativity from the earliest days of our country has been devoted to the pursuit of this goal. Our law has always supported this abundance by supporting the capitalist technology that called it forth. One of the first measures adopted by the United States Congress after its creation was a protective tariff for the encouragement of manufacturing. Early in the nineteenth century, Mill Acts were adopted in many states to enable budding industrialists to exploit what was then our most important energy source—water power—at the expense of their riparian neighbors. Judges in the same period developed new principles of tort law to keep railroads and other new technologies from being unduly burdened by paying for personal injuries. Later in the nineteenth century, accumulations of venture capital for new industrial development were facilitated by increasingly liberal incorporation laws. In more recent times, the flow of capital into high technology has been encouraged in some industries by anti-trust legislation and in others by public utility treatment—depending on whether, in the particular industry, competition is considered good or bad for investment. In our own time, all these incentives to investment are being further supplemented with a sophisticated program of favorable tax treatment.

The infrastructure of industrial and commercial development has long been considered a responsibility of government. Turnpikes and canals, including the highly successful Erie, were built with public funds in the early days of our country. Railroads, although private, were given the power to take land by eminent domain, and, in the West, were given substantial tracts of land outright. With the coming of the automobile, we have gone back to public funding, producing more and more elaborate highways. Communications, like railroads, have benefited from public utility treatment.

Ships and airlines have been subsidized. Much of our foreign policy also has gone into maintaining the infrastructure — witness our concern with freedom of the seas in the nineteenth century, our acquisition of the Panamal Canal, and our present-day concern with sources of oil.

Government has also traditionally taken responsibility for education. The original understanding was that because every citizen in a democracy is in some sense a ruler, the government should concern itself with educating everyone in the same way that the government in a monarchy concerns itself with educating the heir to the throne. But education for citizenship has also been education for work — that is, for participation in the industrial technology on which our abundance is based.

Today our institutional commitment to abundance is so firm that the gross national product can almost be taken as an index of how well our institutions are functioning. Certainly, if we are not satisfied with the continuing flow of goods and services, we invoke the whole machinery of government and the whole process of making new laws to get the economy moving again.

B. OPPORTUNITY

Within this highly productive society, we have expected a range of individual careers to be available offering every person achievements and rewards commensurate with his (and, more recently, her) ability and application. To this end, we have adopted economic policies fostering growth no less than abundance, so that people can all go on indefinitely bettering themselves. We have also adopted patent, trademark, and copyright laws to make sure that enterprising people enjoy the fruits of their ingenuity, and antitrust laws to keep them from blocking the way for others who come after. In the past, our courts often struck down government regulations that restricted access to certain careers; they do so on occasion even today.

Our educational system is of course an elaborate public subsidy for all forms of upward mobility. It is supplemented by actual cash subsidies for entry into certain endeavors, such as small businesses, and by programs like technical training in the armed forces (note the extent to which preparation for a civilian career is used as a recruiting point).

Perhaps our most important legal initiative in support of universal opportunity is the elimination of discrimination on account of race, religion, or, more recently, sex. Legislation for this purpose made an abortive beginning after the Civil War, and a new start after the Second World War. With the recent cases applying the Civil Rights Act of 1964, we seem finally to be on the way to offering the former victims of discrimination the same opportunities that are available to everyone else.

C. FREEDOM

We have conceived of freedom in terms of participatory democracy ("no taxation without representation" "one man one vote") and the absence of restraints upon choice ("It's a free country"). The two conceptions harmonize fairly well, although there are occasions when the courts annul the result of a democratic process because it interferes unduly with choice (note the characterization of the Supreme Court's position on abortion as "pro-choice"), and even a few occasions when interference with choice is rationalized on the ground that it was democratically adopted. There are also cases where conceptions of free choice pull in more than one direction — does the law, for instance, protect the freedom of a black family to choose where to live, or does it insure the freedom of a white homeowner to choose who shall buy his house?

Our preoccupation with democracy and choice has made us tend to be insensitive to some of the things that other societies and other ideologies include in the category of freedom. Much modern economic thought would insist that people are not free if they lack the basic amenities of life — note the inclusion of "freedom from want" among the "four freedoms" for which we professed to be fighting in World War II. Traditional Catholic thought has it that people are free to the extent that they encounter no obstacles to the fulfillment of their God-given destiny. This tradition, which provides the foundation for liberation theology, embraces the concept of freedom from want, but is not limited to it.

The freedom-of-choice approach sometimes clashes with these alternative approaches rather than merely overlooking them. For instance, the freedom of an employer to choose what wages to pay his help may clash with the freedom of his employees to eat what they need. Or the freedom of a person to choose what drugs he will take may clash with his freedom to grow into the person God wants him to be. In all these clashes, we have concentrated on freedom of choice at the expense of other kinds of freedom. Furthermore, within the realm of freedom of choice, we have been much less tolerant of legal or political restraints than of circumstantial restraints. Only recently, for instance, have our courts accepted the idea that "inequality of bargaining position" may interfere with freedom of contract even more than legislation does.

In short, the freedom that constitutes one element in our American understanding of the good life is important but limited. It is involved almost exclusively with minimizing legal and political restraints on freedom of choice, and maximizing participation in the framing of such restraints as we cannot do without.

D. EQUALITY

The principle that all men are created equal has deep roots in Western and Christian thought. As we took it from our ancestors, it had two elements. One was a certain equality of ultimate worth that transcended any differences of economic or social circumstances prevailing in a particular society. The other was equality before the law—the principle that economic or social circumstances are not to interfere with the impartial application of a legal disposition to the cases it purports to cover.

American thought supplemented the tradition very early with an aspiration to equality of opportunity, that is, to a state of affairs in which everyone starting out in life has the same chance for achievement, recognition, and reward as anyone else with equal talent and industry. To establish such a state of affairs, we did away with the inherited forms of distinction that obtained in the mother country. We did not feel free to do away with inherited wealth in the same way, but we tried to spread it around by abolishing primogeniture, and we abolished estates tail and other obstacles to the owner willing it on death to whomever he chose. Thus, we established the law of inheritance as vindicating the power of the decedent over his own wealth rather than the continuity of the wealth in his family.

Allowing everyone to go as far as his abilities would take him was also among the goals of our educational enterprise. The framers of the first constitution of Indiana (1816), for instance, mandated the legislature to provide a program from township schools all the way through universities, gratis and open on equal terms to all. Later generations lowered their aspirations to the point of leaving the university level to the discretion of the legislature, but the ideal of equality was still present.

In more recent times, there has appeared alongside the goal of equality of opportunity, and in some tension with it, a concern with equality of circumstances. For instance, I have referred to the principle, pretty well established by now, that a contract may be vitiated by the "unequal bargaining position" of the parties. Where I need a job worse than anyone needs my services, or I need an apartment worse than anyone needs me as a tenant, the courts today will look very skeptically at any onerous conditions I feel compelled to accept. In 1915, on the other hand, the Supreme Court accepted this kind of inequality with entire cheerfulness:

> No doubt, wherever the right of private property exists, there must and will be inequalities of fortune; and thus it naturally happens that parties negotiating a contract are not equally unhampered by circumstances. This applies to all contracts. . . .

The court could have added that as long as there is equality of opportunity there must also be inequalities of fortune. If everyone has the same chance to achieve in accordance with his ability and industry, those who are more able and industrious than others will achieve more, and will end up having more.

Indicative of our growing concern with equality of circumstances is the generally favorable reception given Professor Rawls's doctrine, to which I referred in the last chapter. It appears to be Rawls's teaching that every inequality of circumstances is *prima facie* unjust, and can be justified only by a showing that it improves the circumstances of those less favored. What is important for present purposes is not so much the way Rawls justifies inequalities as the fact that he finds it necessary to justify them at all. He seems to reflect a widespread assumption that anyone who is better off than other people owes them some kind of explanation, and that being more talented, working harder, or having better luck is not the kind of explanation that is required.

Often, our concern with equality is manifested in the pursuit of a homogeneous lifestyle. Where one person's opportunities or circumstances differ from another's, we have no effective criterion for telling whether the case is one of "diversity," which in theory we welcome, or one of "inequality," which we reject. Only by a broad distribution of similar goods and services in every part of our society and at every economic level; only by putting ethnic traditions into forms like shamrocks and pizza that the whole population can appropriate; only by privatizing religion and other inevitable differences, can we be sure that our people are as equal as it is possible for us to make them.

II. THE TRIVIAL LIFE

In general, then, the image of the good life held out to Americans in the closing decades of the twentieth century is one of widespread material prosperity in which most people have the opportunity to participate in accordance with their ability and industry; at the same time, it is one of an extremely homogeneous but generally tolerant culture, where people are free to choose what they will believe or say, and free to choose how they will live as long as they do not claim any special privileges from their neighbors or their government. The pursuit of the good life understood in this way still retains its attractions, especially when compared to the pursuits that dominate society in other parts of the world. But we have paid and are paying a price for it in the form of a persistent trivializing tendency in our national life. It is this that we have now to examine.

A. STANDARDIZATION OF GOODS AND SERVICES

The discovery that if you make things alike you can make more of them cheaper is popularly attributed to Henry Ford. Its revolutionary effect on American life is well documented. Not only did it put America on wheels; it put America into three bedroom ranch houses with picture windows, and it glued America in front of TV sets. By now, we have become considerably dependent on this discovery and its accompanying technology: if we are to maintain the broadly distributed affluence in which we take such pride, we will have to reconcile ourselves to sharing our tastes with millions of our fellows. Whether it be in silverware, furniture, automobiles, or entertainment, idiosyncrasy has become a prerogative of the rich or the subsidized. When *Look* magazine ceased publication a few years ago, a columnist remarked on the fact that several million readers were not enough to keep such a magazine in business. The situation is often paradoxical. Those who fancy the elegance of artifacts used by the aristocracy of a bygone age can now buy mass-produced imitations at prices within the reach of all but the very poor, whereas those who fancy the clean simple lines of artifacts used by the peasants in those days must now buy them handmade at astronomical prices.

It is the same way with services. Those who go out for a cheap meal do not go to a mom and pop restaurant; they go to Col. Sanders, McDonald's or some other franchise store. The franchisor, by centralizing the administrative tasks, the more intellectually demanding decisions (what color to paint the walls, how many hamburgers to cook at a time, how much milk to put in the milkshakes, how much to charge for the pies), and the purchasing, is able to achieve the coveted "economies of scale" that support competitive pricing for the mass market.

In short, production of goods and delivery of services at broadly affordable prices requires production and delivery for the mass market, and production and delivery for the mass market requires that the goods and services be standardized. It must be added that since the human touch is always a bit idiosyncratic, the standardization seems to impart a slight touch of inhumanity, of plasticity, to everything we use. For a last example, think of one of the more elegant chain restaurants where the waiter comes up to your table with a prepared speech written by someone in the franchisor's office and memorized by the waiter during orientation week.

To insure public acceptance of these standardized goods and services, we maintain a vast and highly compensated advertising industry. There have been various theories put forth as to what effect, if any, advertising actually has on the public taste. Theorists can point to at least one product, Hershey's chocolate, that has maintained an enviable position with the public without advertising, and one product, the Edsel, that was extensively advertised without ever gaining enough public acceptance to break even. The most persuasive theory, in my opinion—that of Martin Mayer in *Madison Avenue, U.S.A.*—has it that advertising imparts a certain quantum of glamour to a product, thereby giving it an edge over another product otherwise indistinguishable from it, but not enabling it to prevail over a significantly better or cheaper product.

I suspect that another important reason why "nationally advertised brands" have more public acceptance than other brands is that only large-scale enterprises can advertise nationally, and the public believes, rightly or wrongly, that large-scale enterprises are run better and are more accountable than small-scale ones. That is, even if I do not believe that Colgate toothpaste will make me more beautiful or give me 40 percent fewer cavities than a brand I have never heard of, I probably believe it is less apt to poison me. Furthermore, if it does poison me, the manufacturer will be in a great deal of trouble with the Federal Trade Commission, and I will have a lawsuit that will set me or my heirs up for life.

In other words, we as a people have come to believe in our high-volume, high-technology, standardized culture, and our advertising is successful because it ministers to that belief. In fact, the advertiser is very apt to deliver on his somewhat antiseptic promise. Take the Holiday Inn chain, for instance, with its slogan that "the best surprise is no surprises." When you go to one of their motels, you are indeed apt to find that all the plumbing works, as does the television set, that there are no bedbugs and that they are not out of coffee. But you are not apt to find cows in the yard, chickens on the doorstep, a proprietor who brings a hot water bottle when your baby cries, a shelf full of forgotten and esoteric books, or a waitress who speaks nothing but Lithuanian and Spanish—all of which I have found in my not terribly extensive travels among non-chain inns and hotels.

B. Routinization of Tasks

To produce a high volume of standardized goods and services requires that the component tasks be standarized as well as the goods and services themselves. Furthermore, as it is easier and quicker to do the same thing over and over than to do a series of different things in a sequence (another discovery popularly attributed to Henry

Ford), we have tended to seek improved production by breaking down tasks into ever-smaller components.

As a result, a great part of our work force has been condemned to dull and repetitive work, sometimes under severe time pressures. Even when the work is not repetitive, it is apt to be dull because the creative decisions about how it is to be done have been made by someone other than the person doing it. I have referred to the waiter in the franchise restaurant with his set speech. More elaborate routines seem to be common in door-to-door and phone sales. The breakdown of mechanical operations into numbered steps and of school curricula into predetermined syllabi and lesson plans are manifestations, more or less all-encompassing, of the same process at work.

The more mindless a task is at the operational level, the more supervision those engaged in it must have if they are not to deviate from it. Thus, the routinization of tasks has played a significant part in the rapid growth of bureaucratic organizations. This is especially true in the private sector, where the process of bureaucratization has attracted less notice than it has in government, but is, in my opinion, no less pernicious.

As the process of bureaucratization goes on, middle management and lower executive jobs tend to become as dull and mindless as are those on the production line. They involve less and less the making of decisions and more and more the implementation of routines worked out by other people. My father tells a story of a large American corporation that owned a warehouse full of equipment in a city in North Africa. The roof blew off the warehouse on a weekend, and could not be replaced because the local manager had no authority to spend more than $100 on anything not represented by a line item in his budget.

C. SUPERFLUOUS CONSUMPTION

High volume technology requires a great deal of capital, and once the capital has been invested it cannot be recouped except by using it for high volume production and selling the product. Furthermore, as I pointed out in the last chapter, we are not technologically static. We continue to develop new and more capital intensive technology which will produce massive unemployment unless we support it by ever increasing levels of production. To the extent that we have no colonies and are not at war, the only thing we can do with all this production is to consume it ourselves. We have found it imperative for our national prosperity, therefore, to match our high and increasing levels of production with correspondingly high and increasing levels of consumption.

I remember a science fiction story involving a society in which economic premises like ours were found to require punishing people who failed to consume enough. In our own society, however, we have thus far found social convention plus the natural tendency of human beings to emulate one another sufficient to dispose of all our production—though we have occasionally been reminded of a patriotic duty to buy.

Aside from habit, we have three main social incentives to high consumption. The most important is probably advertising. Here again, what advertising actually accomplishes is problematical. It does seem, however, to play a significant part in informing people of how other people live. Its effect in raising the expectations of the poor has often been noted. It probably has a similar effect in telling the borderline affluent what to expect if they grow rich. It probably also establishes conventions for the recognition of social status through consumption. In general, it gives us reasons for buying things in addition to personal taste and untutored enjoyment.

A second major contributor to our high level of consumption is our system of consumer credit. We are constantly being urged to buy what we feel like and take our time about paying for it. We respond so well that the amount of consumer credit outstanding is increasing by some billions of dollars every year. This increase is just as inflationary as a corresponding increase in the amount of cash in circulation. This inflation gives further impetus to the tendency to consume more: in a time of inflation, the safest thing you can do with your money is spend it.

The third, and most controversial, of our social incentives to consumption is planned obsolescence. Not only do we make things that wear out sooner than they would have to if we used our technology to make them last longer; we design them in such a way that they are extremely hard (and expensive) to repair, and we change designs so often that after a few years they cannot be repaired at all. Personal experiences of mine in this regard, which are not unusual, include having to replace the entire steering column on my car because a bolt had sheared on the old one; being unable to get a new speaker to fit a five-year-old television set; and being unable after some hours of work to replace a simple drive belt on a washing machine.

D. QUANTIFICATION

Given our commitment to equality of opportunity, we are generally not content with the reflection that the race is not to the swift or bread to the wise or favor to men of skill, but time and chance happeneth to them all. We expect anyone with the power to bestow advantages not only to use some rational criterion in bestowing them, but also to be accountable for the manner of applying that criterion. As a result, we have fallen into the habit of quantifying measures of worth or achievement, and using them extensively in the distribution of amenities or rewards. We admit people to colleges and graduate schools on the basis of a combination of grade-point averages and scores on various multiple-choice examinations developed by a mysterious organization in Princeton, New Jersey. We distribute jobs and promotions on the basis of rather similar tests (often "batteries" of them) plus various performance records (number of accounts serviced, policies sold, employees supervised, new customers brought in, etc.) and form evaluations ("In comparison with all the junior executives you have known, would you rate the applicant () in the top 5%; () in the top 20%. . . .").

The principle extends to all walks of life. Advertising agencies evaluate media in terms of statistics like cost per thousand. Voters evaluate candidates in terms of their liberal ratings as compiled by the Americans for Democratic Action or their conservative ratings as compiled by Young Americans for Freedom. Indeed, the habit of quantifying measures of achievement has become so ingrained with us that we do it even when we have nothing in particular to bestow on account of it. We are constantly comparing football players on the basis of how many yards they gain, books on the basis of how many people buy them, businessmen on the basis of how much money they make, movies on the basis of how many nominations for Academy Awards they elicit, television programs on the basis of what percentage of a predetermined sample turn them on, countries on the basis of gross national product or per capita national income.

What could be a mere harmless eccentricity in our national character becomes dangerous when we take these quantified measures so seriously as to pursue them instead of pursuing genuine achievement. Unfortunately, a good many of us do just that. Professors all know students who spend four or even seven years picking their way through an elective curriculum to pursue a grade point average instead of an education. We all know of cases where a person will leave a job he likes in favor of a better-paying job he likes less, even though he does not need the money and most of it will go into taxes—simply because salary is the only measure of achievement operating in his culture.

The tendency of large corporations to go after the largest share of the market instead of looking for needs that they are uniquely able to fill seems to be an example of the same phenomenon, as does the tendency of our whole people to think of prosperity in terms of gross national product instead of the more intangible satisfactions that go with a free and fraternal society.

E. VENDIBILITY

The tendency of goods and services to flow in the direction of maximum financial return seems to be a product of our tendency to quantify. People either are themselves subject to that tendency, are under moral and financial pressure from others who are subject to it, or are caught up in institutional patterns based on it. Take for example a farmer who raises cabbages on land that a developer wants to use for high-rise condominiums. If he decides not to sell out to the developer, he must reckon first with his own cultural conditioning, which tells him that he is a fool not to take the developer's money, second with his friends and neighbors, who tell him the same thing, and third, in many places, with a real estate tax based on the amount the developer is willing to pay, and sometimes amounting to more than his cabbages will fetch on the market. Similarly, a television programmer who has come up with a program that twenty-five percent of the viewers want to watch is under internal pressure from his peers, and pressure from his advertisers to drop that program and go out for the other seventy-five percent of the market.

The most important victim of this tendency is the spice of life, variety. The sources of enjoyment are more varied than the sources of money, and the sources of money are more varied than the sources of more money. Thus, the desire for maximum return adds to the effect of the other sources of standardization in American life. Specifically, it keeps entrepreneurs all competing for the same 51 percent of the market, rather than spreading out to meet as many different needs as possible. If nine people out of ten wash with Soap A, and the tenth person with Soap B, it does not occur to the manufacturers of Soap B to congratulate themselves on making it possible for ten percent of the population to wash themselves in the way that they like best. Rather, the manufacturers of Soap B try to do over their product to make it more like Soap A, and thus gain some of Soap A's customers. If the project is successful, the two soaps will become indistinguishable, and the ten percent who preferred the former Soap B will no longer have a soap to their liking. This process is, I suspect, responsible for the phenomenon noted by the columnist Sydney Harris that "if it's any good, they'll stop making it." A wide variety of products are affected by the process, the most prominent being television programs.

F. EXTRUSION OF QUALITY

The pursuit of the largest possible share of the market is less a matter of eliciting enthusiasm than one of not eliciting aversion. Enthusiasm is apt to be idiosyncratic, while toleration is often fairly broad. So, when products are standardized for mass production or mass marketing they are generally more inoffensive than inspired. This situation is enhanced by our commitment to equality, which leads us to resent products that it takes more than common sensitivity or erudition to appreciate.

The result is a kind of cultural Gresham's Law. Trivial or sentimental art tends to drive more astringent art off the mass market— witness the unequal competition between Walt Disney's and Ernest Shepard's versions of Winnie-the-Pooh. Similarly, bad imitations of highly decorated styles—baroque, Victorian, and the like—tend to drive simple craftsmanship off the mass market. Try to buy a plain, well-made cylindrical coffee cup without a perfunctory floral pattern or something worse painted on it: it can be done, but it is not easy, and it will probably cost you some extra money.

This tendency is nowhere more perniciously at work than in our educational system. Here, everything seems to militate in the same direction. Because we are committed to equality, we are reluctant to mount an elitist program of education: whatever we teach anyone we try to teach everyone. Because we are committed to freedom, we try to teach people what they want to learn. Because our resources are limited, we tend to limit our offerings to those that have many takers, so we end up teaching people what large numbers of other people want to learn. But what people want to learn is drastically affected by what they already know. Hence our educational enterprise perpetuates the lowest-common-denominator character of the rest of our culture, and quality education tends to be available only in a few schools catering mostly to the very rich.

G. EXTRUSION OF RELIGION

Religious freedom is an essential element in our conception of freedom, and religious equality is nearly as essential an element in our conception of equality. We have therefore interpreted our national commitment to freedom and equality as requiring extreme caution, not to say timidity, in matters of religion. Public measures, whether practical (support for church-related schools) or symbolic (Christmas cribs on the steps of city halls) are apt to be protested if they favor one religious group over another, or even appeal to one religious group more forcefully than to another.

It follows that the way to keep out of trouble is to avoid bringing up any matters on which religious groups in our society disagree. This means that questions like why we are in the world, whether there is a God, and, if so, how we can commend ourselves to Him, what we owe other people, and whether there is any point to going on living are systematically excluded from any examination in our national life. The exclusion is most vigorous and advertent in the public schools, but it spreads out from there into every aspect of our public affairs. Indeed, even the attempt to introduce moral principles into the national life is resented if those making the attempt seem to find any support for their moral principles in their religion. This whole situation is characterized by many people as an establishment of secular humanism. I am not sure it is that, but it is certainly an establishment of triviality.

III. A PROGRESS REPORT—SUCH AS IT IS

These patterns of trivialization are widely perceived, but little has been done about them because they seem inseparable from the conception of the good life as I have been describing it. Our various manifestations of national malaise have made a few incidental inroads, but the patterns are in general as solidly rooted as ever. We seem on the whole resigned to their remaining so.

In the first place, standardization, routinization, and superfluous consumption seem essential to the economic growth on which we depend for the widely distributed abundance and opportunity that belong to our vision of the good life. We have made only the most tenuous steps away from any of them. Experiments have been undertaken in a few places to see if production units can be redefined for greater job satisfaction without destroying high-volume production (it appears that they can). In some places the high-volume technology itself has been curtailed for environmental reasons. The antitrust laws have been interpreted to require some decentralization of dealerships, thus allowing for some creativity at the distribution level. Also, some small businesses with creative opportunities have been developed for repairing and servicing the products of mass production. These, however, are being eroded by the tendency of mass production to come up with larger and larger components, which cannot be broken into except at the factory.

Quantification, aside from being deeply rooted in our culture, has often seemed to us to be the only sure way to avoid arbitrary decisions. If we can point to a set of objective measurements on which A scores higher than B, we can show that we are not favoring A over B because of race, religion, or sex, or as a retaliation for an exercise of constitutional rights, or for some other capricious or impermissible reason. To some extent, this confidence in numbers is being undermined by a series of civil rights cases in which it has been shown that the numerical measures are themselves sources of racial or other bias. How we will cope with this discovery has yet to be determined.

While we have begun subsidizing a few businesses that are not self supporting, such as mass transportation and public broadcasting, we continue to feel as a general matter that both progress (i.e., continuing abundance and opportunity) and freedom (giving people what they want instead of what other people think they want) require vendibility. Indeed, we sometimes impose vendibility in the name of progress even at the expense of freedom — witness the broad range of projects to which we accord the right of eminent domain.

On the other hand, we have taken some steps to eliminate taxes that impose vendibility. Forty some-odd states make some provision for taxing agricultural land at what it is worth for agricultural purposes rather than at what developers or speculators are willing to pay for it. Since 1976, the federal estate tax laws have made similar provision. A few states extend the same relief to forest land, wildlife preserves, or even land used for recreational purposes (a provision that seems to do more good for the owners of golf courses than for anyone else). These provisions, while useful, are not as broad as the problem. Some of them have limited eligibility, some require long-term commitments that few farmers are willing to make, and some do not apply to land that the zoning authorities would like to see developed. Nor would any of them protect a residential neighborhood against taxation based on its value as a place to put office buildings.

We set a few additional limits to the vendibility of land through restrictive zoning. These limits, such as they are, tend to be eroded through a political partiality to variances. They also have against them that they are often used to keep poor people out of rich neighborhoods, and the courts are sometimes skeptical about them for that reason.

The lowest common denominator approach that I have characterized as an extrusion of quality seems to be perceived as the best alternative to quantification in the preservation of equality. For instance, in the realm of education, our national debate focuses around the options of having special classes for children with high I.Q.'s, making the best education available to the children of the richest parents (a particularly obnoxious form of quantification), and giving all children the same education — necessarily one that the least apt among them will be able to absorb. The options in television programming and book publishing tend to be seen in a similar way.

To be sure, some of the more obvious ethnic and religious minorities have found legal support for distinctive cultural elements that are neither quantifiable nor common. The Supreme Court has held that people are entitled to maintain their own schools if they can afford them, or even to forego schooling if that is what their religion teaches them. If they speak a language other than English, they have a right to schooling in that language, and at least some right to have that schooling at public expense. They are also entitled under our anti-discrimination laws to "reasonable accommodation" for their religious practices. But these concessions do nothing for the rest of us, whose unique qualities and concerns do not fall into line with well-defined religious or ethnic subcultures.

Religion is of course the special domain of the lowest common denominator approach at its most banal. We have still found no way to institutionalize the respect that people of serious and divergent religious commitments ought to (and often do) feel for one another. So, year after year, when the time comes for celebrating the birth of Christ, the triumphs of the Maccabees and the winter solstice, our schools, our parks, our courthouse steps, and our mercantile establishments continue to offer us no common ground except Rudolph the Red Nose Reindeer.

IV. A LEGAL AGENDA

The aspiration to the good life as I have been describing it and the legal dispositions supporting that aspiration constitute an example of a set of claims on history, with laws being used to articulate the claims and to mediate history's response. The ensuing historical development has evinced the ambivalence of all history, but I think we will have to say that it has brought us on the whole more good than ill. The evils I have been pointing out here seem not so much inherent in our historical pursuit of the good life as responsive to that pursuit having run its course. Abundance, opportunity, freedom, and equality are no less attractive goals than they were when our country was founded. But the expedients we adopted at the time have brought us as near to these goals as they are able to bring us. They will turn destructive unless we adopt new expedients or new goals.

So a legal agenda to deal with problems of trivialization is more a matter of claiming and mediating new historical turns than one of confronting either history or power. There are some residual confrontations to be sought, mainly with the force of ongoing technology, which is less baneful in this context than in the context of the previous chapter, but is still in need of a check, and with the power of people committed to ideologies which have been or should have been discredited by experience.

A. LIBERATING THE LAND

Our present approach to land, the one mediated in our laws on the subject, can be called one of controlled development. Without challenging the basic assumption that the community is to "grow" and land is to be "developed," the laws aim at seeing that growth and development take place in such a way as to preserve and distribute amenities as well as possible. Our typical zoning law is set in motion through the adoption of a "development plan." We try to build highways, airports, and even parking lots as fast as anyone wants them, acquiring the necessary land by eminent domain, and exercising control not in terms of whether we need them, but only in terms of whether we can afford them and where to put them so they will do as little harm as possible.

In the same way, we build electric power plants and the like to meet new "demand"—which may or may not correspond to need. The builder may have to get a "certificate of convenience and necessity" from a regulatory agency, but the certificate will be issued if the demand is shown and there is no better way to meet it. The possibility of not meeting it at all is not considered.

Our environmental law is based on the same assumption of controlled development. Its main requirement is that "environmental impact statements" be prepared on various projects so that the pros and cons of different projects and their alternatives can be weighed with regard to their effect on the environment. But it does not undertake to label any particular quantum of environmental damage as unacceptable. As a general matter, environmental considerations do not kill a project (except through the cost and delay of preparing statements) unless some environmentally superior alternative can be found.

Individuals who do not choose to subject their land to the prevailing pattern of development can be brought into line by eminent domain in many cases. Even where eminent domain does not apply, there is the property tax. If land is taxed at a market value based on what it is worth to a developer, it may become prohibitively expensive to leave it undeveloped. As we have seen, the measures for protecting landowners from this kind of pressure are far from complete.

What I would like to see the law mediating instead of development is humane use. That is, the uses most conducive to human satisfaction should be encouraged over other uses, and people who enjoy their land should be favored over people who want to make money from it.

The simplest reform along these lines would be a change in the tax laws so that all land rather than only certain farms or forests would be valued for tax purposes at what it would be worth if restricted to its present use, or at what income it presently produces, rather than at what a developer is willing to pay for it. This would reduce the financial pressure on the owner of a stand of woods to break it into house lots, or on the owner of a house to give it up for a shopping center.

A more radical measure to reduce the financial incentive to development would be the nationalization of development rights as such. Britain's first Labor government after the Second World War adopted such a measure, but it was repealed by the ensuing Conservative government before it could be fully implemented. It has since passed in and out of the statute books with the varying fortunes of the Labor Party. The theory behind it is that a landowner has done nothing to bring about patterns of settlement that make his land valuable for development, so he should not reap a windfall profit from developing it. My own interest is somewhat different. I would like to see considerations other than monetary determining what people do with their land.

In some cases, it might be desirable to go further and subsidize uses that are thought to be especially conducive to personal satisfaction. Family farms are the prime example: they need help if they

are to compete with more efficient and less humane ways of growing crops. Home ownership and perhaps some forms of recreational
use might also be effectively subsidized.

Supporting the humane use of land is an interest of the community as well as of the owner. Everyone's land is part of everyone
else's surroundings—Constable did not paint pictures of his own
property. Much of our contact with beauty and our contact with
nature depends on how other people use their land. So to mediate
a principle of humane use, we must not only relieve pressures on
those who choose to use their land humanely; we must impose limits
on those who choose to do otherwise.

One simple and direct device for doing this is the purchase of
"conservation easements." An easement is a right of one person in
another person's land, and a conservation easement is the right of
a neighbor or of the whole community to have someone's land con-
served in its present use or otherwise not developed. Such easements
have been proposed in the literature for some time, although they
are not yet in use on any substantial scale. There would seem to
be no obstacle to the creation and purchase of such easements if
a landowner is willing to sell. The use of eminent domain might
require legislation in some states. In any event, the community interest in preserving the ambiance would support both the enactment of any necessary legislation and the spending of any necessary
public funds.

Of course, the primary vehicle for implementing community
interests in land use is the zoning laws. What needs to be done with
these laws is to shift their emphasis away from controlled development in the direction of no development at all. That is not to say that
there should never be any development, but that non-development
should be one of the options under consideration, and under some
circumstances should prevail. Green belts and historic districts are
examples of areas which the law protects fairly stringently against
new development; both, especially the former, should be extended.

Similarly, some restraints on environmental damage should be
made absolute. We do not have and are not likely to acquire the
self-discipline necessary to give proper scope to environmental considerations in the cost-benefit analysis contemplated by our present
environmental impact statement practice. This is especially the case

when the alternative to preserving the environment is developing new sources of energy.

In addition to laws, which we already have in some places, setting absolute limits to pollution of air and water, we need effective strip mining legislation which will establish that there are some lengths to which we will not go in tearing up our landscape to extract minerals from it. We also need to change our policy with respect to certificates of convenience and necessity in public utility regulation to recognize that some new facilities will be neither convenient nor necessary even if we would like to have more of whatever form of power or transportation they provide.

B. LIBERATING THE WORKER

As we saw in the last chapter, the laws that we have for the benefit of working people are generally concerned with wages, hours, working conditions and security. That is, they mediate the traditional value of abundance, with its ancillaries in the way of security and comfort. We have seen that this mediation is still badly needed. The new mediation I am proposing here, one based on job satisfaction, is a complement, not a substitute. I include under the head of job satisfaction the sense that one's facilities are creatively engaged in one's work, the opportunity to develop further skills, an identifiable and useful work product or other result in which the worker can take pride — in short, all the things that are negated by the standardization and routinization of work.

In the familiar mass-production environment, the first order of legal reform would be an extension of occupational health and safety laws to cover enervating conditions of employment and an extension of workmen's compensation laws to cover psychic damage resulting from such conditions. They would not have to be extended terribly far. Regulations under the federal Occupational Safety and Health Act (OSHA) already cover in tedious detail many aspects of many industrial processes. These regulations have been heavily criticized, but more for their scope and their manner of enforcement than for their basic format. There seems to be no reason why the format should not be maintained and put to further use in limiting the breakdown of industrial tasks into mindless components.

As for workmen's compensation, many states are already awarding compensation for mental breakdown due to extraordinarily stressful work situations. It would not be a terribly innovative step to go on and compensate people who are gradually worn down by the ordinary stresses of their jobs, just as coal miners are compensated for the gradual onset of black lung disease.

It does not seem to be customary for unions to include job satisfaction among their negotiating objectives. My impression is that vendibility is so entrenched in our national life that working people will put up with almost anything as long as it is adequately compensated and does not unduly impair either safety or job security. If they were to begin pursuing less material goals, they might not get much support from the law. Such goals would intrude heavily on what have been considered management prerogatives, and might well not be regarded as mandatory subjects of collective bargaining under the Taft-Hartley Act. Management might be within its rights in refusing to talk about such matters. Worse, a union might be in breach of its statutory obligation to bargain if it pressed such a matter to the point of rupture when other matters had been settled. The law on this point should be either reinterpreted or amended.

Outside the mass production process, what is needed from the law is more support for the smaller enterprises in which the individual worker is more apt to function as a human being, or less apt to feel like a cog in a machine. I mentioned in the last chapter the possibility of modifying government regulations so it would be less costly for small businesses to comply. Perhaps this kind of support could be supplemented with direct subsidies in some cases.

Particularly in need of direct subsidies are the craftsmen who have begun trying to compete with mass production in such businesses as ceramics and woodworking. With a program of modest subsidies, or even tax deductions, it should be possible to offer people a wide range of handmade artifacts at reasonable prices, and to keep more and more people creatively occupied making them.

Finally, laws could be made to keep manufacturers from adopting technologies that wipe out the service occupations. Manufacturers could be required to keep spare parts on hand for a certain number of years, and required to build units capable of being broken down in a shop. These requirements might make units more expensive, but they would last longer and be less wasteful of irreplaceable resources.

C. LIBERATING THE CONSUMER

What our laws presently aim at mediating to the consumer is an abundance of risk-free and affordable goods and services. The antitrust laws and the laws governing public utility rates are calculated to prevent the formation of monopolies capable of limiting supply or raising prices, and to prevent inherent monopolies from taking advantage of their position to charge unconscionable prices. Laws governing advertising, consumer credit, door to door sales and the like are calculated to keep people from being defrauded or financially overreached. Other laws aim at keeping harmful or dangerous products off the market, or at making the manufacturers and distributors of such products pay compensation for the damage they do.

The abundance supported by these measures involves no particular quality beyond reasonable acceptability. Nor does it involve great variety or responsiveness to any but the most widely distributed tastes. For consumers, a liberating mediation would support quality, choice, and responsiveness to particular needs and desires. Most of the legal measures for such a mediation have already been mentioned in other contexts. A reduction of the scale of production and an increase of local control over all forms of business would be as conducive to greater variety in the things produced as it would be to more and more interesting work. Measures to support individual craftsmen and measures to discourage planned obsolescence and non-repairable units would enhance the quality of products as much as they would the quality of work.

It would be desirable, but perhaps impracticable, to aim for a more drastic alteration of the psychic rewards of industry. It is not strictly true that the mainspring of capitalism as we experience it today is the desire to maximize profit. While no one in business wants to go broke, most business executives, once the economic survival of their enterprise is assured, are more interested in expanding its contribution to the national abundance than they are in making more money. Even when they do profess an inordinate concern

with profit, they are apt to do so in response to what they suppose
to be a moral imperative (we are not free to be charitable with other
people's investments) than out of simple greed. The point is that
business executives, like anyone else, are apt to take pride in performing well whatever it is that they have been taught to regard
as their function. It would seem to follow that if they were praised
for turning out quality as they are now praised for turning out quan-
tity, quality is what they would turn out. The change might be liberating to designers and engineers as well as to consumers.

D. LIBERATING THE CULTURE

The law's approach to our culture has generally been one of
mediating our aspiration to homogeneity—*e pluribus unum*. This
has meant first of all support for a unitary system of public schools,
coupled with an interpretation of constitutional church-state doctrines to exclude any support for the most usual alternative schools.
Our courts and to some extent our legislatures accept the interpretation of our history that sees the public schools as the primary vehicle for acculturating immigrant populations, and the ideology that
sees other schools as divisive.

Similarly, when the law comes to deal with the education of
ethnic and linguistic minorities, its approach is to break down the
distinctions as far as possible. School district boundaries are altered
and pupils reassigned for the purpose of breaking up concentra-
tions of blacks and achieving racial "balance." Now that it is considered unconstitutional to ignore or suppress the use by Hispanics
of their native language in school, attempts are being made to establish bilingual programs for everyone. The general principle is that
the educational system supported by the law should be exerting itself
to make our citizens alike.

Our laws governing the media also make their contribution
to the homogeneity of our culture. In the first place, the First Amendment makes us charier than we should be of interfering with the
way the media are organized. Hence, their pursuit of the mass market continues relatively unchecked. Such regulation as we do undertake tends also on balance to favor homogeneity. While the Federal
Communications Commission imposes a certain amount of local
programming that would otherwise be displaced by network shows,

its doctrine of fairness tends to exclude controversial programming from the airwaves, and with it much that would be interesting or unusual.

What our laws ought to be mediating to our culture is quality and pluralism. What this would mean in the schools is support for a variety of programs. Where students share a common tradition, their education should include an exploration of that tradition in its uniqueness. Where several traditions are represented, each student should be encouraged to develop what is uniquely his or her own, while approaching other traditions with interest and respect. Private schools should be subsidized to the extent necessary to meet the needs of particular groups. Nor should we be afraid of neighborhood schools, even if they sometimes suffer from racial imbalance. If all of the races and cultures that have entered into our heritage are precious to us, we will not have to feel that a concentration of one of them in a school is an unqualified disaster.

In the media, there would seem to be a need for public support for programs and projects that appeal to particular groups. Most specialized interests are able to publish magazines and books, but few are able to broadcast. Most broadcast time today is either bought and paid for or distributed according to someone's opinion of what will appeal to the mass market. In addition, a certain amount of material appealing to a more highly educated element in the mainstream of the population finds its way onto the public channels. But material of really limited interest is discouraged by the pressures of the market, by the fairness doctrine, and by the general ethos of federal regulation that all broadcasters should serve all the public. Religious broadcasts, despite (or perhaps because of) the devotion of their followers, have come under particular attack under this principle that all broadcasters should serve everyone. Perhaps the solution would be a law requiring a station to make time available for any program petitioned for by a sufficient number of residents of the broadcasting area.

V. RETHINKING THE IDEOLOGIES

This, as I have said, is not a confrontive agenda. It is aimed at mediating new goals in about the way our present goals have been mediated in the past. But it may require some confrontation in the realm of ideology. If we continue to understand abundance, opportunity, freedom, and equality in the same way we have done in the past, we will naturally implement them in the same way and achieve the same results. To achieve a new and liberating understanding of these traditional values, we may have to meet a few cherished principles head on.

A. ABUNDANCE AND OPPORTUNITY

Thanks to Keynesian economics, we have conceived our pursuit of abundance and opportunity in terms of the continuing development and distribution of new goods and services. I have tried to show in the previous chapter some of the reasons why this does not work very well now, and will not work at all in the future. If we keep up a geometrical expansion of production and consumption, we will eventually reach the limits of our resources, our ability to consume, or both.

To understand abundance and oppportunity in a less wasteful fashion, we must see what human goals they really serve. Take abundance first. It is hard to see how a Christian can suppose that any truly human purpose is served by the indefinite accumulation of consumer goods. To grow and prosper as loving beings and children of God, people need enough to eat, clothes, a roof over their heads, a modicum of leisure, and a modicum of space. If they need anything more, it is because their culture makes it necessary. In other words, beyond the basics, human needs are culturally determined.

Expanding what is available tends to expand what is desired, and ultimately what is needed. In the process, what happens to the capacity of goods and services to show love, bestow honor, and afford comfort is what happens to money when there is inflation. It takes more and more to fulfill the same human purpose. Consequently, an examination of our society in terms of real human purposes may be expected to show that much of our vaunted abundance is illusory, and that it would cost us nothing of real value if we were to aim at making broadly available a selection of quality goods and services rather than at force feeding the economy with more and more standardized goods and services of dubious quality. The culture that has been gradually schooled to expect the one could eventually learn to demand the other.

As for opportunity, the human purpose behind this aspiration is surely not so much that ability and industry be more munificently rewarded as that faculties be creatively engaged in serving the community. It is serving this purpose that constitutes the real moral basis of the free enterprise system: people can, without resort to any higher authority, support themselves by discerning and meeting their neighbors' needs.

Opportunity as thus understood is diminished when the scale of economic enterprises is increased: a system in which most enterprises require accumulations of capital beyond most people's reach may be called capitalistic, but it cannot properly be called free enterprise. Measures to reduce scale will enhance opportunity by making it possible for more people to embark on new enterprises or continue old ones.

In short, if we can come to look at abundance and opportunity as human values instead of quantified fetishes, we will find them enhanced, not diminished, by the measures proposed in this and the previous chapter for limiting the scale of our production and delivery of goods and services.

B. FREEDOM

As regards the ideology of freedom, the chief villain in my view is John Stuart Mill, to whom is generally attributed the absolutizing of freedom of choice. It is his formula that everyone should be allowed to do exactly as he pleases, subject only to the limitations imposed by allowing a like freedom for others. The formula has become vastly popular in recent years, and has given rise to such illusory concepts as the victimless crime and the consenting adult.

The point is that Mill, thanks to a highly transitory conjunction of historical circumstances, was able to think and write in a social vacuum. Shielded by extravagant economic privilege against any social forces that had not been effectively internalized in the course of a rigorous education, the upper middle class Englishman of the mid-nineteenth century could really suppose that all his decisions were rational and independent, and, worse, that everyone else's were equally so.

The major manifestation of Mill's doctrine in his own time was laissez-faire capitalism. It was the Millian conception of liberty that supported the inalienable right of the British or American worker to accept starvation wages or to sign a yellow dog contract. It is odd that a resurgence of the doctrine today should coincide with the definitive repudiation of its principal application. Somehow the perception that choices about wages, hours, and working conditions are not made in perfect freedom under modern industrial conditions has not been carried over to other situations.

In fact, the relation between choice and social context is all but universal. The consenting adult who chooses a personal lifestyle without regard to society is as rare as the free worker who chooses a job in the same way. Our situation in society and the attitudes society presents to us are constantly influencing both our options and the way we exercise them. Most people need support from society if they are to lead virtuous lives. Hence the current apotheosis of Mill tends to erode private virtue throughout our society by cutting away its social support.

If the concept of freedom is to be truly liberating, it cannot be as abstract as Mill makes it. It must be understood with respect to at least a hope as to what people will do with it. God made people not to be consenting adults but to grow in love and knowledge. Freedom is important not because it is nobody else's business what people do, but because people need to be free if they are to grow in love and knowledge as God intends them to. If we keep this in mind, we will recognize that a commitment to freedom does not require us to maintain our legal and social institutions in a posture of strict neutrality as to all the significant choices with which a human being is faced. Freedom rightly understood is derivative from the respect that human beings owe one another. It cannot be carried to the point that human beings are bereft of respect. It should present no obstacle to the measures proposed here for reversing the trivialization of our national life.

C. EQUALITY

I think that most of our problem with equality comes from the failure, alluded to earlier in this chapter, to distinguish between inequality and diversity. I suspect that failure of being a reaction against certain aspects of medieval thought. Medieval philosophers and theologians accepted a kind of hierarchy of being whereby if two things were different one of them had to be in some way nobler or more perfect than the other. In taking this view, they were not consciously seeking to justify the hierarchical society in which they lived; they were trying to discern the underlying order of creation. But they gave powerful support to opinions concerning the superiority of whites over blacks, aristocrats over peasants, priests over laymen, and men over women. In our time, they give corresponding scandal to those who are concerned with the emancipation of blacks, peasants, the laity, or women.

However, much of the thrust toward emancipation has taken the form of an attack on differences as such, rather than on the metaphysics by which those differences are turned into degrees of perfection or evidences of inferiority. The results of this attack we have seen at various points in this chapter—the smoothing away of ethnic or religious subcultures, the spread of uniform ignorance in lieu of education, the pervasive quantification and vendibility of life, the standardization of goods and services, and the extrusion of religion.

Since differences between people are so intractable, and the results of trying to do away with them so baneful, it would seem that we should take another look at the metaphysical approach that turns all differences into inequalities. On examination, it appears pretty vulnerable. Both modern philosophy (or a Christian reflection on it) and Pauline theology suggest that perfection for each person or thing is a matter of being what God intended that person or thing to be—so that if things are living up to their own particular ends or people to their own particular vocations, there is no basis for saying that one is nobler or more perfect than another.

Against this background, we can assert that equality, like freedom, is not a goal in its own right, but is derivative from respect. Human beings, whoever, wherever, whatever they are, are equally precious to God and equally worthy of respect from other human beings. This respect on particular occasions may best be manifested in equality of opportunity, equality of circumstances, or equal distribution of particular social amenities. But the only thing that is always and everywhere required for a Christian and a liberating pursuit of equality is that we be committed with equal passion to affording every person in his or her existential situation whatever is necessary for that person to become what God intends. Equality understood in this way should be enhanced by the measures proposed here.

D. RELIGION

The points that have just been made about freedom and equality need to be made with special emphasis as they apply to religious institutions and commitments in our national life. The prevailing interpretations are nowhere more ingrained or more harmful than they are here, and nowhere more deeply imbedded in our constitutional and legal doctrine. It is current judicial doctrine that public measures which favor one religion over another or all religions over none are unconstitutional under the non-establishment clause of the First Amendment, and that measures which tend to make followers of a particular religion or of no religion feel uncomfortable are unconstitutional because of their "chilling effect" on the "free exercise" guaranteed by another clause of that amendment.

It has even been argued, successfully in some cases, that the things we do to make our national life tolerable to minority religious groups—giving preference to Seventh-Day Adventists in allocating Saturdays off, exempting Jehovah's Witnesses from jury duty, exempting various fundamentalist groups from joining unions (sharing the yoke with unbelievers)—are unconstitutional as establishments of religion. Further, some civil liberties groups seem to have embraced a principle that any moral agenda whose adherents are religiously motivated is ipso facto excluded from having legal effect.

Other manifestations of the same thinking seem to be trying to drive religion into the closet. The same court system that holds that a state educational institution cannot refuse to grant a gay rights organization the same benefits it grants to other student organizations, holds rather more than half the time that it may or perhaps must withold such benefits from a religious organization.

Whatever all this is, it is obviously not respect. Not only does it tend to trivialize our national life in ways I have been pointing out, it tends also to demean every citizen who takes religious questions seriously. It is hard to see as a pursuit of freedom measures that inhibit anyone seeking to live out his deepest commitments in our midst, or to see as a pursuit of equality measures that selectively drive religiously committed people to the margins of society. If freedom and equality are to be related to respect, as I have been suggesting that they are, we will have to find new ways of applying them to our religious situation.

The new ways are not hard to find; I have proposed a number of them in this chapter and one or two in the previous chapter. They have in common that they take as their starting point respect for real people in their existential situations. From this starting point, the normal relation between religious groups, which society should aim at and which the law should support, would not be mutual embarrassment or suppression of differences; it would be dialogue. And the educational and charitable activities, even the celebrations, of different religious groups would be equally supported by the community and the law, instead of being equally ignored.

VI. THE CHURCH AND THE VISION OF FULFILLMENT

It will be hard to make of the church a sign and celebration of freedom from the trivializing forces in our national life, because the forces are so pervasive and the church is so much subject to them. As Tocqueville put it:

> All American clergy know and respect the intellectual supremacy exercised by the majority; they never sustain any but necessary conflicts with it. They . . . readily adopt the general opinions of their country and their age; and they allow themselves to be borne away without opposition in the current of feeling by which everything around them is carried along.

Still, the "necessary conflicts" excepted by Tocqueville from his gloomy analysis (gloomier to us perhaps than it was to him) have left room for some sections of the clergy to play a creditable part in some of the controversies of the past. These offer a few helpful analogies. We might, for instance, hope for the Catholic hierarchy to support the humanization of job structures and land use as authoritatively as they once supported collective bargaining and the just wage. We might hope to see trivial affluence and the lifestyle based on it denounced from the pulpit as effectively as race discrimination, drunkenness, and pornography were once denounced. We might hope that initiatives like the Catholic Action programs of a generation ago could be developed to foster cooperatives and other ways of bypassing our standardized system of production and distribution.

Along somewhat different lines, it might be possible for the church to resume in some measure the cultural leadership it had in earlier ages. There was a time when the Bible and the liturgy constituted the standard for English prose, and the best art, music, and architecture that society had to offer were enlisted in the service of the church. I can sympathize with the modern view that the church has to take people the way it finds them, and cannot articulate its message in forms that are over their heads. Still, it can be questioned whether a total acceptance of the prevailing tackiness is an effective witness to what God means human beings to become. The church need not attempt to elevate the public taste by imposing esoteric or even especially elegant material on its congregations, but a firm commitment to honest craftsmanship and straightforward expression would do a great deal to lead our culture in the right direction.

Here as in the previous chapter, it is appropriate to end with a plea for restructuring the religious life. One of the functions of religious communities in the church has always been the structuring of a sign of contradiction, a witness against the prevailing vices of the time and place in which the community is set up. Part of the witness they should be providing in our society today is against the consumerism in which so many of the rest of us are trapped.

It is unfortunate, therefore, that religious tend to look more affluent than laypeople—indeed, more affluent than they themselves really are. This is because they have reasonable sums spent on their food, shelter and clothing, and have no responsibilities requiring them to divert either time or money to other purposes. They lack many things that others enjoy, but they usually lack them privately. They seem never to have the slightly scruffy look that parents and other family people occasionally have. It would seem that to bear an effective witness in favor of simplicity and against consumerism, religious should be subject to some kinds of sumptuary rules that would affect their public stance as well as their private condition. I recall once on a road outside Oxford picking up a man in a Franciscan habit who was hitchhiking. He turned out to be an Anglican friar pursuing the usual way for members of his order to get from one place to another. It may be a rather flamboyant way to save only a little bit of money, but I was edified by it.

Religious might also go back to doing their own farming and

their own crafts. Here at Notre Dame, some of the best buildings were built by Holy Cross brothers, using their own bricks. Other brothers fed most of the University at one time with the food they grew on their farms. In other places run by religious, one can be shown the furniture that the religious made in the early days, or the ovens where they used to bake their own bread. With the growth of affluence and specialization, more and more of the goods religious used to make are being bought on the market and more and more of the work they used to do is being hired out.

To be sure, a revival of the tradition of religious doing their own work should not be undertaken without a careful look at the class distinctions that existed within the religious life when the tradition was at its height. Many brothers and sisters have achieved real holiness through service as hewers of wood and drawers of water to the priests, the contemplatives, and the educators in the religious life, but it seems likely that this generosity at the bottom has contributed to a good deal of *embourgeoisement* at the top. What is really needed at the moment, I believe, is for the priests, the educators, and the contemplatives to hew some of their own wood and draw some of their own water. This is being done in some places, and has enhanced the reputation of the religious involved without seriously impairing the leisure they need for intellectual and spiritual achievement. I recall the admiration with which someone described visiting a certain Jesuit house and finding one of Europe's foremost theologians repairing the plumbing.

4

Powerlessness

I. THE PROBLEM

People feel powerless when the interventions of others in their affairs impinge on them in such a way as to belie their adulthood. It is hard to bring under a single formula the different kinds of intervention that have given rise to this feeling in different times and places. It appears that the exercise, even the meticulous exercise, of authority is never enough by itself. It is always a matter of authority coupled with insensitivity, stupidity, capriciousness, or self-dealing, and usually an ironclad intransigence as well.

In the past, this kind of authority has been exercised most often by landlords and employers, although schoolteachers, social workers, and policemen have also been involved. In any event, the form of powerlessness resulting can be characterized as feudal or dependent. There is a particular person on whom you are dependent for your livelihood, your shelter, your physical security, your freedom, or whatever, and if that person chooses to be insensitive, stupid, capricious, or self-dealing in granting or withholding what you need, there is nothing you can do about it, because law and society offer no effective way of restraining such a person or calling him to account.

The literature of the nineteenth and early twentieth centuries abounds in examples of this feudal or dependent powerlessness— the suspect who gets worked over by the police; the factory worker twisting his cap while his employer lectures him on the virtues of thrift; the family thrown out on the street for complaining about the heat in their tenement; the migrant workers milling about the gates of a farm where some few of them may be hired to pick grapes; the salesgirl fired for resisting her supervisor's advances; the schoolboy caned for wetting his bed. The quintessential example, to my mind—its very triviality seems to enhance its outrage—is the one Orwell gives of a village cricket match where the players are tenants of the local squire. When the umpire calls the batsman out, the squire rebukes the umpire and sends the batsman back to his wicket. The game continues as if the umpire had never made the call.

Most of the victims of this kind of powerlessness are poor, and some of the measures mentioned in chapter two have brought about considerable improvement. In particular, we have looked at the growing body of legal protection against arbitrary or vindictive treatment on the part of landlords or employers. Other legal developments have given much better redress against teachers and policemen. Since the Agricultural Holdings Act of 1948, the English village cricketer need no longer show unseemly deference to the squire.

It would be rash to say that these mitigations have made feudal powerlessness a thing of the past in our society. Still, they have taken a good deal of the edge off it. I cannot see that we need any new legal initiatives, beyond those suggested in chapter two, to deal with such manifestations of it as remain. The form of powerlessness that is now pervasive in our national life is somewhat different. It depends not on individuals dealing insensitively, stupidly, capriciously, or selfishly with other individuals, but on institutional structures coming up with insensitive, stupid, capricious, or self-regarding interventions because they are programmed to do so and nothing or no one is set up to stop them.

We can call this kind of powerlessness structural, because it depends on interference by structures rather than by individuals. Here are some of the types of interference that evoke a feeling that we are powerless before our own structures. As with the case of the squire and the cricketer, it is often the most trivial interferences that seem the most outrageous.

First, there are cases where institutions seem to be interfering gratuitously in matters perceived as inappropriate for institutional concern. A farmer is in trouble with the United States Department of Agriculture for growing grain on his own land to feed to his own livestock. A householder must take out an Employer Identification Number and deduct Social Security payments from the money he pays his babysitter: otherwise he will be violating federal law. The town fathers descend on a parent who builds his children a treehouse without a building permit. The Department of Health, Education and Welfare suppresses the traditional Father and Son Dinner in a local high school because it is a discrimination on the basis of sex. The Occupational Safety and Health Administration threatens an employer with stiff fines if he does not move all his fire extinguishers a few inches lower on the wall.

Next, there are cases where institutions seem to impose impractical or financially exhausting requirements without regard for how they are to be met. A storekeeper building a small building is required to make alterations in the plans that will almost double his cost, so that if a person in a wheelchair is caught on the second floor during a fire, he will not have to take the elevator. A worker with a family to support has to wait two weeks for his pay while a computer error is rectified. A private school turns out pupils with consistently better test scores than the public schools, but the state education authorities propose to close it down because it does not have as large a gymnasium or as many certified teachers as state regulations require. An employer is told he must provide reasonable accommodation for drug addicts among his employees, because drug addiction is a handicap and employers must provide reasonable accommodation for handicapped employees. A drug that shows great promise in treating a painful disease is not manufactured because there are not enough people suffering from the disease to pay for the testing the Food and Drug Administration will require before allowing the drug to be marketed. Public agencies, and some of the larger private businesses as well, demand information and distribute forms with apparent disregard for who is to pay for the time and effort involved in assembling the information and writing it down in the blanks.

Next, there are the untraceable decisions that seem to emerge from the depths of an organization without any human being taking responsibility for them, but with all the resources of the organization arrayed in their support. There is the case of Ellen Knauff, who married an American soldier in Europe during the Second World War, and was never told why the Justice Department was so anxious to keep her out of the United States. She suspected a former girl friend of her husband of planting an anonymous tip against her. There is Robert W. Black, who contributed to Social Security for years, and found that the government wanted to deprive him of his benefits because his employer had embezzled his contributions. There is Morris D. Solow, whose enemy entered false and derogatory information in his personnel records, but who could not sue the employer for disseminating the information because the person who put it in the records had no authority, and the person who copied it out had no malice. There are in addition all the people who cannot find out what happened to the merchandise they ordered and paid for, or who cannot stop the computer that keeps sending them dunning letters for merchandise they never ordered and never saw.

Finally, there is the unresponsiveness of the political process. On the whole, unless we join a single-issue lobby, we will not have much luck either as individuals or as groups in getting public officials—even elected ones—to adopt measures we like or refrain from adopting measures we dislike. If we do join a single-issue lobby, we may gain some influence as to the single issue we choose, but only at the cost of forfeiting all influence on other issues. Indeed, if we wish to have any real impact concerning our one issue, we must give our unstinting support to every candidate that goes our way on it, regardless of how outrageous his views are on everything else.

As to most things, therefore, most of the time, public officials are able to do pretty much as they please, even if a considerable majority of their constituents would rather have them do something else. The example that comes most readily to mind is metrication. I know of no survey on the subject, but insofar as I am able to judge the sentiments of the American people through being one of them, I believe that a referendum would reveal overwhelming support for retaining our present system of measurements. On the other hand, I think most of us believe that metrication will inevitably come to pass. This may or may not be a good thing, but it suggests important reservations about the ability of the democratic process to give

us what we want or spare us what we do not want. We wonder
sometimes if a war can come upon us in the same way as grams
and kilometers will.

II. THE UNDERLYING VALUES

Unlike vindictive landlords, tyrannical employers and opin-
ionated squires, the people whose decisions and interventions create
the patterns of structural powerlessness are *principled*. That is, they
act not on impulse but on principle. The Secretary of Agriculture
is able to explain (and get the Supreme Court to agree with him)
that a farmer who feeds his own grain to his own livestock is contributing to the depression of the corn market by not buying any
feed. The town building commissioner will point out all the evils
of letting people build without permits, and will defy you to show
why a treehouse should be an exception. An employer can show
how he will inevitably go broke if he pays his workers before the
computer says to. The Food and Drug Administration will tell you
about thalidomide, which produced deformed babies all over Europe, but was never cleared for marketing in the United States. They
will insist that any drug that has not been through their testing procedures could be another thalidomide.

But these appeals to principle do not in the particular cases
allay our feeling that the decisions we are looking at are stupid,
insensitive, capricious, or (in some principled form) self-dealing.
The question comes up, then, where do these principles come from —
principles so wise in some applications, so asinine in others, or principles so beneficial on paper, so baneful in the real world? I see them
as derived mainly from three major values.

A. INTERDEPENDENCE

The first is interdependence. If, as Donne puts it, any man's
death diminishes me, so does any man's being illiterate, not having
enough to eat, living in a substandard building, or blowing two
fingers off with a firecracker on the Fourth of July. From this awareness has come much good legislation and many decent and compassionate administrative interventions. The problem is where to

stop. If you accept as a principle that I have a stake in my neighbor's well-being, then, in principle nothing is private. It is not possible to draw a principled distinction between what is and what is not my business.

What has to be done in deciding how far to carry a principle is not to explore the limits of its applicability, but to weigh it against competing principles that also apply. Here, the competing principle is that human beings need for their well-being a certain scope for making their own decisions about their own affairs. This principle has also been run into the ground in its time. To keep such competing principles in balance requires discretion, or common sense — the intuitive understanding of the game of life that goes with being one of the players. The absence of this kind of common sense or the failure to use it has a lot to do with our present disaffection toward the principled manifestations of interdependence.

B. ORGANIZATION

A second major value is organization. We are constantly encouraging one another to get organized, or commiserating with one another for failing to do so. All the great technological enterprises on which our affluence depends require a high degree of organization; so does keeping them under control. Being organized, living by flow charts, computer printouts, and forms with carbon paper ingeniously folded in so they can be executed in quintuplicate with one stroke of the ball point pen, is a characteristic not only of government agencies, but of business corporations and labor unions as well.

The primary means by which organization is achieved are *routinization* and *accountability up*. That is, tasks are broken up into components which are assigned to different people in the form of prescribed routines. Supervisors are then assigned to make sure that the routines are followed. Only at the topmost echelons can anyone's performance be measured in terms of contribution to the overall mission of the organization; others are praised or blamed according to how well they implement the prescribed routines. I discussed this situation in the previous chapter with respect to its effect on workers. Here, we must note its effect on those who have to deal with the organization.

In the complexities of a large organization, mistakes (i.e., slip-

ups in the application of routines) and failures of common sense
(i.e., adherence to routines despite intuitively unacceptable results)
are easy to fall into and hard to rectify. Because of routinization,
it may be extremely difficult to determine how the situation came
about, or how it may be rectified without total disruption of the
rest of the operation. Because of accountability up, the person most
responsible for the situation will often have a powerful stake in not
rectifying it — rectifying will mean admitting to his superiors that
something for which he is responsible has gone wrong. Even a person who is not responsible for the situation will hesitate to take
steps to rectify it, because his superiors have assigned him a routine,
and he cannot be sure how they will react to his departing from
it. In short, when you are complaining to a large organization, you
are never far from the knowledge that you are not the one whom
the person you are addressing has to satisfy.

C. EXPERTISE

A final value, perhaps the most important in the principled
imposition of powerlessness, is expertise. We need experts to control our different technologies as far as we do control them. We
need experts also to plan for the future in government and industry
alike, to provide for an effective deployment of social amenities,
and to render competent professional services in law, medicine,
education, counseling, and the repair of automobiles, vacuum cleaners, and television sets. Our institutional commitment to expertise
is especially manifested in the tremendous growth of administrative
agencies since the inauguration of the humble railroad and warehouse commissions of a century ago. The whole object of placing
a matter in the hands of an administrative agency is to have it handled
through an exercise of discretion (here meaning not simply common sense, but common sense augmented by expertise in the particular field involved) rather than through the application of rules
and principles articulated in advance. Almost all of our economic
and social legislation is based on a perception of this kind of discretion as a panacea.

Our commitment to expertise is also reflected in licensing laws
whereby not only doctors, lawyers, and engineers, but also barbers,
plumbers, funeral directors, real estate brokers, and sometimes even

dry cleaners, have to undergo a prescribed course of training and demonstrate their mastery of a prescribed subject-matter before being admitted to work at their chosen callings. Requirements of this kind are nothing new — witness the medieval guild system — but in a period of economic and social change they raise problems that were not raised in earlier times. One thinks, for instance, of the time not so long ago when restricted access to the real estate broker's profession contributed a good deal to segregated housing in the United States. One could think also of the arguments being made at the present time to the effect that the teachers who come best through the certification process are often not those best able to teach.

The laws establishing job security and promotion routines for civil servants are another development attributable in part to a concern with expertise. To the extent that a person needs specialized knowledge to fill a position, neither election nor political appointment seems a very good way to fill it. Not too long ago, in my own city, all the police captains became sergeants, and many of the sergeants became captains, whenever one party replaced the other in the mayor's office. Most of us felt that this was not the way to assure to our city the most competent police captains. The city has since adopted a "merit system" for police promotions. The terminology indicates both what we hope to achieve with the new system and what we thought was wrong with the old one.

Even those positions that we do not entrust to experts, those filled by election, tend to become affected by the prevailing commitment to expertise through the increasing use of staff personnel. On issues that do not call forth anyone's deeply felt political concern — that is, on most issues — elected officials are more and more apt to depend on their staffs for their understanding of what is at stake, and often for their actual decisions as well.

All these manifestations of expertise have in common their resistance to lay accountability. The limitations on the scope of judicial review of administrative agencies, the concentration on prescribed training courses and peer review in licensing and certification decisions, the insistence on tenure for civil servants, the fight against curriculum decisions by elected school boards, are all examples of the resistance I have in mind. Because the field of learning of the expert is complex and difficult to master, it is hard for the expert to explain to laypeople what he is about. The benificent purposes he is supposed to serve will be frustrated if laypeople are constantly looking over his shoulder.

The clashes produced by resistance to lay accountability are many and varied. Sometimes the result is a fairly straightforward body of legal technicalities, such as those governing judicial review of administrative agencies. Sometimes the result is hostility between the members of a politician's staff and the members of the press, with the politician caught somewhere in the middle. Sometimes it is a matter of a battle between an elected school board and the professional educators who work for the school system, resulting in either a lawsuit or a teachers' strike. A particularly difficult clash arose in connection with the federal anti-poverty programs of the sixties. The law required representation of the poor on the governing bodies of the different agencies involved — a requirement which the education and social work professionals (to say nothing of the lawyers) regarded as an intolerable interference with their getting on with the job of deploying essential services.

In these clashes, whether by legislation, judicial decision, or mere attrition, the experts have generally won. As a result, there is a broad and on the whole broadening area of our national life where experts operate without lay accountability in situations where the rest of us would like to call them to account.

III. THE QUEST FOR ACCOUNTABILITY

Developing institutions to control other institutions is a bit like setting a thief to catch a thief, or perhaps like hiring a wolf to take care of the sheep. While our experience of institutional checks and balances is happier than the experience of other societies where the structures tend to be monolithic, we cannot really claim that our institutions are sufficiently checked and balanced. The problem is that to check or balance an institution requires the same kind of organization and expertise that are needed to keep an institution in business. As a result, our controlling institutions tend to become indistinguishable from the institutions they are supposed to control. Their personnel go to the same schools, are hired on the same job market, hold conventions in the same hotels, and, not surprisingly, approach things with the same mindset. This state of affairs has been noted in a good deal of the literature on regulatory agencies, where it is referred to as "capture" of the regulators by the regulated. The relation between union leadership and employers has not been as much written about, but it was the subject not long ago of a bitter election campaign in the United Steelworkers (the candidate who claimed that his rival was too cozy with management lost). Also, a couple of recent films about union organizing campaigns have depicted top union officials as generally unhelpful to the efforts of the rank and file.

In general, then, our institutional checks and balances, while they are better than no checks and balances at all, are of severely limited effectiveness in making the whole institutional complex accountable to the real people whose lives are affected by it. More interesting for our present purposes are institutions that might be called not checks or balances, but points of entry—places where real people can have an opportunity to penetrate the whole complex without being filtered through an organization or examined by an expert.

A. POINTS OF ENTRY

One point of entry in our tradition is the law, as administered by an independent judiciary. The law sets limits to every kind of power, and confines within predetermined and philosophically coherent bounds anyone's capacity to intervene in anyone else's affairs. Through the courts, conceived as in but not of the institutional structure of society, every citizen can invoke those limits and enforce those bounds.

A second point of entry is politics. Through the right to vote, and through the constitutionally protected power to address other voters or to petition government, people with grievances or proposals may hope to have their concerns fully debated, and, if they persuade enough other people, to have their grievances redressed or their proposals implemented. The best example of the way the process is supposed to work is found in the triumph, first over public opinion, then over the authorities, of the people who opposed our military enterprise in Vietnam.

The principles of shareholder democracy and the operation

of the market provide additional points of entry applicable to the private sector. A large corporation whose stock is traded on the open market should number a fairly broad segment of the community in the body of its shareholders—not including, of course, the poor, but usually including some of their partisans, as well as some institutions devoted to their service. Thus, to be answerable to a body of stockholders is in some measure to be answerable to the community.

To have customers to satisfy is in still greater measure to be answerable to the community. No business can survive on the free market unless it fills some kind of need, and fills it at least as well as its competitors do. Every time you buy one product or refrain from buying another, you are excercising control over the business enterprises of our country.

B. THE FLAWS

Needless to say, none of these points of entry affords the citizen as effective an ingress into the institutional structure as it is supposed to afford. Each is impaired in its own particular ways.

Between the citizen and his vindication through law, there is always the delay and expense of going to court. Even in Shakespeare's time, the law's delay was high on the list of things that might lead a man to make his quietus with a bare bodkin. The law has not gotten a great deal quicker since then; nor has it gotten any cheaper. The possibilities for delay and expense are particularly colorful when an ordinary citizen is litigating with a large corporation or with a government agency. Reams of interrogatories, hours of deposition taking, days of pretrial motions and conferences, weeks of trial, and mountains of exhibits await anyone who sets out to confront our institutional structures through the courts.

Also, such a person may find in the courts an ideological bias in favor of the very things he wishes to confront. Judges are shielded against many of the pressures and temptations that affect other public officials, but they are not immune to the philosophical attractions of interdependence, organization, and expertise. The reported cases are full of clashes between citizens' privacy and social necessities, between moral or philosophical intuitions and empirical data, between stockholder interests and management prerogatives, between individual claims and administrative finality. In at least half of them, in my opinion, the wrong side wins.

It is said that under the old ward system an individual citizen could make his wants felt in politics because he had access to a precinct worker who needed his vote. Looking at the whole range of nineteenth and early twentieth century legislation instead of at who got a turkey for Christmas, one can be a bit skeptical about this claim. But even if politics used to work that way, it no longer does. Votes today are gathered not by the diligence and service of precinct workers but by the careful orchestration of campaigns in the media. Such campaigns require, naturally, a high level of organization.

Once a person is elected through this process, he becomes further dependent on organization and expertise for his decision making. It is the expert staffs and the organized lobbies that bring matters before public officials ready to be acted on. An ordinary citizen has but little hope of making his concerns felt without filtering them through one or another of these.

Under the American constitutional system, the effectiveness of the political process in vindicating citizens' concerns is also limited by the power of the courts to supersede political decisions that conflict with prevailing ideologies. This power is generally regarded as one that protects individual citizens in confrontation with institutional structures, but it has the opposite effect in a significant minority of cases. The great corporate entrepreneurs of the nineteenth and early twentieth centuries found in the courts an extremely effective shield against the political process. The courts are providing nothing quite so far-reaching today; still, they are giving a good deal of protection to secular public schools against political action aimed at supporting alternative educational enterprises. They also give some protection to those substantial business organizations that keep softcore pornography within the reach of every citizen and his children. And they have provided an all but insuperable obstacle to any use of the political process for protecting the unborn.

As a point of entry into the structure of business, the market is flawed by the fifty-one percent philosophy to which I alluded in the last chapter, and by the fact that the motivation of businessmen to maximize profit is not as great as has sometimes been supposed. A businessman who is competing with reasonable success for a conventional clientele, and is making a reasonable profit, is not apt to take on something new simply because there is a demand for it.

Shareholder democracy as a point of entry has been vitiated in some part by a tendency of courts and administrators to feel that shareholders should not concern themselves with anything but making money. This tendency is changing, as we shall see, but it is still not certain that shareholders who oppose a point of corporate policy on moral or social grounds will be allowed to put their concerns effectively before their fellows.

Shareholder democracy is further vitiated by the tendency of shareholders who disapprove of management policy to sell out rather than exercise their franchise. Selling out may be effective as a symbolic protest, but it does not seriously challenge management. Rather, it assures management of a sympathetic, or at least an indifferent, set of shareholders. I find it unfortunate, therefore, that proponents of socially responsible stands on some issues — notably, investment in South Africa — have regarded selling one's shares in the offending companies as an acceptable alternative, or even as a moral imperative.

C. PALLIATIVES, SOME WITH POTENTIAL

We have not been entirely oblivious to the erosion of these points of entry. We have adopted various measures to keep them effective. That is more than any such measures can be expected to accomplish. Still, a number of them are, or can be, helpful.

In the realm of litigation, we have done a good deal in recent years to improve our small claims procedures. These procedures make redress possible in cases where ordinary citizens would otherwise be victimized with impunity because the amounts involved are too small to make it worthwhile either for the victim to hire a lawyer or for a lawyer to volunteer his services. The commonest case of this kind is that of the landlord who refuses to give back a deposit when the tenant leaves. The plaintiff is not always successful in these small claims cases, or even in the ones he deserves to win. The defendant, even if he does not have a lawyer on retainer, may have a managerial employee who can impress a judge. Still, it costs more to defend a court proceeding than to snub an outraged citizen in one's office or toss his complaints into the wastebasket.

In cases that do not call for small claims treatment, the ability

of some citizens to resort to the law has been greatly enhanced by
the multiplication of legal services organizations since the sixties.
Government funding of such organizations has had its ups and
downs, but on the whole it has made a great difference. In South
Bend, Indiana, for instance, in 1965, there was one full time legal
aid lawyer, and he was not terribly busy. Now there are five or
six and they cannot handle all the work that is brought to them.
The whole program has not only given more people access to the
courts, it has encouraged more people to seek such access.

So-called legal clinics have done a certain amount to open legal
redress to people not poor enough for legal services and not rich
enough for the major law firms. These organizations provide ini-
tial consultation with a lawyer at some affordable price (generally
not more than twenty-five dollars). They cannot actually take cases
to court without charging much more, but they make it possible
for a client to find out if he has a case worth spending money on,
and so encourage people to seek redress who would otherwise give
up. The Supreme Court, by abolishing on free speech grounds the
old prohibition against lawyers advertising, has enabled the public
to find out about these clinics and invoke their services.

Hardly innovative, but still important in giving ordinary citizens
access to the legal process is the jury. This venerable institution has
been castigated many times on the reasonable ground that it is not
very good at doing what it is supposed to do, which is to weigh
the evidence at a trial and determine the true facts. On the other
hand, at vindicating people against organizations, or at providing
support for the victims of misfortune, it is fairly effective. Without
it, for instance, we would feel much more keenly than we do the
absence of an adequate program of social insurance.

Access of citizens to the political process is enhanced in some
states by the three devices of initiative, referendum, and recall,
elements of direct democracy introduced early in this century. Initiative involves the adoption of legislation, referendum the rejection of measures adopted by the legislature, and recall the removal
of elected officials before their terms have expired. In each case,
a proposal supported by a petition with a specified number of voters'
signatures must be put on the ballot at the next election, and implemented if a majority votes for it. Well known examples of this
process in recent years include votes abolishing throw-away bot-

tles in Oregon, limiting property taxes in California (Proposition 13), repealing the gay rights ordinance in Dade County, Florida, and removing a judge in Wisconsin who thought rape victims had it coming because of the way women dress nowadays. These ventures in direct democracy are occasional affairs; they cannot be a substitute for an adequately accountable set of representatives. But they sometimes bring forward the concerns of people who would not otherwise have been considered politically influential.

In the way of making representatives more accountable, we have developed various provisions for open hearings and other kinds of public scrutiny or constituent contact. Our most recent efforts along these lines are the "sunshine" laws requiring deliberative bodies to deliberate in public, and the freedom of information laws that make the records of most government agencies open to the public. Whether these laws make public servants more accountable or just more cautious about what they say or write is still being debated. It is hard to go through a whole deliberative process without saying or writing something that looks idiotic in retrospect, and I am not sure that those who succeed in doing so are the ones whose decisions are best in the end.

While trying to bring more public influence to bear on the political process, we also try through the regulation of lobbyists to bring less private influence to bear. The basic approach of our laws on the subject is to assimilate advocacy before a legislature to advocacy before a court. The lobbyist is typically required therefore to register with the body before which he is appearing, to state for whom he is acting, to limit himself to considerations addressed to the reason and understanding, and often to open his financial dealings to some kind of scrutiny. All these rules are more stringent on paper than they are in practice.

In the private sector, we have a few laws calculated to enhance the operation of shareholder democracy. Perhaps the most important of these is Rule 14a-8 of the Securities and Exchange Commission, which requires management to include on its proxy solicitations to the shareholders any proposal put forward by a shareholder, with a hundred word statement in its support and a box where the recipient can check off a vote in favor of the proposal. The SEC was inclined to limit the application of its rule to cases where the proposal concerned conventional business goals, but the courts now tend (and the SEC has largely acquiesced by amending the rule) to allow social concerns to be included if they are within the power of the corporation to implement. Other forms of access are more problematical, however. There is a leading case on the books that says that a shareholder is not entitled to a list of his fellow shareholders in order to canvass them on behalf of a slate of directors who favor his social policies.

IV. TOWARD CONFRONTING POWER

A. MEDIATIVE APPROACHES

Behind our failure to maintain fully effective points of entry for our citizens into our institutional structures lies our overall commitment to interdependence, organization, and expertise. This commitment will have to be confronted if the power of the citizen is to be effectively established. As with other matters we have considered, our present legal approach is mediative rather than confrontive. That is, our laws presuppose a continuing commitment to interdependence, organization, and expertise; their aim is to make that commitment as fair and as beneficent as possible in its impact on individuals.

It is in this spirit that prevailing legal opinion understands the relation between interdependence and traditional personal rights. Following John Stuart Mill, judges and theorists of this persuasion see liberty as a principle governing those aspects (and only those aspects) of human life which are not subject to interdependence. Hence the increasing concern with "privacy" as a fundamental — or perhaps *the* fundamental — right. As I have pointed out, there is not really any aspect of life that is not subject to interdependence. Accordingly, the boundary between the realm of privacy and that of interdependence ("compelling state interest") cannot but be arbitrarily drawn. At the moment, it seems to put too much sex and too little of anything else on the private side.

The right of property is related to interdependence through the principle of just compensation. If somebody wants my property for a government or government-supported project, there is not much of anything I can do to hold onto it. I can, however, make them pay me for it. If they take the whole thing, I am entitled to whatever it would have fetched on the market, as determined by a jury after listening to real estate agents or other experts. If they take only part of my property, I am entitled to the market value of what is taken plus something to make up for the diminished value of what remains (as where they take a strip out of my farm, depriving me of access to my back forty, or cutting off my cows from their drinking hole).

The principle of just compensation also prevents any "confiscatory" regulation. There is almost no limit these days to the way government can require me to use or not use my property, except that if they make it impossible for me to put it to any profitable use at all, they have taken it away and they must pay for it. In practice, rather than pay, they will generally withdraw the offending regulation. Some forms of zoning and some forms of price-fixing have been ruled out in this way. But the basic principle is still one of unrestricted power to interfere with property rights, as long as payment is made when appropriate.

Recently, a few courts have moved toward a new approach to interdependence, by mediating it in terms of cost-benefit analysis. That is, in deciding whether a particular regulation is acceptable, a court will weigh the detriment to the person regulated against the benefit to the person protected or helped by the regulation. As the factors to be weighed are usually incommensurable (what risk of occupational cancer is worth how many dollars increase in the price of a gallon of paint?), the weighing process has necessarily an air of unreality about it. The intuition that people should neither risk serious harm to avoid petty discomforts nor undergo major disruption to avoid trivial or conjectural harm is probably a sound one, but it does not lend itself to quantification. The latest Supreme Court decision on the point has gone so far as to say that a government agency must find a serious, rather than an insignificant harm to be averted before it imposes a regulatory standard. But the court expressly refused to require a cost-benefit analysis as such. This is all to the good, but it leaves the mediative approach firmly in control. It admits of protecting an individual against spurious or insubstantial claims of interdependence, but if interdependence is seriously established, personal considerations must give way before it.

Organization and expertise are mediated in the law through

the ubiquitous requirement of procedural due process. This venerable concept has been given new scope through the modern development of administrative law, culminating in the federal Administrative
Procedure Act of 1946 and its numerous progeny in the states. This
legislation, with its provisions for notice and hearing, for separating
investigative from decision-making functions, for broadly distributed
opportunities to submit data and arguments, for requiring that decisions be supported by a record, bespeaks two fundamental concerns —
that organizational patterns be established and adhered to, and that
expertise be properly informed.

In more recent decades, these concerns of administrative law
have been carried beyond the agencies to which they were first applied, and brought to bear in contexts where decision-making had
previously been pretty much unstructured and intuitive. The courts,
drawing on the due process clause of the Fourteenth Amendment,
have begun to apply standard administrative law doctrines to such
matters as the determination of eligibility for welfare payments and
the disciplining of pupils in public schools. The antitrust laws have
been drawn on to impose similar doctrines in other cases, such as
the processing of applications for membership in trade or professional associations. In some situations, administrative law concepts
are made applicable by statute, as with the termination of automobile
dealerships, or by contract, as with the redress of employee grievances or the tenuring of faculty members. Finally, in many cases
the same concepts are drawn on by people who simply wish to avoid
criticism, agitation, or the appearance of illegality. In this way,
private schools often adopt disciplinary procedures like those imposed on public schools by the Fourteenth Amendment, or non-
union employers adopt grievance procedures like those that appear
in union contracts.

This gradual extension of administrative law concepts to embrace the whole range of decision making seems to be the product
of a widely held belief that organization and expertise really do serve
the ends of justice in most cases. Take for instance academic tenure
decisions. It seems that as time goes by these decisions are involving more and more elaborate tiers of deliberation by faculty and
administrators (organization) and more and more sensitive provisions for peer review (expertise). Most faculty members seem convinced that the continued vitality of this apparatus is their best as-

surance that shortsighted administrators will not be able to get rid
of brilliant but inconvenient scholars by unjustly denying them tenure.
Most administrators seem equally convinced that the same apparatus
is their best assurance that softhearted faculty members will not be
able to eviscerate academic excellence by tenuring incompetents.

It is this kind of conviction that supports the broadly mediative
stance of our law. While the conviction may be well founded in
some cases, it tends to be self-fulfilling. That is, procedures based
on prescribed routines and the rejection of lay accountability naturally produce decisions that commend themselves to the devisers of
the routines and to the peers of the decision-makers. These may
or may not be the best decisions for the community at large.

B. A CONFRONTIVE AGENDA

The claims of interdependence, organization, and expertise are
so far-reaching and so plausible that the mediative approach adopted
in our law cannot be expected adequately to vindicate the need of
ordinary people for a measure of control over their own affairs.
As long as we take as given that these claims when plausibly made
must be accepted, nothing we can do to mediate their impact on
individuals will be sufficient. We must find points at which these
claims can be directly confronted.

We might begin by limiting the scope of interdependence. As
I have pointed out, there is no theoretical limit to interdependence.
Thus, the limits we set must come from an intuition of noninterference rather than from any theoretical absence of a community
stake. I believe that there are intuitions of this kind, and that they
should be respected. The facts and figures that show inescapably
how consumption of grain on the farm where it is grown affects
the national market may lead us to suppress our intuition that what
a farmer grows for consumption at home is his own business—but
they cannot make us comfortable with the result. Letting the farmer
alone may reduce the effectiveness of a price stabilization program,
but maybe it is worth the price. Similarly, one cannot deny the
possibility of a treehouse being ugly, dangerous, or both; still, we
are not comfortable requiring a householder to submit plans and
take out a permit before he builds one. Somehow, the Norman
Rockwell scene offers no place for a building inspector.

In many cases, the intuition goes more to bureaucratic supervision than to legal restraint. For instance, it is one thing to make me take down my treehouse if it offends my neighbors, but quite another to make me get a permit before I build it. Similarly, if I sell a toaster at a yard sale without letting on that it gives people shocks when they use it, I ought to get into some kind of trouble — but it does not follow that I should be made to get a retail merchant's license before I hold the sale at all. We might almost state as a general principle that private — i.e., non-commercial — transactions should be subject to law, but not to administrative intervention.

But it is not enough to adopt principles of this kind. We need a different approach to the whole subject. We are in a realm of paradox here. The arguments supporting noninterference and those supporting interference are both valid from their own standpoints. Which will prevail depends on which standpoint we choose. The mediative standpoint is that if the claims of interdependence are made out (as they always will be) they must prevail: all that can be done about them is to make their impact as painless and as equitable as we can. The confrontive standpoint would be that the intuition of noninterference, if it is strong enough, must be respected, and the claims of interdependence met only as far as they can be met without violating it.

The famous and controversial Proposition 13 is a fairly crude example of the confrontive standpoint. It is a limitation, embodied in the California state constitution by an initiative measure, on the amount of real estate tax that any property owner can be made to pay. It is confrontive in that it was adopted not on the basis of a cost benefit analysis, and not because of any particular objection to the things being done with the money, but simply on the ground that the taxes were more than anyone should be obliged to pay. I am of two minds about Proposition 13, because it is, as I say, crude (though perhaps no cruder than the use of real estate taxes to finance all the activities of a modern local government). But whether or not it is a step in the right direction, it starts from the right place — that is, from a perception that interdependence is being carried too far.

An area in which it would be particularly useful to apply this approach is that of eminent domain. As the law now stands, any private property, however important to the owner, may be taken for any public use, however unimportant to the public, as long as just compensation is paid. There are limitations, more in some states than in others, on what may be said to constitute a public use, but it is hard to give these limitations an adequate theoretical basis. Since there are no theoretical limits to interdependence, there is no theoretical limit to what use of property can be called public.

The uses of eminent domain that are experienced as oppressive are generally those linked to some form of development. Someone's house is taken to build a cloverleaf on a highway. A line of trees in front of the house along a road is chopped down to widen the road for easier access to a shopping center. A delicatessen and a drugstore are removed to make way for a redeveloped downtown. A farm is flooded for hydroelectric power. Some of these takings are stopped by the courts because they are overly involved with the private sector. For instance, the Supreme Court of Florida held that a local government could not take land for a parking garage merely to accommodate the private developer of a shopping center. There was a strong dissent, though, on grounds that might have prevailed in another state.

While I favor the result reached in this case, I do not find the reasoning all that persuasive. What is important to my mind is not that a private developer is involved, but that we do not need shopping centers badly enough to justify taking away people's property to encourage one. In other words, the real distinction is not between public and private uses but between important and unimportant public uses. In addition to adopting this distinction, I would consider what the owner is doing with the land as well as what the taker proposes to do with it. I would require a more important public purpose to take a home than to take a parking lot or a junk yard. In short, the question should be not the mediative one of whether a case can be made out for a public purpose, but the confrontive one of whether in this case the public purpose deserves to be implemented. This is not a matter of quantifying costs and benefits; it is a matter of determining that some uses are qualitatively superior to others.

There is some argument among scholars in constitutional law in favor of applying similar considerations to the power of the federal government over interstate commerce. Just as there is no theoretical limit to interdependence of people, so there is no theoretical limit to interdependence of states, and therefore no theoretical limit to the commerce power. If there is to be any limit at all on federal power, it will have to be because certain measures, however plausible, take away too much from the states and the people—because it is perceived in a given case that the government is going too far.

A confrontive approach to organizations involves attacking the two principles of routinization and accountability up. Measures must be taken based on the results the organization achieves, rather than on whether prescribed routines are followed or whether the lower echelons obey the higher ones. It should be made clear that organization people will get into more trouble and bring down more trouble upon their organization by following prescribed routines with baneful results than by not following them. Provision should be made for evaluating the whole organization in terms of what it is accomplishing, rather than in terms of its own routines. People aggrieved by organizational action should be given some kind of recourse outside the organization.

In the case of government organizations, measures calculated to further these ends include zero base budgeting, which requires each agency to justify its entire budget in every fiscal period (instead of using the previous year's expenses as a starting point), and sunset laws, which require certain agencies to justify their entire existence at regular intervals. We have yet to gather enough experience with these devices to know how well they accomplish their purpose. They have tended to be adopted in the jurisdictions where they are least needed. Indiana, for instance, whose citizens have seldom felt the hand of state bureaucracy, has had a particularly elaborate sunset law since 1978. Its most prominent victim so far has been automobile safety inspection, which, as it used to be administered, probably did more good than harm, though not a great deal of either. At any rate, if these devices were to be zealously applied to the federal government or to some of the more heavily regulated states, they might have a real bite.

Government agencies have experienced some check from the Supreme Court holdings that they must have warrants in order to make routine inspections of private property for the purpose of seeing whether the laws they administer are being complied with. But the holdings are not as broad as they have sometimes been painted; in fact, they are more mediative than confrontive. They grant that a showing that entry is sought pursuant to a reasonable plan of routine inspections will be a sufficient ground for issuing the warrant. A really confrontive holding would require a showing of probable cause to believe that the law is being violated on the premises in question. We may be ready for such a holding with respect to some agencies, but probably not with respect to all of them. It is significant that the latest Supreme Court case on the subject — which many people applauded supposing that it went farther than it did go — involved the nit-picking and unpopular Occupational Safety and Health Administration (OSHA).

Meanwhile, it is not insignificant, and it is at least somewhat confrontive, for agency inspection routines to be subject to judicial scrutiny, as they are under the current decisions. This scrutiny makes the agency accountable outside its own structure: it imposes what might be called lateral accountability as opposed to the standard accountability up. Certainly, the government opposed it vigorously enough.

A proposal that I have already mentioned a couple of times might provide another kind of outside accountability. This is making government agencies pay the cost of complying with some of their regulations, or at least the cost of furnishing them the information they demand, and, above all, the cost of successful litigation resisting their demands. If a government agency needed a higher budget to order people about than to let them alone, its people might reflect in an entirely new way on whether the public really needed a proposed regulation.

It would seem that government may be more accountable to ordinary citizens on the state or local level than on the national level. There is less media involvement, and less opportunity for candidates and officeholders to interpose organizational checks and staffs of experts between themselves and their constituents. It would follow that a transfer of functions from federal to state or local government, and from state to local, would enhance the power of ordinary citizens over their affairs. This observation is a form of the "principle of subsidiarity" familiar to the followers of recent Roman Catholic social teaching. Some legislative initiatives, especially in the area of welfare and economic development, are based on it. I would like to see these initiatives carried further.

I would also like to see a number of functions transferred from the municipal to the neighborhood level. Matters that could be effectively dealt with in this way include education, public housing, welfare administration, streets, parks, and libraries, enforcement of zoning regulations and building codes (along with some voice in their enactment), consumer protection, legal and medical services, some aspects of police and fire protection (especially general orders governing police discretion), and perhaps some kinds of judicial business involving local residents. Various programs connected with the federal anti-poverty legislation have put a number of these functions, or at least a concern with them, onto the neighborhood level in one place or another. These tend also to be the concerns which voluntary neighborhood associations have taken up in places where they exist.

What seems to stand in the way of this kind of localization of functions is a feeling that functions ought to be controlled on the level at which they are paid for. As long as this is our feeling, the poor neighborhoods that are most in need of localization will be the ones least apt to achieve it. There is of course something attractive in the original idea behind the feeling—the idea of a sturdy yeomanry handling their own civil affairs out of their own resources without asking leave of any central authority. But the idea loses some of its attractiveness when it translates into an insistence that New Rochelle and the South Bronx should each take care of its own poor. Or that if the resources of the South Bronx are not adequate to the needs of the local poor, then those poor must be cared for out of Washington, Albany, or lower Manhattan.

The English, from whom we have derived our local government law, have in this, as in many other areas, abandoned anachronisms to which we resolutely adhere. Their agencies of local government have a major discretionary role in many programs adopted and funded at other levels. Also, at least in London, they have made effective provision for decentralizing city government. The thirty-two London boroughs exercise a wide range of functions, either exclusively or concurrently with the Greater London Council.

Localization of functions will be only a theoretical source of accountability, however, unless more people participate in local politics. It is interesting that the administrators of the federal anti-poverty program—which calls for developing a number of federally funded programs administered at the neighborhood level—gave up on holding elections as a means of securing neighborhood participation, because they were getting less than five percent of the eligible voters to turn out. Instead, they established committees of representatives of the different community organizations active in the areas they were trying to serve.

The general experience of community organizers is similar. They have often been successful in developing a cadre of residents concerned about community affairs, in providing increased outreach for public and private programs, and in organizing for effective presentation of grievances. But in their efforts to politicize the rank and file of their constituents, they have on the whole been disappointed. Perhaps, though, their experience depends on the kind of neighborhoods involved and the kinds of politicization envisaged. Presumably, a set of neighborhood officials nominated and elected in the same way as other elected officials would get voted on to the same extent as the rest. And presumably, the more power they had the more carefully people would choose them.

Confronting large business organizations involves holding them accountable to the market, to the general public, and to their own shareholders. I have suggested some of the reasons why such organizations are not made adequately accountable to the market simply through individual customers electing to take their business elsewhere. Organized boycotts can of course be more effective. The consumer boycott is analogous to the strike, by which workers have succeeded very well in calling businesses to account. Consumer boycotts in recent years have had a good deal to do with the acceptance of the United Farm Workers by grape growers in California, the modification by J.P. Stevens of its intransigent labor policy, and Nestlé's change in its ways of marketing milk substitutes in poor countries. Another such boycott was mounted for some years against Campbell's and Libby's because of their treatment of farm workers in Ohio; it appears that a settlement has just been reached.

One device for public accountability that has been talked about a good deal is having outside constituencies represented on corporate boards of directors. I gather that something of the kind has been done in Germany with considerable success. But experts in American corporation law tend to be skeptical. They believe that any outside constituency with a stake in corporate affairs can vindicate that stake better by confronting the corporation or negotiating with it than by helping to run it. Workers will do better through collective bargaining, consumers through boycotts, and government through law making than any of them will do with votes on the board of directors. For my own part, I am inclined to agree with this criticism.

One form of outside accountability that is growing all the time is that administered by the civil and criminal courts. Thus, an employer has long been liable, regardless of fault, for on-the-job injuries to his employees. The cost of insuring this liability, which increases with unfavorable experience, has provided a powerful motivation toward making workplaces safer. The growth of products liability litigation, and the size of the jury verdicts, has had a similar effect on manufacturers. The increasing possibility of punitive damages or criminal liability tends to prevent proposals for safer or healthier products from falling victim to cost benefit analysis. Punitive damages and criminal sanctions are more apt than they once were to be imposed for other improper business practices such as trademark infringement and violation of the antitrust laws. Occasionally, top management personnel have even gone to jail.

At one time, the courts were on the way to providing a broad range of corporate accountability to stockholders. The Supreme Court held in a number of New Deal cases that a stockholder could sue to keep a corporation from entering into illegal transactions, or even from complying with unconstitutional laws. But this line of authority had the immense prestige of Justice Brandeis against it, and it seems now to have given way before the principle that management decisions, if made in good faith and on reasonable grounds, are not to be questioned in stockholders' suits. It might be appropriate at this point to revive and embellish the earlier principle.

The law concerning the right of a stockholder to call management to account before the whole body of stockholders is better than it has been, but not as good as it might be. We have already looked at it. At present, under federal law and SEC rules, a stockholder may, at the expense of the corporation, put before his fellows any proposal that the stockholders have power to adopt and the corporation has power to implement, together with a hundred word statement in support of the proposal. He can also prevent management from stating unfairly or untruthfully its case against the proposal. On the other hand, if he wishes to put up candidates for the board of directors, he must print his arguments himself and pay

the postage for sending them out. Under federal law, he can probably make the corporation use its addressing equipment to send out
his material. Federal law, however, does not entitle him to his own
copy of the stockholder lists, and the courts in some states will not
entitle him to a copy if his purpose is to impose some form of social
responsibility on the corporation. These lists should be available
to any stockholder who wants to address other stockholders concerning corporate affairs (some restrictions are required to prevent
their falling into the hands of direct mail advertisers). In addition
the SEC regulations concerning stockholders' proposals should be
expanded to cover stockholder candidates for the board.

A more radical form of stockholder accountability would be
provided by a law requiring a corporation to buy out at an appraised
value any stockholder who disapproves of management policy and
cannot persuade management to change. At present, the law makes
provision for buying out dissenters in this way only in the case of
mergers or, in some states, other organic changes. The right to be
bought out is generally considered an inadequate vindication of the
dissenter's stake in the corporation. At the same time, it is a burden
to management because if enough stockholders exercise the right
they will drastically impair the corporation's liquidity; hence, a
relatively small percentage of the stockholders may be able to veto
management policy by demanding to be bought out.

But consider the problem of the person with a serious objection to management policy. Say that I have just taken charge of the
portfolio of a certain religious institution, and am horrified to find
a substantial block of International Knout Corporation, which has
a heavy investment in segregated facilities in South Africa. By holding
onto this stock, I seem to be condoning the racist policies of the
South African government. On the other hand, how am I to get
rid of it? To sell it on the market will not convey much of a message
to management. Also, if there is a moral objection to investing in
International Knout, my selling the stock would make me a party
to the morally objectionable conduct of the buyer, and therefore
would constitute morally objectionable conduct on my own part.
To burn the stock would convey a windfall benefit upon the corporation, as well as costing me a great deal. So the best way to handle
the situation would be to make the corporation buy me out.

A law imposing such a requirement would have to be heavily

qualified, or it would place every business at the mercy of any crank who was able to buy a large block of stock in it. This is not the place to develop all the nuances of such law, but I think it would be possible to distinguish serious moral dissent from mere captiousness. Also, weight could be given to the purposes for which the corporation was founded. It has been suggested that the remedy of being bought out should be available whenever the corporation departs substantially from the expectations the stockholders had when they first invested. The principle could be extended to moral expectations as well as economic.

Confronting the power of labor unions is a problem in our society, because unions operate in two different historical contexts. In some places and in some industries, the union is still what it was early in this century, the only effective device for confronting management on behalf of workers, and liberating workers from the feudal powerlessness that was once their condition everywhere. In other places and other industries, though, the union has become part of the complex of organizations responsible for the structural powerlessness of individuals.

Because of this ambiguity, persons concerned with social justice have generally (and, in my opinion, rightly) refused to support "right to work" legislation, which is probably the most powerful protection that can be afforded the individual worker against the power of a union. This legislation prevents "union security" provisions in collective bargaining agreements—that is, provisions which maintain the position of the union by requiring continued support of the union as a condition for continuing to work in the bargaining unit. Such provisions prevent a newly established union from being undermined by the fickleness of its members or the glibness of their employer. But they also prevent a corrupt and sclerotic union from being replaced by disgusted workers.

Current federal legislation reflects an ambivalent attitude toward union security. It permits some forms of it, forbids others, and leaves still others up to the states. Where the question is left up to the states, those with the most backward conditions of employment and the most oppressive employers have the most restrictive legislation. It seems to me that the character of the collective bargaining relationship should be taken into account in deciding what form of union security is acceptable. I might, for instance, favor doing away with union security in any plant where the same bargaining agent has been representing the employees for twenty years, and the median hourly wage is at least twice the statutory minimum.

The main thrust of our labor laws has been to protect the individual worker by redressing his grievances concerning the way the union is handling his affairs, rather than by letting him opt out and handle them himself. The courts impose on every union a duty of "fair representation." A union cannot allow (much less require) an employer to make unreasonable and invidious distinctions among classes of employees; nor may it capriciously refuse to support an employee's grievance against the employer. This duty, which was first developed to prevent race discrimination on the part of a union, has been extended far into other areas, while race discrimination itself has now been brought under the various civil rights laws, which apply to unions as well as to employers.

Other laws have been adopted either by courts or by legislatures to protect the right of the rank and file to vote for union leaders and engage in other political action, to protect them against arbitrary or unfair use of union disciplinary proceedings, and to prevent various kinds of corrupt dealing in union funds. All of these measures are vitiated in some part by a confusion of jurisdictions between the National Labor Relations Board (NLRB) and the courts. Whether to initiate a proceeding before the NLRB is always discretionary with the General Counsel, so a personal right enforceable only before the NLRB is not exactly a right at all. I think we now need a broad definition of the rights of union members, together with provision for their enforcement in court.

Confronting experts outside of their organizational context is mainly a matter of enhancing their sources of lay accountability. The most popular new way of doing this is by subjecting them to malpractice suits. For some time, the courts drastically restricted such suits by requiring the plaintiff to introduce expert witnesses from within the defendant's profession to show what the defendant did wrong. Thus, the malpractice suit was another form of peer review rather than a form of lay accountability. In the past few years, this requirement has been dramatically attenuated. It is now often held that the public knowns enough about medical procedures and the like for a jury to decide for itself such questions as whether radiation treatment for Hodgkin's disease can cause paralysis in the absence of negligence, or whether the paralysis is itself sufficient evidence of the negligence. Or whether, if even a carefully administered treatment causes paralysis once in a while, the doctor should not have warned the patient in advance. Once a jury gets its hands on a case like this, the outcome is apt to reflect the built-up anger of ordinary citizens at their sense of powerlessness in the face of our society's commitment to expertise. Doctors have been the first to feel this anger in the form of high jury verdicts, but other professions, including my own, are not far behind.

I think that a good deal of the atmosphere of vindictiveness that these suits (or the threat of them) tend to generate is due to the persistent claim of experts to be free from any form of lay accountability, and the success with which, until quite recently, that claim had been asserted. We can hope that before too long everyone will calm down, and we will reach a general consensus on what ordinary citizens are entitled to expect of professional people. When that happens, malpractice litigation will be a useful adjunct to other forms of professional discipline, and professional people will have been liberated from pontificating, as others will have been liberated from being pontificated at.

Enhancement of lay accountability in the professions will probably require some check to the exuberance of the devices for peer review that are now found in the law (thirty-nine articles in the Indiana Code, from Accountants to Water Well Drilling Contractors). The typical statute forbids engaging in the business without a license, sets up standards of education, financial responsibility, and sometimes equipment for would-be licensees, and establishes a board of practitioners to issue the licenses and police the conduct of licensees. Standards of professional "ethics" are set, partly by statute and partly by the various boards. These embrace obvious forms of dishonesty, and cover kinds of offensive conduct that a layman might not have thought of (e.g., an embalmer using obscene language in the presence of the bereaved). They also tend to limit competition, fix prices, restrict advertising, and impose a uniform mindset on the profession. In some professions, private organizations impose more elaborate requirements for membership than those that are laid down for licensing under the law. These requirements generally stick, because practitioners are under a good deal of economic and social pressure to keep up membership.

In the past few years, the Supreme Court has invalidated blanket restrictions on advertising under the First Amendment and the setting of minimum fees under the anti-trust laws. This is helpful, but it is not enough. Standards of professional ethics should be reviewed across the board to eliminate requirements that restrict competition or enhance pomposity rather than serving the public.

Requirements for entry into the different professions need also to be reviewed. It does not make sense to impose a course of education and an examination on someone before he can aspire to be a dry cleaner. People will find out soon enough whether a dry cleaner is competent or not. A dry cleaner is not like a doctor. Before I find out that a doctor is incompetent, I may be dead. But if a dry cleaner ruins my suit I can always make him buy me a new one.

There are some cases also where a legal standard of competence is desirable, but there seems to be no reason for excluding a person who fails to meet that standard from rendering services to anyone who chooses to employ him. It is important, for instance, that there should be certified public accountants; but there seems to be no harm in letting other people keep accounts for anyone who chooses to hire them, as long as there is no misrepresentation involved. Indeed, I am not sure there is any harm in letting a layman give legal advice if he does not hold himself out as a lawyer.

The point is that reducing the power and the mystification of these structures of peer review can subject experts to the lay accountability of the market. If you are dissatisfied with the services of your doctor, lawyer, beautician, or plumber, you ought to be able to take your business to someone else, and advise your friends to do the same. To re-establish at least the theoretical possibility that a professional person who gives no satisfaction will get no business seems essential to liberating the general public from its powerlessness in the presence of any form of expertise. I am reminded in this connection of a *Punch* cartoon from the First World War. A somewhat pompous medical officer is looking severely at a soldier and saying, "Young man, in civilian life you would surely not have come to me with an ailment like this?" The soldier replies "No, sir; I should have sent for you."

C. CONFRONTIVE LITIGATION

Some of the confrontations envisaged here will put additional strain on the already tenuous devices for giving ordinary citizens access to the courts in cases where organizations and experts are on the other side. The problem is, in a word, money. The ordinary citizen does not have enough of it to pay out of his own pocket the legal fees required for a major courtroom battle. But where a case has important political and social implications, none of the devices we have for enabling the citizen to pursue it at someone else's expense works quite satisfactorily.

A number of legal services programs have oriented themselves toward social change, rather than toward simply rescuing one private litigant after another from his immediate problems. Often such programs have been able to develop a sophisticated agenda for confrontive litigations, and carry through a good deal of it in spite of the resulting pressure from politicians to cut off their funding. The trouble is that lawyers with the ideological intensity to pursue such an agenda successfully tend not to be content to follow the instructions of their clients. They develop the same organizational structures and the same resistance to lay accountability that characterize the people with whom they are litigating. In such a litigation, the ordinary citizen, chosen by the lawyers to make an appealing client, is apt to be relegated to a peripheral role. An example of what this kind of thing can lead to is provided by the case of *Natonabah* v. *Board of Education*, a spectacular decision won by a consortium of agencies devoted to rendering legal services to Indians against a school board that had been discriminating against Indian students and misapplying federal funds meant for Indian education. But it appears that just when the suit was getting started, the local Indians had made it pointless by winning an election and taking control of the board.

The class action, another device that can often be used to good effect in calling large organizations to account, is subject to similar problems regarding the accountability of the lawyers in charge. Through this device, a particular aggrieved person can bring suit on behalf of everyone who has a similar grievance. The recovery will then be divided among all the people so aggrieved. The court may determine the value of the lawyers' services in bringing about the recovery, and may order them paid a suitable fee off the top. Where there is a large class, the stake of each individual member may be very small, while the recovery on which the lawyers' fee is based may be very large. Again, therefore, the client tends to be relegated to a peripheral role in the lawsuit, and the lawyers give the impression of pursuing an agenda of their own.

This situation should probably be dealt with in the lawyers' Code of Professional Responsibility (the absence of adequate provision for it is far from the most glaring of the gaps in that Code). Certainly, the Code, along with all the other material on legal ethics, envisages a lawyer representing a client, and pursuing the client's purposes insofar as they may legally and morally be pursued. It does not envisage the case with a strong ideological element and a peripheral client. I think I would add a requirement that a lawyer not undertake a class action or a suit for the purpose of improving the economic or social condition of a group except at the request and under the instruction of someone whom he reasonably supposes to be representing the class or group.

There are some situations where lawyers' fees are provided for. In damage suits, including those for professional malpractice, the lawyer will be compensated out of the recovery. In civil rights cases, antitrust cases, and a few others, such as cases under the federal Truth in Lending Act, the governing statute provides for adding reasonable lawyers' fees to the recovery. It is this provision for statutory fees that seems best calculated to support litigants in taking on major defendants without losing control of their cases. I have already suggested that such statutory fees should be provided for a successful litigant resisting government regulation. It would be hard to know just how far to go in providing them also for people resisting the power of corporations or labor unions, but I think a considerable extension would be in order.

VI. THE CLASS ENEMY

To confront our society's commitment to organization and expertise is, naturally, to confront organization people and experts. There is an extensive literature studying organization people; particularly notable is William H. Whyte's famous study, *The Organization Man* (1956). Some of Whyte's findings about personal lifestyles and family relations would have to be updated today, along with the sex designation in the title. Still, the main point is as true as it ever was. There is a large and growing class of people who find comfort, security, material reward, a prospect of advancement, and a sense of purpose in participating in an organization, following its routines, and abiding its provisions for accountability up. Lateral accountability and evaluation by results are threatening to these people; doubly threatening if they threaten the organization itself.

There is a price to be paid for all the *gemütlichkeit* in the organization, and insiders can on occasion feel just as powerless as the outsiders do. Whyte, in a judicious concluding chapter, argues that the people he studies are deluded in supposing that it is possible to abolish the tension between the individual and society. Their betrayal of themselves lies not in accommodating themselves to the demands of interdependence, the needs of others, or the exigencies of the organizations through which they make their contribution to the world, but in allowing the organization to determine for them what form that accommodation shall take and how far it shall go. It is at this central point in their personalities that organization people may be liberated by a curbing of the power of their organizations.

The major adverse consequence for them would be some loss of job security. An organization that is accountable outside its own borders may have trouble shielding team players from the consequences of their own incompetence. On the other hand, not everyone is incompetent. Most of the team players no doubt possess real skills for cooperative activity and management of high technology. Nothing proposed here (and nothing that is likely to happen) will make those skills superfluous. We may expect that new forms of accountability will eventually be taken in stride.

Also, along with more lateral accountability and concern with results, we may expect a shifting of responsibility toward lower echelons in the organization. A consequence will be more opportunities for more people to deal creatively with the real world. For instance, if school teachers are evaluated on what their pupils have learned instead of how the higher administrators like their lesson plans, they will have more chance to do creative teaching.

Experts, like managers, are not about to become superfluous in our society. The measures I have proposed here may deprive some of them of the power to restrict additions to their ranks, but otherwise they will not be much hurt. The imposition of new forms of lay accountability may be disconcerting to them, but it should prove liberating in the end. In my own profession, which is at least as infected as any other with the *delectatio pomposa*, the arrogance of expertise, there is a great deal of self-study intended to teach respect for and cooperation with the people served:

> The average prosperous law office suite is an engine of one-upmanship . . . . Lawyers meet people in coat and tie, sit behind massive desks in massive chairs, and barricade themselves with superior demeanors, and yellow pads fourteen inches long, and gadgets like "squawk box" telephones. Our heady language suggests that all communication is what Berne would have called from parent to child. The atmosphere . . . is a mighty nonverbal claxon directed at clients: "SIT UP AND PAY ATTENTION: I'M IN CHARGE HERE". . . .
>
> The alternative is to learn non-competitive strategies, as a valid and important professional preparation for dealing with clients. What we have to be able to say, verbally and nonverbally, to clients is: "There is no need to compete in this office. I am your companion on a journey which I know to be strange and anxious for you. . . . "

This is taken from a widely circulated textbook on legal counseling. I believe it has its counterpart in the literature of other professions. The approach described as the alternative to the parental or intimidating stance is obviously more conducive to a loving and helpful relation with the people one is supposed to serve. Measures that provide new incentives to adopt that alternative will make lawyers, or doctors or whatever (I know a furnace repairman who powerfully embodies the way an expert should treat his clients) more fully human — will help to liberate them from their status as an oppressor class.

VII. THE CHURCH AND THE VISION OF POWER

The church has sometimes been characterized as a state within a state, and has sometimes been likened to a multinational corporation. Neither analogy is altogether persuasive. Like the state, the church has courts, lawyers, bureaucracies, public figures, and pageantries, and it commands loyalties not altogether rational. But it lacks the crucial power of the state, which is to implement policy by exercising physical control over persons and property. If the church ever had powers of this kind, it had them in subordination to secular rulers with agendas of their own. Now, it does not have them at all: it can no longer even deliver a bloc vote at an election. Like a multinational corporation, the church has a world-wide reach, a central direction, a range of different activities, and a good deal of money. But it has no control over the supply or production of anything, the flow of capital from anywhere to anywhere else, or the price of anything on the world market.

In short, the church maintains a great deal of the apparatus of power, but on the whole, very little of the reality. The apparatus can sometimes be turned to enhancing someone else's power, but it cannot exercise any significant power of its own. It is this quality of the institutional church that gives it a unique potential for dealing with some of the situations considered in this chapter. Being relatively powerless, it can become identified with people who lack power. At the same time, it has the juridical and corporate forms to provide coherence and legitimacy to confrontations with power. I have alluded in other chapters to some of the forms that such confrontations could take.

First, though, the forms have to be separated from their alliance with the people and organizations that they should be confronting. Effecting such a separation is not quite the problem in this country that it appears to be in some others, notably in Latin America. Our first settlers were in large part English Protestant Dissenters, people whose church polity was informal and who rapidly developed a tradition of letting a clergyman do just about anything his congregation would put up with. The Anglicans were not allowed to establish their hierarchy on this side of the Atlantic until after the Revolution, and took care not to adopt the pretensions to power of their colleagues in the old country. Other Protestant church administrators—Methodist bishops, Presbyterian moderators, Lutheran superintendants—tended also to keep a low profile. It is not that these groups have failed to identify themselves with the powerful in our society. But there is no great weight of institutional inertia to be overcome if particular ministers or churches should be minded to reorient themselves.

Roman Catholics, meanwhile, with their complex and highly visible institutional forms, have until quite recently maintained an underdog role in our society. Mostly late-arriving and poverty-stricken immigrants, often from what were regarded as inferior ethnic groups, always subject to mistrust arising from the religious conflicts of the sixteenth and seventeenth centuries, they slipped easily into a posture of powerlessness. In this posture, they were proud of being able to build splendid churches and effective schools. They also cherished a certain loftiness in their clergy as a challenge to the power and complacency of the dominant classes in society.

The clergy, for their part, knew how to take confrontive stands without relinquishing the role of underdog. They gave a good deal of support to the labor movement and organized boycotts on occasion to support such agendas as the suppression of pornography and the muting of anti-Catholic propaganda. Occasionally, for similar purposes, they delivered or threatened to deliver a bloc vote, or drew on the growing power of their parishioners in local politics. They were able to keep being underdogs through all this because, until the time of the Kennedys, Catholics, for all their upward mobility and political clout, were not really accepted into the elite. People might complain about the growth of "Catholic power" in American society, but it was always apparent on a little reflection that the people complaining had more real power than the people they were complaining about; they just wanted to keep it that way.

The 1960 election, the Second Vatican Council, and the ecumenical movement all came to pass in a remarkably short space of time. Among the results has been a rapid absorption of Roman Catholics into the mainstream of American life at every level, with everything good and bad that that mainstream affords. A certain amount of the apparatus, naturally enough, has been coopted along with the members, so that some of the old potential for official confrontation has been lost. The recent endorsement of the J.P. Stevens boycott by the bishops of the southern states argues, though, that a certain amount remains.

Within the apparatus itself, some people were affected in the old days by the kind of feudal powerlessness described at the beginning of this chapter. Innovative clergy, and the few laypeople who took an active and innovative part in church affairs were the main victims. Others ran afoul of the apparatus only by being at once insubmissive and unaware of their rights. Such people, although not subject to physical coercion, could be placed in a position where they supposed (erroneously) that they had been read out of a status required for their salvation.

The waning of the feudal style is all to the good, but it has left the church open to the national commitment to organization and expertise. Other churches, lacking the feudal tradition, have found it even easier to go the same way. Many of our most important religious projects, from the elucidation of Scripture to the organization of relief work, have come to be dominated by an ecumenical network of religious organizations and theological experts working more or less independently of the rank and file of believers. The theologians and the people who staff the organizations are often canonically lay, but occupationally and psychologically they are clerical, i.e., insiders when it comes to ecclesiastical affairs. Indeed, their insistence on the rights of the laity sometimes seems intended more to support their own insidership than to give new power to outsiders.

The network is in some tension with all forms of ecclesiastical authority. For the organizers, the intervention of such authority is a form of lateral accountability—since their own structures are ecumenical. For the theologians, accountability to any church authority is a form of lay accountability—the paradox is merely one of terminology. At the same time, the authorities are apt to see resistance as an imposition of lateral accountability on their own structures, and to react accordingly.

If the church is to enhance, or even retain, its usefulness in confronting organization and expertise in the secular world, it must also confront them here. It cannot do so by reviving the feudal style of a generation ago. What is needed is a more rational and dignified style, one both authoritative and pastoral. Organizations must be taken into account as they appear on the scene, and at the same time their activities or the participation of church members in them should be subjected to defined limits. Similarly, the role of professional theologians in the church should be spelled out, and at the same time limited. The need for a theological enterprise in dialogue with the teaching authority has been articulated, but never given legal content.

Here again, the church is meant to be a sign and a celebration of our liberation. It is by clothing the victims of powerlessness in our society with the symbols and structures of a higher power, by identifying with the powerless and articulating their claim to power, that ecclesiastical authority plays its part in manifesting that sign and carrying on that celebration.

5

Rootlessness

The Merriam Webster Unabridged Dictionary defines "rootless" as "lacking a tie or sympathetic relationship with or in the social environment." This use of the term is of fairly recent origin. The Oxford English Dictionary has only one entry in which people are characterized as rootless; that is an 1869 description of man's condition when separated from God. In the Merriam-Webster usage, the term seems to answer to the French *déraciné*, which the Supplement to the Oxford English Dictionary defines as " 'uprooted' from one's (national or social) environment." This definition is supported by entries beginning in 1921. Cassel's New French Dictionary treats *déraciné* as a noun, and defines it as "one torn from his (or her) native country." The general idea behind these definitions is that people are rootless when they lack a sense of belonging somewhere.

Americans are, almost by definition, torn from their native country, or uprooted from their national or social environment. They or their relatively recent ancestors have had the experience of trying to adopt a new native country and construct a new environment in forms assimilable by their children and grandchildren. To the extent that their children are not lacking a tie or sympathetic relationship with or in the social environment, it is because the endeavor has had a good deal of success. Still, except in a few isolated groups or places, the ancestral expedients hardly did away with the endemic rootlessness of American life. Now that these expedients are being eroded (along with more venerable ancestral expedients elsewhere), a growing tendency to rootlessness is all but unchecked for great numbers of our people. I propose in this chapter to consider what it was that was supposed to provide roots for

Americans in their new country, how it has been undermined, and how law can contribute to freeing our people from the ensuing drift.

I. AMERICAN ROOTS AND ROOTLESSNESS

Those who came here from Europe in the century or century and a half following independence found waiting for them a tradition, new-minted but already powerful, and either a supportive community or the intellectual and emotional tools for constructing one. The tradition was made up of a history, an ideology, and an aspiration — a past, a present, and a future — ready to be appropriated by the newcomer.

The history was articulated in terms of freedom under law. It was the love of freedom that had brought the Pilgrim Fathers to the stern coast of Massachusetts, and the love of law that had led them to sign the Mayflower Compact when they got there. The same combination was ringingly set forth in the Declaration of Independence, and fought for in the Revolution and, later, in the Civil War. In this context of ideological euphoria, a thing could become history almost as soon as it happened. The apotheosis of Washington began even before his death; that of Lincoln not long after his.

The ideology took up the same themes of liberty and law, with political democracy as a kind of corollary. There is a right way for people to live. That is the way most of them will choose to live when they are set free from meaningless inherited institutions and restraints. What laws and institutions they require for their protection and for the pursuit of their common concerns they can be relied on to establish for themselves by common consent. This ideological foundation — a simplified version of traditional natural law doctrine — supported a rapid political development in the newly founded settlements, and a rapid advance of new arrivals to full participation in the community. At the same time, the emphasis on the ideological underpinnings of our burgeoning institutions tended to obscure the extent to which those institutions depended on their historical context — the English (and to some extent the common European) legal and political tradition, and the rise of capitalism in the seventeenth and eighteenth centuries.

The aspiration can be described as upward mobility. However

much the new arrivals sought freedom and other intangibles, the prospect of economic and social betterment was seldom far from their minds. The concern took on a moral dimension because it validated the ideology: we never tired of flaunting before Europeans how our nurturing climate of freedom and democracy was making doctors, lawyers, scientists, and bank presidents out of the wretched refuse of their teeming shore.

By appropriating this tradition, the newly arrived American was able to achieve a substitute for the longer history and less amorphous culture he had left behind, and to think of himself as belonging to a nation different from other nations, including the one that was formerly his own. It remained to provide him with a substitute for the close-knit social fabric in which he had grown up, and from which he had torn himself in pursuit of a new life in a new country. This was constructed upon the common experience of being newly arrived. In the pioneer community, the new arrival was another pair of hands, another crack in the surrounding isolation, another assurance of the community's survival and growth. In the settled community or urban neighborhood, the new arrival was a potential voter, a potential spouse, a recruit for the ethnic group or the church. In either case, he found people who were glad to include him in their number and to share with him their newly acquired experience of how to get along.

As the experience of one generation became the history of the next, the tradition of shared assimilation and mutual support became identified with the rural settlement and the urban neighborhood. The tradition rapidly became embodied in a variety of institutions. Schools, churches, ward and precinct political organizations, lodges, Granges, and *Turnverein* provided ensuing generations with identification and support, all upon a fairly narrow geographical base.

This combination of ideology and neighborliness was not exactly the equivalent of a millennial history and an ordered society where everyone had a place. But it did give people a general idea of who they were and where they were coming from. Its power in the lives of our people is attested to by the sense of tragedy or at least nostalgia that goes with its loss or abandonment.

At this point, though, it is not the loss or abandonment of the supportive background by individual tragic figures that we have to contemplate. We are close to witnessing its loss or abandonment by the entire society. Not only have uprooted individuals become so numerous that it is hard to go on thinking of them as tragic; the national tradition and the supportive community are becoming ineffective as sources of rootedness for anyone. A number of forces have been at work in bringing this situation about.

First, there is a kind of disappropriation of our history. The so-called revisionist school of historians has taken a new look at much of our past, and found it seriously lacking in the moral qualities we have tried to claim for it.

The indictment is impressive and well-documented — the venality and corruption lurking behind our most ringing vindications of personal liberty, our persistent cheating of the Indians, our looking the other way while the slaves were brutalized and their descendants lynched; the violence and cynicism of so many of our industrial leaders; the miscarriages of justice, Sacco and Vanzetti, *Dred Scott*, and the rest.

These moral barriers to the comfortable appropriation of our history have been reinforced in recent years by the growing awareness of elements in our population who were on the wrong side in some of the crucial events. To look at plantation life through the eyes of a black person, at the Alamo through the eyes of a Mexican-American, or at the Winning of the West through the eyes of an Indian is vastly to complicate the process of identifying one's own roots through appropriating American history.

The ideological and aspirational elements of the national tradition have suffered in much the same way as the historical. The failure of our enterprise in Vietnam following a decade of growing perception of failure at home led many thoughtful Americans to wonder if their institutions were really as universally responsive to human needs as the traditional ideology supposed them to be. At the same time, our intellectual life came to be more and more dominated by doctrines that question the existence of any universal human qualities of which laws or institutions can take account. The result has been a tendency to think of our democratic institutions as a mere set of procedures, of marginal relevance to our own problems, and no relevance at all to other people's. If institutions are understood in this way, there is very little they can do to enhance anyone's sense of identity or belonging.

Other sources of disillusionment I have dealt with in previous chapters. For many of us, the hope of upward mobility is shattered by the reality of poverty. For others, the experience of upward mobility has proved more trivializing than fulfilling. For most of us, democratic ideology has been flawed by our sense of powerlessness before the different forms of organization and expertise that seem to be in control of our destinies.

It appears to be a combination of individualism and uniformity that is eroding the supportive community. Our culture recognizes no community loyalty that transcends the opportunity of the individual to find economic betterment or enhanced self-fulfillment by going somewhere else. A young person who turned down a well-paid or psychically rewarding job simply in order to remain a part of the community in which he grew up would be regarded, even within the community itself, as either a coward or a fool. As a result of this attitude, the tendency is for our supportive communities to lack a secure place in our national life. We think of them as having no purpose except to feed new arrivals or their children into the deracinated mainstream.

The mainstream, once entered, resists most forms of residual identification with the community left behind. The combination of high geographical mobility with uniform economic and social conditions tends to impose a homogeneous lifestyle, and most forms of personal uniqueness are seen as a threat to what social cohesiveness there is. Unique religious traditions, which were thought to be more durable than ethnic or geographic differences, have also become attenuated. The traditional Protestant-Catholic-Jew identification persists, but there seems to be less and less difference in attitude or lifestyle between one identification and another. The growth of fundamentalist and other non-mainstream congregations may change the situation before too long, but at the moment our social mainstream is almost as homogenized and deracinated in its churchgoing as in its television watching.

II. LEGAL CONTRIBUTIONS TO UPROOTING

I have already referred to the place of law in the democratic ideology of our people. Our law was conceived of as a witness to the immutable moral principles underlying our newly-formed and rapidly changing society, as a guarantee of the personal worth of every citizen, as a safeguard of our freedom to pursue new achievement, and as a support for the civility of our living together. It was also an essential element in our supportive communities, connecting them with the wider society, establishing the forms and rituals of personal participation and mutual expectation within them, and sometimes protecting them against invasion or overreaching from without. In view of the part law has played in the establishment of roots for our society, it is not surprising to find law playing a key part now in their attenuation.

A. DISMANTLING THE TRADITION

The idea of an immutable natural law came out of the nineteenth and early twentieth centuries with a bad press. It was not scientifically demonstrable, it was irreconcilable with prevailing philosophies, and it had been persistently used in the courts to protect oppressive capitalist institutions against reform legislation.

To replace the immutable, undemonstrable, and unhelpful principles of natural law, legal theorists came up with doctrines characterized by the technological metaphors to which I referred earlier, by a reductively pragmatic approach to legal phenomena ("law is what the judges say it is"), and by concern with professional expertise. From an embodiment of the higher aspirations of our people, the law became only a sophisticated way of getting things done.

This pragmatic approach has had some successes to its credit. It put an end to a number of useless or pernicious dispositions. It supported legislation abolishing the yellow-dog contract and the twelve hour workday. It freed the urban slum dweller from the feudal principles that made it possible for a landlord to collect rent without fixing the toilet. Its stern critique brought about a total remodeling of civil procedure. In many ways, in short, it has served us well.

In the end, though, the unremitting exposure of the legal system to a pragmatic critique has to be destructive. Inevitably, the ability to perceive defects and inefficiencies is more widespread and more far-reaching than the ability to cope with them. Inevitably, criticisms pile up more rapidly than reforms. From being seen as a way of getting things done, the law comes to be seen as a way of not getting things done, or as a way of getting them done badly. If you see law as nothing more than a useful tool, you will come to see it as a failure, and eventually as an obstacle.

In a country where people's ideological underpinnings are heavily dependent on law, this process is obviously disorienting. I read of a judge who refuses to recite the Pledge of Allegiance because he is unwilling to assert that this is a nation "with liberty and justice for all." If he is right in regarding the words as an empirical statement, he is of course right in refusing to recite them. Even those who take a relatively complacent view of our legal system do not claim that everybody, without exception, enjoys liberty and justice under it. Those of us who are content to keep reciting the pledge are bestowing our allegiance not on what we see but on what we hope for. It is this allegiance based on aspiration that gives us roots in our law, and that is undermined by an uncompromisingly pragmatic approach.

Law has ways also of turning the national ideology against itself. It is through law that freedom is translated into pluralism and pluralism into non-discrimination. The ideology of freedom necessarily entails freedom even for those who reject the ideology; this paradox has been with us from the beginning. But if we move from freedom to non-discrimination, we cannot content ourselves with leaving in peace those who reject our ideology. We must do nothing to make them feel less fully accepted, less fully citizens, than we. Such a requirement militates against any public affirmation of our ideology at all. We have pretty well travelled this route in connection with religious affirmations; we seem in the process of travelling it with respect to sexual standards, social conventions, language, and most other things. While we can still affirm a commitment to freedom itself, we can no longer attribute that commitment to any profound conviction about what human beings are and are meant to be. It follows that there is not much of anything the community can offer its members as a contribution to their sense of identity.

As a further development, law not only undermines ideology, it replaces it. Since law is inherently common to the whole population, and people are discouraged from asserting that anything else is, concern for the common good becomes concern for the law and for the processes by which the law is made and applied: legality becomes a substitute for civic virtue. People are urgently instructed that it is their duty to lay aside their moral concerns and follow the law. Lawyers are exhorted to follow their high calling by implementing their clients' wishes as far as the law permits. We are told that if we do otherwise our free pluralist democracy cannot survive.

Law thus understood has little power to hold the community together. People cannot find in it an adequate matrix for their responsibilities to one another; nor can they feel the moral force of the community behind its dispositions, or perceive that being a good neighbor or a good citizen has anything to do with living by it.

For an example, take our attitudes toward the cohabitation of the unmarried. The legal institution of marriage is intended to set the terms for the participation of a man and a woman in society as a couple—both their social responsibilities and their sources of social support. In other times, when a couple lived together without being married, it was either because they could not meet the legal conditions for marrying one another, because they disapproved of the incidents attached to the marriage relation by law, or because they did not choose to participate in society as a couple. The typical unmarried couple today is quite different. They could marry if they chose, and may eventually do so. Their involvement in one another's economic and domestic affairs is at least as convoluted as what the law requires of a married couple, and about as hard to disentangle if they should separate. They are willing, and often eager, to participate in society as a couple. They keep their money in joint bank accounts. They buy furniture and sometimes even houses together. They take joint responsibility for raising their children. They expect to be jointly invited to social events. They complain of discrimination if society or particular members of it are reluctant to accept these patterns of joint participation.

It seems to me that their reason for not marrying is not so much to flout society as to flout the law. They are willing to accept social responsibilities, willing to demand social supports, but they cannot see the law as either defining the one or providing the other. The law for them has become so attenuated that it cannot speak with the moral force of the society in which they live.

That couples live together without bothering to marry is only one of the consequences of the demythologizing of law. When legality is put forward as a substitute for civic virtue and fails to gain acceptance in that capacity, what ensues is not a return to civic virtue, but a vacuum. If law does not embody the moral force of society, the moral force of society will probably go unembodied. Virtue will be entirely privatized, and people will not know what to expect of one another or of society, or what society is entitled to expect of them. And without some guidance on these matters, they will find no roots in the society or its traditions.

B. Dismantling the Supportive Community

I have described the impermanence of the supportive community in terms of a tendency to feed people into a homogeneous, eclectic, and deracinated mainstream. This phenomenon is of course not new. What is relatively new is the encroachment of the mainstream upon the communities that formerly fed into it — an encroachment largely either initiated or backed up by the legal system — so that people who have not chosen or are not ready to enter the mainstream find the mainstream forced upon them, and people who do enter the mainstream find their origins pulled out from under them.

The most obvious, the most legal, and the most vigorously protested of these encroachments involves the destruction of the geographical base of the local community. In the city, there is urban renewal and there is highway construction, both supported by tax money and by the power of eminent domain. Both tend to split or flatten neighborhoods, scatter the inhabitants, and move the social amenities out of reach. New housing is put up for people from somewhere else to live in, local shops give way to shopping centers along the newly built highways, and local schools are abandoned in favor of educational complexes characterized by fast buses and enormous gyms. Meanwhile, the corresponding rural community, under pressures described in an earlier chapter, is being turned into a suburb with relatively transient inhabitants whose roots, if any, are elsewhere.

These processes are reinforced by our concern with racial integration, and by our legislative and judicial measures to meet that concern. We are all familiar with the problem. Cohesive traditional neighborhoods tend to be racially segregated. It follows that neighborhood schools tend to be segregated schools. It also follows that building housing for poor people in the neighborhoods where they already live tends to perpetuate patterns of residential segregation. So do zoning restrictions that limit development—i.e., that prevent people from moving to new places where no one is living now. As regards schools, the remedy of choice has been to expand the districts and gerrymander the boundaries for racial balance: it is referred to as busing because the newly expanded districts are not compact enough for all the children to walk to school. As regards housing, the remedy of choice has been to scatter individual units, or, if need be, whole projects in neighborhoods where there have not previously been any poor people, especially poor people of a minority race.

The law has also contributed to the erosion of the political base of our supportive communities. I alluded to this process in the last chapter. Of course, we cannot blame on the law the replacement of precinct workers by spot commercials as the chief means of attracting voters. But the system of neighborhood politics has been powerfully affected by civil service laws that eliminate the patronage on which neighborhood political workers depend for their pay, and by social welfare laws that give people benefits administered by bureaucrats instead of favors administered by politicians. As regards the delivery of public services, and perhaps even as regards the integrity of the democratic process, these developments are all to the good. But they have eliminated one of the cohesive forces of the old neighborhood, and one of the sources of rootedness in neighborhood life.

III. THE CLASS ENEMY

A. THE ORGANIZATIONAL ELITE

William H. Whyte's *The Organization Man*, to which I have already referred, has a chapter called "The New Roots," in which he argues persuasively that the people he studies have found roots or a substitute for them in the sharing of their very rootlessness. Here again, Whyte's details and emphasis need updating, but his

basic conclusion seems valid. There is an organizational and professional elite in our society who have come to terms with the deracinating forces I have been describing, and who are consequently
comfortable with the status quo. Barring occasional moments of
nostalgia, they have gotten away from the need for a sustaining tradition. They are able to maintain the necessary sense of identity and
self-esteem under positivistic or pragmatic forms. They are able to
keep up with ongoing organizational values and measures of achievement. They have the material and intellectual resources to control
important aspects of their lives. With their vibrant organizations
and their developing skills, they find the present so challenging and
the future so open that they can afford to put up with the dismantling
of the past.

They are also independent of any geographical base. Whether
they work for one large employer or a succession of small ones,
their career commitments move them about and rub off any local
idiosyncrasies in their accent, their appearance, or their lifestyle.
Wherever they go, they fall into and out of interchangeable communities composed mostly of people transient or transplanted like
themselves. Wherever they go, they have more in common with each
other than with the rest of the population.

Culturally, they are homogeneous. They are products of a
generally uniform educational experience, administered by members
of their own class, and constituting both their socialization and their
ticket of admission to that class. Such diversities as there are reflect
not so much different cultural heritages as different curriculum options. A Chicano from a Los Angeles barrio is no more apt to read
Cervantes than is a German boy from New Ulm, Minnesota, who
is no more apt to read Goethe than is a French-Canadian from
Maine, who is no more apt to read Racine than is one of the Boston
Irish, who is no more apt to read Yeats than. . . . The point is that
the education is always indifferent to the heritage, never built on it.

The uniform culture is also supported by uniform patterns of
consumption, based on similar economic circumstances, similar
tastes updated by a common experience of the media, and generally similar needs. All of this is being passed on to the next generation through schools, either private ones or public ones in suburbs
where members of the elite can control the school board and have

an adequate tax base. These superior schools tend to be in the hands of educators who belong to the same class as the parents and share their outlook on life.

B. Mediation and Struggle

It seems farfetched to cast these friendly, sophisticated, competent, and well-intentioned people in the role of a class enemy, but that is in fact the role they often play. They do not sufficiently realize how much their adjustment to chronic rootlessness depends on economic, social, educational, and personal qualities that not all Americans possess. So whether they are liberals or conservatives, whether they are judges, teachers, government officials, academics, clergymen, social workers, or business executives, they tend to universalize upon their own experience, and to set social agendas accordingly. As they have more than their share of the altruism in our society, and a near monopoly of the power, money, and expertise, the social agendas they set are usually all the ones there are.

These agendas, wherever they appear on the political or ideological spectrum, tend to be ruthlessly pragmatic, and therefore to leave out of account the delicate fabric of community and tradition on which some people's sense of well-being depends. They tend to suppose that a suitable opportunity to participate in the national mainstream is all that an individual requires for personal indentity and fulfillment. Liberal agendas based on centralization and redistribution of social amenities and conservative agendas based on freeing the forces of the market for maximum production have both these tendencies in common. They mediate the adjustments of the organizational and professional elite at the expense of people who cannot achieve those adjustments, or who would prefer others.

As I have said, the elite are well-intentioned. Most of the harm they do is done through inadvertence. It arises largely from their persistent failure to realize how different they are from the rest of the population. The situation bears out with poignancy the liberationist's insistence that to ignore the class struggle is to side with the oppressor.

The converse may also turn out to be the case. These people do not want to be oppressors: if they realize what they are doing, they may have both the motivation and the resources to stop. There is in fact some indication that this is beginning to happen. Some social agendas—notably the razing of slum neighborhoods and the construction of highrise housing for the poor—are beginning to be abandoned because the same expertise that devised them is now showing how destructive they have turned out to be. Indeed, the very pragmatism on which all these class agendas depend seems to be drawing itself into question. That is, experiences like "Watergate" are perceived as pragmatic demonstrations of the inadequacy of pragmatism, and the weakness of a social class that has no more than a pragmatic justification for its own preeminence. The elite are attempting to fill the resulting gap by drawing on their own expertise for a supply of "values."

Their pragmatism is also teaching them that absorption into the mainstream is not an answer to everyone's need for identity and self-esteem. They are coming to accept agendas that admit of autonomy and cultural identification for certain groups in society, notably, blacks, Hispanics, and Indians. This acceptance has been hard come by. The first manifestations of the black power movement met with total bewilderment and considerable hurt feelings on the part of those members of the elite who had been contributing their professional and organizational skills to civil rights. The complaints of Mexican-Americans about forced acculturation in the schools were hardly noticed for some time after the black power advocates had succeeded in making their point. The abolition of Indian tribal institutions was barely halted in time.

Because these concessions are pragmatically based, they do not offer much in the way of new principles. It seems that every group that opts out of the mainstream has to make its own case for doing so. The lesson that the mainstream is presented too coercively across the board has not yet been learned. Similarly, the quest for values, because of its pragmatic origin, has failed to produce results commensurate with the effort it has evoked. To abstain from bribery, theft, and the corruption of public officials—the moral lesson of the Watergate fiasco—is important, but hardly an adequate orientation of one's life.

In sum, the pragmatic altruism of the organizational and professional elite is now being seriously challenged on its own terms. Those who have found in it a substitute for the traditional roots are not yet ready to give it up, but the more thoughtful among them are experiencing more and more discomfort in maintaining it. An acceptable alternative could free them from many pressures.

IV. A LEGAL AGENDA

A. RECOVERING THE TRADITION

I have suggested pragmatism and disillusionment as the forces primarily responsible for dismantling our national tradition. The disillusionment is largely responsive to the pragmatism: what disillusions us is not our aspirations but our experience of failure to live up to them or to achieve them. The failure is real enough; the disillusioning experiences are not going to go away. It follows that the triumphalism of the New Right is not an adequate basis for recovering what we have lost. What is needed is a new — and much humbler — way of relating our successes and failures to our aspirations.

I proposed earlier the replacement of technological metaphors by verbal ones to describe what law is about. The replacement would disarm much of the destructive pragmatic critique from which our laws have suffered and would open the way to a realistic understanding of the place of law in our social fabric and in the appropriation of our history. We could see, say, the Fourteenth Amendment or the National Labor Relations Act as a witness to our common suffering rather than a support for our common complacency. Laws like these are made for use, and we often use them to good effect, but it is not their effectiveness that gives them their places among the spiritual roots of our people. They are claims to justice written in the blood of our citizens — at Cold Harbor and Shiloh, in Watts and Selma, in the Chicago Haymarket and Harlan County, Kentucky. Whether we or our ancestors played a noble or an ignoble part in these confrontations, they are part of our national heritage, and the law stands witness to them.

To make the most of this witness involves replacing our pragmatic jurisprudence with a jurisprudence of aspirations. As we have seen, the pragmatic jurisprudence begins by seeing law as a tool or instrument for the achievement of justice. From there, the progression is almost inevitable to law as failure, and then to law as obstacle. On the other hand, if our law is a witness to our aspiration to justice, we can regard it as a protector and vindicator to the extent it is successful, and as a fellow victim to the extent it fails.

A restored jurisprudence of aspirations will enable us to take a new look at the old problem of "legislating morality." There are important moral principles that cannot appropriately be enforced with the full power of the state, but that a legal system worthy of a decent society cannot ignore. These are not all in the realm of sex. Our antitrust laws, multiple dwelling laws, stock promotion laws, and especially civil rights laws all have dispositions whose reach exceeds their grasp. Without them, the laws would be severely impaired in stature, and far less worthy of respect.

It is its moral stature that gives the law much of its power to support, vindicate, and protect. The law's massive witness against the criminal does as much to deter crime as does the fear of punishment. Poor people need the community concern expressed in our welfare laws almost as much as they need the money. These are two particular areas in which the pragmatic approach has proved especially destructive, offering fear without moral suasion in the one case, money without compassion or respect in the other.

A jurisprudence of aspirations will not only prevent the development of some destructive elements in the law; it will also give people a way of coping with the destructive elements that inevitably do arise. Even without accepting the traditional theory that an unjust law is no law at all, we can see the unjust use of legal forms or legal apparatus as a wound or a violence inflicted on the law. Brutal policemen, inept and uncaring bureaucrats, venal legislators, corrupt judges make of the law not an accomplice, but a victim.

A once-important school of jurisprudence, at present somewhat out of style, sees law as an emanation of the spirit of a particular people (*Volksgeist* to the German authors who originated the theory) as manifested in their history. The approach cannot be used in isolation, because the making and application of law raises moral questions that cannot be answered by an appeal to authenticity alone (slavery and the lynch mob are probably as authentically American as the Fourteenth Amendment). But combined with a morally or religiously based jurisprudence of aspirations, it can offer us a way of valuing our laws and institutions without being triumphalist about them. Our moral and spiritual roots as a people are expressed in our laws, such as they are. And our laws, whether they work well or badly, bear witness to an American Dream that has more to do with liberation than with two Cadillacs in every garage.

B. RECOVERING THE SUPPORTIVE COMMUNITY

If we are to have supportive communities of the kind we once had, the first thing we must provide is a geographical base. The least we can do is maintain those geographical bases that still exist. Fortunately, the tendency to tear down and replace people's houses indiscriminately seems to have run its course. But we have still not halted all the destructive forces at work in our neighborhoods, let alone established constructive ones.

For one thing, old houses, if they are left standing long enough, become historic houses. They then become attractive to members of the elite who choose not to live in suburbs. They are bought up, restored physically, and coopted culturally. Any house thus dealt with becomes an alien penetration of the neighborhood to which it belonged. A neighborhood subjected to many such penetrations will eventually extrude its former inhabitants, who will be both financially and culturally unable to keep up. The end result will be a lovely and congenial neighborhood, but not for the people who used to live there.

Many of the legal initiatives that have replaced the former scorched earth version of urban renewal tend to result in this kind of restoration. For instance, in the *Community Renewal Foundation* case, upholding Chicago's landmark program for putting substandard buildings into receivership, the receiver had taken possession of a substandard building worth $25,000, evidently housing more than one family, and proposed to turn it into a single family residence worth not less than $50,000. There is no indication of what became of the people who were living there before the receiver was appointed. A number of commentators on the receivership program have noted this effect and suggested that it be countered through rent subsidies applicable to the rehabilitated premises. Given the prevailing vendibility of things in our society, and the affluence of the elite, it is clear that subsidies of some kind will be required if traditional neighborhoods are to be preserved. Perhaps subsidies for existing tenants who wish to buy and restore their own homes would serve better than subsidies for new tenants coming in after a period of receivership.

Another device that has rather the same drawbacks as the receivership program is that of "urban homesteading." The idea here is for houses that have come into the possession of government agencies, usually through default on government-guaranteed mortgages, to be turned over at a nominal price to people who will repair them and live in them. These properties typically fall into default because they cannot fetch enough rent on the market to recoup the cost of making them habitable. Thus, they may be said to have no economic value, and a fair price for them is no price at all. The problem is that by the time they have gone through the necessary procedures to establish that this is the case, the people who were living in them have probably moved out. The people who take them over are apt to be strangers to the neighborhood. Here again, arrangements to turn the property over to the original tenants when it falls into this situation would do more for preserving neighborhoods.

At another economic level, housing that does not need rehabilitation may be in danger of succumbing to the current fashion of turning multiple dwellings into condominiums. A condominium is theoretically co-owned by the people who live in it. That is, each tenant owns his apartment outright, and is a co-owner of the buildings, the grounds, and the common spaces. You buy your apartment in the same way you buy a house, and, in addition, you pay an assessed share of the cost of maintaining the building, running the elevators, and paying the doorman. When the owner of a building decides to stop being a landlord and become the manager of a condominium, he sells all the apartments for whatever the traffic will bear. Generally, the traffic will bear a good deal more than the present tenants can afford to pay. Transformations of this kind, which provide the landlord with a windfall profit at the expense of his tenants, ought to be restricted by law. Other countries, including Great Britain, have a broad statutory protection for tenants who wish to go on living in their homes. I suspect this protection has something to do with the greater stability of neighborhoods in, say, London than in, say, New York. There is no reason why similar measures should not be adopted here.

Cohesive neighborhoods can be disrupted by the indiscriminate

introduction of the poor, as well as of the rich. With the abandonment of the highrise ghettos of the fifties and early sixties, a number
of public housing projects have turned to "scatter-siting" or putting units of low-income housing in among other kinds of housing.
Nowadays, most cohesive neighborhoods are only tenuously so, and
it does not take very many outsiders coming in at once to disrupt
them. At the same time, poor people are not apt to be comfortable
moving into middle-class neighborhoods at government expense
without the support of a few other people in the same condition.
Add to this the fact that it is cheaper to build large units than to
build small ones, and you have a scatter-siting program that is as
apt to scatter the original inhabitants of the neighborhood as to scatter the poor among them.

This problem is not easily solved, because the poor have to
live somewhere, and if they are not to be segregated they must be
introduced into places where other people are now living. Building
them new housing in the places where they already are is objectionable because it perpetuates patterns of race segregation, and impractical because existing buildings must be torn down before new
ones can be built on the site. Upgrading existing buildings for the
present inhabitants is useful, but it is not a complete solution,
because overcrowding is a serious problem in the slums, and cannot
be dealt with unless more units are built. Some people have proposed giving rent subsidies to the poor and letting them live wherever they please. The theory is that this will encourage private enterprise to put up more housing, because there will be more of a
demand. The Rand Corporation has recently finished running a ten-
year experiment for the government to see if this will in fact happen; the results are inconclusive. Of course, if the private sector
were to embark on a wholesale erection of new units, it would have
the same siting problems the government has now.

The upshot of all this is that we probably cannot develop a
housing program that will cure the erosion of social cohesiveness
in our neighborhoods, but we can develop a set of preferences that
will make it possible for people to stay where they are if they wish.
We should prefer upgrading existing units over building new ones.
We should prefer upgrading plans that protect the present occupants
over plans that call for a change in occupancy. Other things being

equal, we should prefer to site new housing with some regard for the present geographical connections of the people who are to live in it.

Neighborhood cohesion is threatened by the loss of social amenities, as well as by population shifts. Stores, movie houses, and even restaurants tend to give way to larger, more up-to-date, and, alas, cheaper operations on the outskirts of town. People perforce reorient their lives around their automobiles, and do their shopping and take their entertainment among strangers instead of neighbors. Changes in the law might reduce some of the burden of taxation and regulation for neighborhood businesses, and thus support their competitive position, or at least keep them from closing on account of prohibitive overhead. Some of the measures I proposed earlier for encouraging small business units might also help to counter the trend to desert the neighborhood, but on the whole the units in question would not be that small. A supermarket may be big in comparison to a neighborhood grocery store, and still be small in comparison to Gulf & Western.

One neighborhood social amenity for which the law bears the chief responsibility is the public school. Much has been said about the effect on neighborhoods of moving children out to go to school in central complexes or in other parts of town. If the law were to opt for neighborhood schools, it could do a great deal to maintain social cohesion in neighborhoods.

Indeed, education is only one of a broad range of matters that the law could return to neighborhood administration, and even to neighborhood control. I mentioned a number of others in the previous chapter. Transferring functions to the neighborhood level might not only maintain social cohesion in neighborhoods, it might help to impart such cohesion to neighborhoods that presently lack it. Whyte has pointed out how the sense of community is enhanced where people can get together for civic purposes as well as for recreation, and he shows how one of the residential developments he studies gains in social cohesiveness by being a municipality in its own right instead of a corner of a larger municipal unit. Community organizers and founders of neighborhood associations, even when they have failed in their immediate political objectives, have found a heightened sense of local identity resulting from their efforts. It would seem, then, that giving neighborhoods a political structure and assigning them important governmental functions to perform, as suggested in the previous chapter, might help people to recover supportive communities, whether or not it enhanced their political power.

C. TRADEOFFS

Unfortunately, the deracinating forces taken up in this chapter have often been the very forces we have most relied on to overcome poverty and to lower racial or ethnic barriers. In movies and novels, and to a great extent in real life, the path out of the home town or neighborhood into the cultural mainstream has also been the path of upward mobility. The child who emerges from the warm, supportive, socially cohesive family and community to seek his fortune in the great uncaring homogeneous mainstream ends up not only more rootless and alienated than his parents or his schoolmates who stayed behind; he ends up richer.

Similarly, according to the folklore about "Americanization," the shift from the Old World culture of one generation to the national culture of the next almost always involves both a geographical and a cultural dislocation. The generation that speaks English without an accent, that eats hamburgers in preference to tacos or gefilte fish, that is brought up on cherry tree and log cabin legends, and wonders why the old people were so excited about Parnell or Garibaldi is the same generation that moves from South Boston to Brookline, from Bleeker Street to Central Park West, from Skokie to Evanston. The appropriation of an American national identity seems inextricably related to the erosion of the supportive community.

Also, we have long relied on "integration," that is, a purposeful mingling of races, as our prime means of overcoming the injustices suffered in our society by racial minorities, especially blacks. Many black leaders are persuaded that the authorities will never spend enough money on a public school unless there are substantial numbers of white children in it. Similarly, it is felt that in housing projects and workplaces blacks will be individually mistreated if there are too few of them, collectively mistreated if there are too many of them. The loss of geographical and cultural roots has generally been regarded as an unavoidable price for the integration we so urgently require.

I have suggested that it is of the essence of liberation theology to eschew cost benefit analysis. God calls us to cast off our burdens, not to prioritize them. It will not do to ask questions like how much additional poverty or racism we will put up with in order to feel a little more rooted. On the other hand, rootlessness is only one of the things from which we would like to be liberated, and there is no theological mandate for different kinds of liberation to get in each other's way. We ought to be able to look beyond the clash of competing values, and find a point at which the values are not competing but complementary.

In fact, it seems to me that the clashes I have been describing all arise from a certain timidity of purpose. They are a product of pusillanimous notions of how to run a society. Here are the observations on which they seem to rest:

1. Upward mobility is the normal escape from poverty. That is, the remedy for elitism is to join the elite.
2. Appropriation of the national identity involves a suppression of the ethnic heritage. That is, the way to become what you want to be is to forget what you have been. Or the way to get where you want to go is to forget where you are coming from.
3. Racial minorities will be oppressed until they are dispersed among the general population. That is, they will go on being oppressed as long as we have any way of getting at them. They cannot have adequate social amenities unless they take hostages from the general population.

It would be hard to argue that this ungenerous view of the way to survive and prosper in American society is not supported by experience. My point is rather that a liberating legal agenda should confront, not accommodate, the forces that subject us to that kind of experience. Here and in previous chapters, I have tried to develop an agenda that will do just that. Giving people with their different local and cultural affinities a chance to draw sustenance from one another, a chance to reflect together on their origins, their identity, and their place in the national life, and a chance to participate together in the control of their own affairs will not be inconsistent with such an agenda, although it may interfere with some of our cherished accommodations.

V. THE CHURCH AND THE VISION OF ROOTS

For the supportive communities of the past, the local church was a major focus of identity and social cohesion. At the same time, it provided through its theology and polity a bridge between ethnic and local identification on the one hand and national and ideological identification on the other. Each local church had its own way of celebrating the European past—the Yule log, the crown of candles, the statue carried in procession. Each denomination had its own way of appropriating the national history—the Episcopal parish where Washington and Jefferson worshipped, the Congregational or Unitarian churches on the village greens in Massachusetts, the correspondence between George Washington and Archbishop Carroll, the Irish Brigade receiving general absolution before going into battle at Gettysburg, the admonitions of Roger Williams on religious freedom and the separation of church and state. Each denomination had also its own way of appropriating the national ideology, by showing the Catholic philosophical roots of the Declaration of Independence, or the Protestant theological roots of the First Amendment.

Through the 1950s, the church tended to play in the mainstream a role very similar to the one it had played in the peripheral communities. Will Herberg, writing in 1955, pointed to the use of rudimentary religious identifications—Protestant, Catholic, or Jew—to replace ethnic identifications as people moved out of their immigrant communities into the mainstream. Whyte shows how the suburban local church—on an attenuated doctrinal base, to be sure—played a major part in channeling some of the gregariousness of the instant mainstream communities he describes.

In great part, this function of the church was a casualty of the sixties. During that decade, the ecumenical movement progressed to the point that religious identification became virtually useless as a way of positioning people within the mainstream. Liturgical change and theological permissiveness made it harder and harder to find in the church a connection with tradition, heritage, or ideology. In many cases also, the church's moral and social teachings came to be formulated in a way that made them a challenge, rather than a support, to the mainstream.

Like so many of the deracinating tendencies elsewhere in society, these changes were generally presided over by members of the elite, who showed here as elsewhere a good deal of insensitivity to needs and experiences not their own. The agendas for church renewal were characterized by pragmatism, intellectual sophistication, and disregard for the past. The proponents of these agendas, excited about Christian principles long obscured in the popular teaching, and confident of an open future with a major place for their own particular insights, were ruthless in dismantling structures and traditions that stood in their way. They tended to discount whatever opposition they encountered, as based on a perception of the Gospel less acute than their own (as indeed it often was). While they spoke of comforting the afflicted and afflicting the comfortable, they were often themselves comfortable enough in doing so. In their perceptions, and often in their effects, they resembled the people who tore down buildings for urban renewal.

Granted, it is hard to fault a Christian for hoping in the Gospel message rather than the tradition of the church, or for thinking it is more important to be committed to things as they ought to be than to be comfortable with things as they are. Granted also that it is hard to be patient with the people who want to bask in the rich periods of Thomas Cranmer on the rare occasions when they come to church, or to dress up and greet their friends on Sunday mornings without having to worry about social justice. Still, Christ did not come to call the just, and a steady shift toward ecclesiastical forms that demand a high level of spiritual awareness to appreciate may not be quite what He had in mind. Nor does it behoove those who deplore otherworldliness in religion to insist on church forms that ignore what religion is in fact doing for people in this world. In South Boston or Levittown no less than in Soweto or Recife, the church must come to people where they are.

The point is that many changes in church forms and structures, though desirable enough in themselves, have been experienced by rank and file Christians as alienating and uprooting. The task is now to restore as far as possible the traditional sources of orientation and support without obscuring the new light that has been shed on what it means to be a Christian.

With church institutions as with secular ones, it seems to me that the way to proceed is to develop patterns of local identification and autonomy, and to find a non-triumphalist form in which to appropriate the past. Both things can be done. We are already seeing more and more scope given to self-defining and self-governing congregations, even in denominations that have tended to be monolithic and authoritarian in the past. Many Roman Catholic parishes today have elected parish councils with as much power as Episcopalian vestries or boards of Presbyterian elders. Some groups, motivated by common doctrine or common concerns, organize on a non-parochial basis either for worship or for social action, and derive a powerful sense of community from being together. To give these burgeoning communities and shifting organizational structures the broadest possible base among rank and file church members requires, I suspect, a strengthening of both denominational and neighborhood ties. With a little ingenuity and good will, they can be strengthened without giving up our newly developed flexibility and autonomy.

As for the past, it often seems as if what is really important in the Christian religion was discovered in about 1965 — but that is really not the case. We do not have to write off the whole structure of medieval theology because St. Thomas had some bizarre ideas about biology, or because the peasants were superstitious, or because the academic enterprise was supported by skimming off the top of a subsistence agriculture. Nor do we have to write off the Pilgrim Fathers because they kept careful accounts with their London backers or because they were mean to the Indians or because they persecuted Roger Williams. Quite aside from the theological point that Christ's immersing Himself in time makes the past necessarily normative, there is in our religious past much that can be celebrated even if it cannot be uncritically followed. Those who have tried to be Christians before us have left us a past to appropriate. As to drawing doctrinal conclusions from the past, Roman Catholics may have a different approach from Baptists, and Episcopalians a different approach from either, but no Christian body lacks a past, and none has a past to which its present-day members can look with unalloyed complacency. The church is always a pilgrim in this world, but like the rest of mankind it is on a path, not a merry-go-round. A judicious use of traditional polity, traditional liturgy, and traditional art can bring this knowledge and witness, this sign and celebration into sharper relief.

6

Sex

Needless to say, sex, as such, is not generally considered something from which people need to be liberated. On the other hand, sex as it figures among the institutions of our society is often intrusive or coercive, and more often trivialized. For the work of reforming or dismantling those institutions that impede God's initiatives and man's response to them, there is much to claim our attention in the ways that our society deals with sex.

I. A HISTORICAL SURVEY

The concern of the law with the subject is not new. People have almost always felt oppressed or endangered by one aspect or another of sex, and have looked to law for liberation or protection. In our own society, we can discern within the past century or so four different stages in the perception of how sexual matters require the liberating or protective intervention of law.

A. LUST

In the nineteenth century, it was lust that was seen as the problem. During the last half of the century, courts and legislatures both in England and in the United States addressed themselves to this problem with increasing severity and thoroughness. To the traditional laws against rape, sodomy, and public indecency, they added carefully graduated punishments for adultery, meretricious cohabitation, fornication, different degrees of participation in prostitution.

They outlawed contraceptives and abortifacients. They supplemented their measures against infanticide with measures against abortion and concealment of births. They adopted obscenity laws embodying the famous *Regina* v. *Hicklin* test—a work is obscene if it is calculated to incite lustful thoughts in persons whose minds are open to such influences.

In the realm of civil proceedings, they allowed divorce only for adultery, desertion or physical abuse endangering life or health. They allowed a wronged husband and later a wronged wife to sue for criminal conversation (i.e., adultery) or for alienation of affections. They allowed a parent to recover damages for the seduction of a daughter of previous chaste character. The gravamen of these proceedings seems to be for the most part the illicit stirring up of the powerful forces of sexuality, and the consequent disruption of the domestic tranquility of the complaining party.

B. Exploitation

By the turn of the century, a new perception had begun to make its way into the law. That was that exploitation in sexual matters required the law's attention more urgently than did simple lust. This perception entered into the great nineteenth-century feminist agendas. Women seem to have demanded easier divorce laws and more control over their own property less because of an abstract concern for equality than because of an experience of women being exploited to serve the pleasure and comfort of brutal and dissipated husbands.

Women did not get all they asked for—they did not get the vote until 1920—but there were substantial changes along the lines they had in mind. Legislation, mainly in the 1870s and 80s, did away with most (not all) of the contractual and proprietary disabilities of married women. The divorce laws were extended partly by legislatures and partly by the courts to include the infliction of mental distress as a ground for divorce. The 1885 edition of a standard law encyclopedia treats this extension as a desirable reform and the 1904 edition considers it an accomplished fact.

In the first years of the new century, much of the legal material on prostitution was reworked to treat the prostitute as a victim. In 1906, New York abolished both lack of consent and previous chaste character as elements of the offense of placing a woman in a brothel. In 1910, Congress enacted the Mann Act forbidding the interstate transportation of women and girls "for the purpose of prostitution or debauchery, or for any other immoral purpose." The women so transported were referred to as "white slaves," a term borrowed from a treaty on the same subject adopted in Paris in 1904. The states were quick to follow the federal initiative against exploitation:

> Between 1911 and 1915 forty-five states passed laws prohibiting third persons from profiting financially from prostitution, and punishing those guilty of forcing women and girls into prostitution, those guilty of pandering and those subsisting on the earnings of prostitutes.

A parallel development in the same period allowed a woman to bring a tort action for her own seduction if her reluctance was overcome by any artifice or device.

C. REPRESSION

With the popularization of Freud after the First World War, repression and hypocrisy in sexual matters came to be seen as more of a problem than exploitation or lust. Over the next several decades— through the mid-sixties—this perception dominated new developments in the law on the subject. The period coincides with that of interest-balancing in other areas of the law. Among the results of these combined phenomena was the introduction of the concept of redeeming social importance into the law of obscenity. The idea is that honest and liberating communication on the subject of sex can be distinguished from mere titillation ("appeal to the prurient interest"), and that the value of this kind of communication may be weighed in the balance against its potential adverse effect on the public morals.

Another result of the new focus of sexual concern was a shift in emphasis in the divorce laws from cruelty to incompatibility. In some states, this term—interpreted as covering personality clashes so serious as to make fulfillment of the personal ends of marriage impossible—was introduced among the statutory grounds. In others, the courts took the initiative in expanding such concepts as cruelty and desertion to apply to the same situation. If people could not hope within an existing relationship to meet the psychic needs to which the institution of marriage was addressed, it was only right that they should be freed to look elsewhere.

This view of the matter led also to a number of initiatives in the direction of requiring some kind of conciliation procedure before a divorce could be granted. These initiatives generally involved conventional counseling techniques reinforced in various ways with the force of the legal system. In some jurisdictions, statutes required counseling in every case. In others, if one party desired such counseling, the other could be forced to participate. Some courts embodied the results of counseling in elaborate consent decrees, and threatened contempt proceedings against a party who failed to comply. The actual effect of these procedures is debatable, but a good deal of literature, mostly optimistic, was devoted to them in the fifties and early sixties.

In most jurisdictions, the laws against contraception adopted during the anti-lust period were either repealed or interpreted out of existence sometime between 1917, when Margaret Sanger was tried for violating such a law, and 1965, when all such laws were invalidated by the Supreme Court. The typical statute included contraceptives and abortifacients in a general enumeration of obscene writings, pictures, and gadgets all of which it was a misdemeanor to trade in. Typical of the landmark cases in the judicial abolition of this legislation are *United States* v. *One Package* (1936) and *Commonwealth* v. *Corbett* (1940). In *One Package*, the most eminent panel of federal appellate judges in the country held that Congress cannot have meant to deprive the medical profession of the necessary equipment to treat women who had good reasons for avoiding pregnancy. In *Corbett*, the Supreme Judicial Court of Massachusetts held that condoms did not come within the laws against contraceptives, since they could be used for preventing disease as well as for preventing conception. One thing to notice about these cases is their complete disregard of what the nineteenth-century proponents of the laws in question would have regarded as the best way to avoid both pregnancy and venereal disease. It is implicit in both opinions that sexual abstinence is not to be expected of ordinary citizens, and that sexual expression is not to be inhibited by fear of pregnancy or disease.

In *Griswold* v. *Connecticut* (1965) this whole development culminated in an apotheosis of marital intimacy:

Would we allow the police to search the sacred precincts of marital bedrooms for telltale signs of the use of contraceptives? The very idea is repulsive to the notions of privacy surrounding the marriage relationship.

The laws on abortion moved in the same direction as those on contraception. The nineteenth-century legislation had generally forbidden abortion under heavy penalties, making an exception only where the procedure was necessary to save the life of the mother. The leading case on the relaxation of this principle was *R. v. Bourne* (1938), involving a prominent London surgeon who had performed an abortion on the fourteen-year-old victim of a multiple rape, after publicly announcing his intention to do so. MacNaghten, J., instructing the jury in the urbanely tendentious fashion of English judges, pointed out that life-threatening situations cannot be rigorously distinguished from merely unhealthy situations, and then invited the jury to reflect on the traumatic effect on the girl of carrying within her for nine months — and then delivering through less than fully developed pelvic bones — the physical reminder of what she had undergone. The defendant was acquitted with considerable fanfare.

As a result, it became respectable to argue that abortion should be permitted when necessary for the mental health of the pregnant woman — a position that MacNaghten, J., had adumbrated but not exactly embraced. This was the stand taken in the Model Penal Code, which was adopted by the American Law Institute in 1962, and was in the process of being enacted when the Supreme Court took the whole matter away from the legislatures in 1973.

D. CHOICE

Starting in the fifties, the law gradually shifted its emphasis in sexual matters from Sigmund Freud to John Stuart Mill. More and more commentators, judges, and legislators began concerning themselves not with supporting the positive aspects of sexuality, but simply with implementing sexual choices. In England, the famous Wolfenden Report (1957) proposed the repeal of all laws against sexual behavior in private between consenting adults. The framers of the American Model Penal Code (1962) took the same position. As the Code represented a much-needed updating of the general criminal law, it was adopted in many jurisdictions, without much notice being paid to the fact that prohibitions of fornication, adultery, sodomy, and the like were being dropped along with the laws against Sabbath-breaking, medicine shows, and allowing stallions and jacks to run at large.

Where the traditional strictures have not been abolished by the legislature, the courts have been invited to do the job, and, in several cases, have complied. Out of the growing concept of privacy, as set forth in *Griswold* v. *Connecticut*, quoted above, has been fashioned a constitutional doctrine capable of striking down any restriction on the right of our citizens to bed one another at will.

While the Supreme Court has yet to draw all the logical consequences of this approach, it has solidly embraced the approach itself. In *Eisenstadt* v. *Baird* (1972), it held per Brennan, J., that a law permitting the sale of contraceptives only to married people with prescriptions violated the Equal Protection clause of the Fourteenth Amendment by discriminating against the unmarried. This holding represents a departure from the teaching of *Griswold* v. *Connecticut*, which rested the right of married people to use contraceptives on the sacredness of the marriage relationship. *Eisenstadt* rests instead on the principle that the whole subject is one in which the private choice of the citizen, whether sacred or profane, cannot be interfered with by the state. *Roe* v. *Wade* (1973) extended the same principle of free choice to abortion. In the wake of *Roe*, statutes that retain a health criterion for abortion—those governing Medicaid payments are still constitutional—have often been interpreted with so broad a definition of health as to bring them also into line with freedom of choice.

The new emphasis on free choice has led to a rethinking of laws and attitudes concerning rape. It has tended to overcome with respect to this one offense the otherwise prevailing doctrine that the victim has no personal stake in the punishment of crime. It has also drawn into question the traditional legal principle that a husband cannot be guilty of raping his wife.

Free choice in the realm of obscenity has meant that the law has moved away from protecting only material with redeeming social importance, and has begun protecting anything, important or not, unless some "compelling state interest" can be found in suppressing it. An approach of this kind was proposed by Judge Jerome Frank in *United States* v. *Roth* (1956). He argued that appeal to prurient interest is as much within the right of free speech as appeal to any other interest. The Supreme Court did not accept his argument, but in the ensuing decade it imposed such rigorous standards of definition and proof on obscenity prosecutions as to accomplish very nearly the result Frank had in mind. The trend was reinforced by the general hostility of literary and academic people to any kind of obscenity prosecution. There was no work so gross that its publishers could not find witnesses with impeccable credentials to testify to its redeeming social importance.

In 1973, the Supreme Court attempted to restate the law of obscenity. The resulting decisions are not altogether clear, but they do establish that the important question is the motivation of the censor, rather than the motivation of the person uttering the material in issue. What is decisive is no longer the character of the sexuality envisaged by the material, but the nature of the public interest in controlling or suppressing it. You are entitled to freedom of choice as to what kind of sexual material you will distribute or peruse, except insofar as some compelling state interest stands in the way. There is some talk about a state interest in a decent society, but the main concern is with the prevention of antisocial conduct. The empirical basis for attributing antisocial conduct to erotic material is tenuous enough to lead a number of commentators to believe that all laws on the subject of obscenity should be repealed — a position adopted by a government commission that reported in 1970.

The emphasis on choice has by now made divorce available to just about anyone who wants it. Many states have amended their laws to allow divorce on a mere showing that the parties have lived apart for a specified period, sometimes as short as six months. The criterion of "irretrievable breakdown of the marriage," which has commended itself to more and more legislatures since its adoption by the British Parliament in 1969, has been interpreted so perfunctorily as to be meaningless. The criterion was originally conceived during the period before concern with compatibility had given way to concern with choice. It was accompanied by provisions for careful investigation by judges, and often by court-appointed marriage counselors, to see if the marriage had in fact broken down past hope of reconciliation. These provisions failed to achieve their purpose because many judges proved willing to find an irretrievable breakdown with no more evidence than the testimony of one spouse or the other that he or she saw no possibility of reconciliation.

In jurisdictions that have retained the fault criteria for divorce, courts have tended to accept evidence of the small change of marital friction as sufficient to establish cruelty or other statutory ground. They have done this for some time in uncontested cases, but they are now doing it in contested cases as well. In fact, given the prevailing exaltation of choice, it seems to be considered petty and spiteful to contest a divorce. Threatening a contest in order to negotiate a more favorable property settlement is borderline acceptable, but using the law to retain an unwilling sex partner is not.

The current controversies in the realm of sexual choices and the law involve legalized prostitution and gay rights. Neither has made a great deal of headway. Nevada permits brothels on a local option basis, and some cities (including Washington, D.C., and San Francisco) have ordinances forbidding discrimination on the basis of sexual preference. What is most interesting about both these projects is the nature of the arguments they evoke. The proponents of relaxation of the laws talk about not prosecuting victimless crimes and not imposing one person's morals on other people. In other words, they carry out to its logical conclusion the principle of respecting sexual choices. Their opponents, meanwhile, advert mainly to the moral and scriptural principles that condemn the conduct in question—paying little attention to the problems raised by enacting a moral code in the statute books. In other words, they are taking their stand on the nineteenth-century view that the law should condemn lust. What middle ground there is in the debate is occupied by a few people who talk about exploitation, at least in the case of prostitution. Father Bruce Ritter, head of a shelter for runaway children in New York City, where his charges are a hot commodity on several markets, continues to speak of prostitutes as victims. The cogency of Father Ritter's point is not limited to the situation he addresses. The juxtaposition of capitalism and free choice has produced many kinds of exploitation, and many victims besides teen-age prostitutes.

II. THE PROBLEM AS PRESENTLY PERCEIVED

Against this historical background, what can Christians looking at sex in contemporary American society discern as the problem areas calling for legal intervention? I see two such areas. The first is the commercialization, trivialization, and dehumanization of sex through the forces of the media and the mass market. The ideology of unfettered free choice operating in a market economy makes this development inevitable.

It is largely because of the way the market works that the liberation of the arts from the stifling grip of the censor, instead of producing whole generations of Joyces or Lawrences, has produced the skin flick, the *Playboy* centerfold, and ream after ream of paperbacks, written to order at so many sexual encounters per chapter, each differently contorted from the previous one. At this point, serious writers and directors are talking about "obligatory sex scenes" that they have to put into their works in order to sell them.

Similarly, the legalization of abortion as an element in the right to privacy has resulted in nationwide chains of abortion clinics, marketing their product with the usual advertising devices, complete with toll-free numbers and acceptance of major credit cards. If we proceed to legalize prostitution, we shall find the same kind of merchandising used there. In Nevada, home of our only initiatives toward legalization, the corporation commissioner has complained about having to register a corporation called Whorehouse, Inc., or something of the kind. Elaborate statutory provisions are needed to keep brothels from advertising in movie theatres or putting up billboards on the outskirts of town. There is nothing to stop them from taking out two or three column advertisements in the Yellow Pages of the telephone book, as abortion clinics and "adult" bookstores do. Indeed, there is authority from the Supreme Court that could be interpreted as invalidating such restrictions as there are on the advertising of brothels. There may even be a constitutional right for travel agents in other states to stock brochures extolling the facilities available in Nevada.

Part of the problem is that in our zeal for freedom of choice we have entirely lost sight of the economic dimensions of prostitution and pornography. We are able to discern and try to counteract the economic pressures that lead people to accept substandard wages or substandard housing, but we overlook the economic pressures that lead people into becoming prostitutes or acting in peep shows, because we are programmed into thinking of prostitution and obscenity as victimless crimes.

The second problem area is a broad failure of our laws and institutions to encourage the Christian values of premarital chastity and marital commitment. The combination of a libertarian ideology, a consumerist lifestyle, and a judiciary overly concerned with privacy tends to submerge these values in the public consciousness. Marriage is still talked about as a commitment, but living up to that commitment if it becomes difficult to do so is encouraged but little by the media, and not at all by the law. Similarly, if chastity is spoken of as a majority value, it is often only so that the unchaste can be enumerated among the minorities that should not be discriminated against. Much of the rhetoric of sexual permissiveness is borrowed from the First Amendment ("freedom of reproductive choice") or from the civil rights movement ("no discrimination on account of sexual orientation"). The approach can be extended to cover almost anything: on one occasion, the refusal of a college infirmary to distribute contraceptives was attacked as a discrimination against sexually active students.

This legal and rhetorical stand is not without its attractions. It has been effectively, even movingly, advocated by Professor Kenneth Karst in an article entitled "The Freedom of Intimate Association." Karst argues that those who succeed in living by an ascesis of deep intimacy and enduring commitment which they are free at any moment to reject are the only ones who succeed in fully developing the human significance of loving and being loved:

> The value of commitment is fully realizable only in an atmosphere of freedom to choose whether a particular association will be fleeting or enduring.

> The act of marrying . . . undoubtedly carries greater weight as an announcement of commitment when the wife binds herself to a marriage from which exit will be difficult. But from the wedding day forward, there is a progressive decline in that act's significance for the associational value of commitment. What begins to matter more for the husband is not that his wife was once ready to bind herself to him by ties enforceable by the state, but that she remains committed to him day by day—not because the law commands it but because she chooses the commitment. . . . Once the act of marriage recedes into the past, the freedom to leave gives added meaning to the decision to stay.

Of course it does. But Karst and the judges and commentators he so ably analyzes draw more conclusions from this fact than the fact deserves. What they are stating is a corrolary to the rudimentary theological principle that God wishes to be loved and served freely. But it does not follow that He wishes to be loved and served in a social vacuum. The freedom God has in mind is indestructible and there is every reason to suppose that He would like to have people encourage one another to use it well—therefore, to encourage one another to chastity and commitment in matters of sex.

Against this background, the question we have to ask—and to answer in the negative—is whether the law as it is now tending gives those who strive for chastity and commitment the kind of community support they are entitled to expect. The rhetoric of the First Amendment and civil rights is constantly encouraging people to think that the difference between the chaste and the unchaste, the married and the cohabiting, the heterosexual and the homosexual is comparable to the difference between the Catholic and the Protestant or the difference between the black and the white. Building upon this perception, the media, through their choice of situations and role models, tend to convey the message that the chaste or committed alternative is unusual, if not bizarre. Put all this together with the prevailing consumerism and the antipathy of this generation of Americans to any kind of deferred gratification, and you have a situation that is not merely tolerant of sexual alternatives: it is profoundly discouraging to people who choose to live in the way Christians believe God intended.

The situation is particularly distressing in that it affords the least social encouragement to those who are most in need of it. A glance at any period of history will indicate that those who opt for unchaste lifestyles do not need much support from the community to implement their choices, whereas those who opt for chastity need all the support they can get.

The present state of affairs has been referred to as a sexual revolution. Perhaps it is more a revolution in our laws, institutions, and public debate than in our private morals; still, it is a real historical development. I suggest that it is one which Christians cannot but find unacceptable. The persistent trivializing of sex and the persistent discouragement of chastity and commitment far outweigh any new opportunities for intimacy that are being opened up for those who cannot or will not accept the traditional forms. We have reached a point where the real liberation of human sexuality requires a confrontation with the prevailing historical trend—a sophisticated and respectful confrontation no doubt, but a firm confrontation nevertheless.

III. CONFRONTING THE SEXUAL REVOLUTION: A LEGAL AGENDA

A. PRINCIPLES AND DISCLAIMERS

Before considering the legal form that such a confrontation might take, let us take a brief look at the applicable philosophical and theological principles. The most important of these is that of natural law. To recognize a natural law is to accept that moral principles are not merely arbitrary, but respond to basic needs of human nature. Because we are the kind of creature we are, we will be happier and more fulfilled if we behave in certain ways and not in certain other ways. This is true of all people, whether they agree or not. If something is a precept of natural law, any person will be happier and more fulfilled, other things being equal, living up to it than not living up to it.

While the principles of natural law are part of Christian teaching, they are not, strictly speaking, Christian principles. They deal not with how to be a Christian, but with how to be a human being. When God calls on us to live chastely and to commit ourselves when we marry, He is not teaching us how to deny ourselves in order to follow Him. He is not telling us that He hates for us to enjoy ourselves, or that He wants us to pay for present pleasures with future misery. He is telling us that He made us the kind of creatures who will be happy and fulfilled through lives of chastity and commitment.

It follows that a life of chastity and commitment is better not only for those who choose it, but also for those who choose, or would like to choose, a different kind of life. All people share the same nature, and chastity and commitment are what that nature requires. It would seem, then, that a legal confrontation with the forces militating for unchastity and inconstancy should be liberating to everyone in our society.

But that is not the whole story. At least as urgently as our nature requires chastity and commitment, it requires a certain measure of autonomy—of the power to make and implement decisions, even wrong decisions, about our own affairs. Coercion in a matter as close to the core of the personality as sex can be as destructive as wrong decisions. A certain amount of the dismantling of coercive forms that has been going on must therefore be regarded as liberating.

In short, a Christian view of the nature and destiny of human beings can support neither the present tendency toward indiscriminate allowance of sexual choices nor the past tendency toward indiscriminate suppression of sexual immorality. The sexual revolution, like other historical events, is convoluted and ambivalent. It must be confronted because the course it is now running is destructive. But it must be confronted thoughtfully and with balance, because some of the alternatives would be still more destructive.

So it is clear that some things that have been attempted in the past should not be attempted again. Obviously, we should not be trying to ferret out and punish clandestine sexual sins. While, as I have indicated, I cannot agree that such sins are no one's business but the participants', the kind of police work necessary to bring them to light, and the kind of punishments necessary to deter anyone seriously minded to commit them would both be unacceptable in a free and open society.

Nor should we be trying to insure that as many acts of fornication or adultery as possible will be punished with pregnancy. The possibility of conception is, to be sure, a traditional deterrent to unchastity. But it has never been terribly effective, and the results have often been devastating for those who have not been deterred— as well as for their children. Thus, it was probably a bad idea to make contraceptives illegal. The early family planning agenda, which would have made them available only to married people seems wide of the mark also. The married couple who make a responsible decision to limit their family may be more attractive morally than the people who buy contraceptives from the vending machines in the singles bars or the teenagers who are referred to Planned Parenthood through their high school guidance counselors, but the community's stake in their not having children is less.

Related to the practice of denying contraceptives to the unmarried, and equally baneful, is the practice, particularly prevalent in church-related schools and colleges, of routinely firing or expelling any unmarried woman who becomes pregnant. Granted, such a woman's private affairs have inescapably become public, so that there are questions of scandal and bad example to be considered. But these are of secondary importance. To penalize conspicuous pregnancy is not to penalize fornication, it is to penalize not having an abortion.

Another thing we should not be trying to do is compel married people to stay together without regard to their motivations, their grievances, or their circumstances. Still less should we be trying to preserve their legal relationship when that relationship has ceased to have any bearing on the realities of their living arrangements. The divorce laws should insure due deliberation and encourage reconciliation wherever possible. But the Christian teaching that marriage is a lifetime commitment cannot be effectively enforced against people who insist firmly enough on rejecting it. All that can be done is to prevent such people from forming new and stable unions if they are willing to do so. This seems a dubious achievement at best.

Finally, it does not seem that we should be trying to bring about a general cleanup of literature and the arts through the intervention of the police and the courts. I believe that some of the grosser manifestations of media sex can be controlled, but I do not think it is either possible or desirable to suppress everything that an informed Christian conscience would consider it immoral to disseminate. Not possible, because the enterprise of suppression seems inevitably to fall into the wrong hands and to focus on material that is either innocuous if rightly understood, or opposed more for its political than its sexual content, or both. Not desirable because there are people with serious sexual concerns who would be done an injustice if they were not allowed to share those concerns by giving them literary or artistic expression — even if the resulting works are objectively immoral. Art is a way of reaching out, and a Christian view of the human condition must give it a high priority when it is seriously and sincerely undertaken.

B. SUPPORT FOR CHASTITY

Turning to the positive aspects of a legal agenda, I think the most important thing for the proponents of Christian sexual standards to look for in their laws is community support for lives of chastity and commitment, so that people who are making up their minds may be led to choose such lives, and people who have already chosen such lives may be led to persevere.

For this purpose, I would favor retaining or reviving the traditional laws against fornication, adultery, and deviate sexual conduct—not, as I have said, in order to deter or punish these sins as such, but in order to discountenance the claim that they represent acceptable alternative lifestyles in our community. Granted, it would be intolerable if such laws were to be enforced to the hilt. But they have been on the books for centuries without ever being so enforced. The only convictions I have found in recent years involve rape prosecutions where lack of consent is not adequately proved, or else failure to keep private matters private—soliciting strangers, inviting spectators, or distributing photographs. The earlier cases included an additional category of people who added bastards to the relief rolls. They also seem to have required generally more discretion to keep out of trouble than would be needed today. But clandestine sexual sinners were never rooted out and punished, and they are not going to be as long as prosecutors are accountable to the community. Some statutes have always included notoriety as an element of the offense, but I think we can rely on the common sense of police and prosecutors to impose similar limitations whatever the statutes say.

It has been suggested, successfully in some courts, that since prohibitions of private sexual conduct seem to authorize unacceptable intrusions of the state into the bedroom they are unconstitutional even if they are not in fact enforced through such intrusions. This is the argument that prevailed in *Griswold* v. *Connecticut*, where the Supreme Court found in the sacred and arcane intimacies of the marriage relationship a constitutional defense for someone convicted of the public distribution of contraceptives. The same argument was adopted by the Supreme Court of New Jersey in *State* v. *Saunders*, where two men were accused of raping two women in a parked car, and were convicted of fornication because the prosecution failed to prove lack of consent. The conviction was reversed because the statute on the subject was declared unconstitutional.

Other courts have taken what seems to me a wiser view of privacy. They distinguish between the right to make private choices

without the intrusion of public authority and the right to engage
in private intimacies without the intrusion of public surveillance,
and hold that only the latter right extends to the full range of consensual sex. The nuances of this approach are illustrated in the case
of *Lovisi* v *Slayton*, a habeas corpus proceeding decided by the
federal courts in Virginia in 1973-76. Mr. and Mrs. Lovisi were
convicted of sodomy on the basis of certain acts they had shared
with a third person whose acquaintance they had made through
a publication called *Swingers Digest*. The event had been photo-
graphed (evidently by an automatic device, not by a spectator) and
the photographs had fallen into the hands of Mrs. Lovisi's daughters,
then aged 11 and 13. The trial court on the habeas corpus proceeding held that there might be a constitutional right of privacy
for things done in private, even by more than two people, but that
the participants had forfeited their right by allowing photographs
to be taken and left where the children could find them. The appellate court disregarded the photographs and held that the right
extends only to couples (probably only to married couples), so that
the Lovisis forfeited their right by allowing a third person to be present, even as a participant.

Both courts in the *Lovisi* case are doing through constitutional
interpretation the same thing that is done in other cases through
discretionary enforcement. They are distinguishing between private
and public violations of the sexual standards supported by the community. This seems to be an acceptable approach. Note that it recognizes not a right to commit fornication, adultery, or sodomy, but
a right not to be checked up on. The difference is important. The
Lovisis were prosecuted because one of the children brought one
of the photographs to school. But they were prosecuted for the
substantive crime depicted, not for the depiction itself. In New
Jersey, it is hard to see what they would have been guilty of.

Some commentators have suggested a First Amendment objection to distinguishing in this way between public and private
behavior. To punish only for public behavior is to punish people
not for what they do, but for what they communicate. And punishing people for what they communicate is precisely what the First
Amendment forbids. This argument is one of many that treat freedom as a formal principle rather than a human purpose. Communication between human beings is protected by the constitution

because it is essential to their humanity that they relate to each other. The meaning of the constitutional protection should be governed by the reason for its existence. It is not apparent that conducting one's amours without discretion contributes to one's ability to relate to those who learn about them.

A corollary of my view that sexual immorality should remain unlawful is that gay rights ordinances and the like should not be enacted. Here again, it would seem appropriate to distinguish between public and private conduct. If there is a problem of people being harassed because of what other people think they are doing behind closed doors, I can see considerable merit in adopting legislation to protect them—even if their censorious neighbors have guessed right. But that does not appear to be the problem to which gay rights legislation is addressed. Rather, the proponents of such legislation want to "come out of the closet," that is, to have homosexuality accepted as an alternative mainstream lifestyle, one that can be publicly professed without adverse consequences. This I would be unwilling to concede.

For somewhat similar reasons, I would favor curbing the enthusiasm of some groups in our society for non-judgmental sex education and the public distribution of contraceptives. It is fair enough that those who cannot be dissuaded from illicit sex should be taught to avoid as many as possible of the tragic consequences. In the long run, though, the constant hawking of contraceptives to the young will surely have more far-reaching effects than that. The line between encouraging illicit sex and encouraging those who opt for illicit sex to use contraceptives is hard to draw, but I think it should be drawn. My tentative solution would be to limit the distribution of contraceptives, and also to limit some of the more resolutely clinical forms of sex education to doctors or other professional advisers—that is, to make them private rather than public.

The distinction between public and private is particularly difficult to apply in the increasingly common case of unmarried couples who cohabit. Many of these lead lives of estimable domesticity. While their sexual relationship is publicly professed, their lack of marital status is private, or at least not flaunted. Their not wearing wedding rings or not using the same surname does not at all prove that they are not married. You may know about their status only from the way they refer to each other, or you may not find out unless you ask. And you may have to ask still more before you find out what difference it makes. With divorce as easy as it is, they may be more deeply committed to each other than many married couples are. From a standpoint of encouraging chastity and commitment, it is hard to know how the law should treat these couples.

At one time, most states had laws against this kind of cohabitation, punishing it somewhat more severely than simple fornication or adultery. In some states, these laws are still in force, although I have found no recent case of anyone being punished for violating them. The principle that the relationship is unlawful in the sense of officially discountenanced seems still to prevail everywhere, whether or not there are criminal penalties provided. This principle complicates the legal disposition of the parties' affairs when they split up or when one of them dies. The law generally does not recognize rights founded on unlawful transactions (for instance, a murderer cannot inherit from his victim, and if a bank robber cheats his partner of his share of the loot, the courts will give the cheated partner no redress). Hence the laws protecting family relationships are generally not applied to cohabiting couples, nor are contracts enforced between them regarding their relationship.

A mitigation of sorts is the common law marriage. This is simply a normal marriage created by vows exchanged in private, rather than before a clergyman or magistrate. It was abolished by the Roman Catholic Church in 1563 and by the British Parliament in 1753, but it existed in most American jurisdictions well into the twentieth century, and exists in a few of them still. The common law marriage, like any other marriage, is created not by living together but by exchanging vows. Many courts tended, however, to infer the vows from the fact of cohabitation, and thus to bestow rough justice in some cases.

Another mitigation is the enforcement of collateral contracts. While sex cannot be part of the consideration for a contract, it will not invalidate a contract for something else. A lease or a construction contract will not be avoided simply because the parties are illicit lovers; nor will a man who seduces his housekeeper be automatically excused from paying her the agreed-on wages for keeping house.

It was on this contractual doctrine that the Supreme Court of California built the famous case of *Marvin* v. *Marvin* (1976). They held that the agreement of the parties to live together and pool their earnings was collateral to the illicit sexual relation between them, and could therefore be enforced. The premise seems far-fetched, whatever one may think of the conclusion: considering the terms of the agreement and the circumstances of the parties, one would be hard put to believe that anything but sex induced Mr. Marvin to enter into it. Furthermore, it is the sexual relation that makes us feel (if we do feel) that the result is just. We expect a certain economic reciprocity between business partners that we do not expect between sex partners. We do not find it in this case. The popular wisdom is probably correct in seeing *Marvin* as an abandonment of the doctrine that contracts based on illicit cohabitation are unenforceable. Indeed, the Supreme Court of Oregon explicitly abandoned the doctrine in a decision that came down at the same time as *Marvin*, but got no publicity because the defendant was neither an actor nor a particularly wealthy man.

A number of commentators have extrapolated upon this line of cases to project a future when couples (and trios or larger groups for that matter) may contract for whatever sexual and accompanying economic arrangements they choose. This probably goes farther than the cases will support, but I think there is enough of a trend in that direction to warrant mounting some resistance. If we accept that the natural law calls for sexual relations to be accompanied by personal commitment, we cannot take kindly to the idea of putting them all into contractual form. The essence of contract is negotiation, *quid pro quo, do ut des*, whereas open-endedness is of the essence of the commitment that is meant to go with the sexual relation.

The reason for giving some legal recognition to cohabiting couples is that they have in fact made open-ended commitments—often more open-ended than they realize. If the law does not do something for them, they will be hurt. The most attractive of them will be hurt not because their contracts are unenforceable, but because under the circumstances they have not thought to make contracts.

Accordingly, rather than the approach taken in the *Marvin* case, I would favor the approach taken by the drafters of a proposed new Civil Code for the Province of Quebec. They recognize a status of de facto consorts—couples who, without being married, live as married couples do in a stable union. Such couples owe one another an obligation of support as long as their relationship endures, and a court has power to continue the obligation after they break up. The presumption of legitimacy and parentage applies to children born during the relationship in the same way as it does to children born during a marriage. In case of intestacy, one consort can inherit from the other. No provision is made for a distribution of property on breakup, but one could be added without disturbing the basic scheme of the draft.

This draft is fairly radical on a number of family law topics; I would expect it to have some trouble in the legislature. The drafters report considerable controversy over whether it is right to institutionalize in this way a basically illicit relationship. To my mind, however, the draft is on the right track. The values in Christian marriage seem to be enhanced, rather than detracted from, by providing that people cannot embark on a continuing sexual relation without taking a modicum of responsibility for one another.

C. RESISTING COMMERCIALISM

In addition to giving generalized support and encouragement to chastity and commitment, the law can focus specifically on certain areas that call for more forceful interventions. One of these is commercialism in sexual matters, beginning with prostitution. The laws on prostitution are still dominated by the nineteenth century concern with lust and the early twentieth century concern with exploitation. They punish the prostitute (somewhat halfheartedly) for stirring up lust among respectable citizens, and they punish the procurer for luring virtuous maids into prostitution. The applicable statutes are often old ones, and the fines they impose are nominal, or have become so through inflation. Even where the statutes have been updated (as in New York), enforcement continues to follow old and perfunctory patterns.

The problem with enforcement is that the original purposes of this body of laws are not taken seriously any more. The ideology of free choice has undermined our concern with lust, and the conditions of modern life have made our picture of betrayed and exploited innocence look quaint. The findings of the social scientists also indicate that the old emphases are misplaced. They indicate that the typical customer of a prostitute is not a man driven by ungovernable lust, but a man who has weighed the costs and benefits of a personal relation with a woman and has opted for a commercial relation instead. Similarly, the typical prostitute has not been lured or betrayed; she has coolly weighed the alternative ways of making a living and has chosen this one. To be sure, some of the child prostitutes (the constituency of Fr. Ritter whom I have already mentioned) seem to have been betrayed in the old way, usually by pimps who befriended them when they ran away from home. Many of these, though, are in prostitution because they feel they have no practical alternative. They are too young to get jobs, and they have been abused at home. In a way, they are more victimized by the economic and social system than by their pimps. At any rate, these young victims are overlooked in the routines of a prosecutorial and court system geared to the perfunctory processing of consenting adults.

In short, prostitution as we experience it today is a quintessential capitalist enterprise, founded on cost benefit analysis, and eliciting the venality and vendibility that are endemic to American life. It cannot be countered under legal categories based on lust and betrayal. We need instead to take measures geared to the actual economic forces at work.

The place to begin is with the customer. He is the most vulnerable element in the enterprise. To attack the purveyors and ignore him is, as Karl Llewellyn puts it:

> to leave the demand vibrant and profitable, while seeking to choke off the supply. It is a curious piece of legal engineering. It is a charmingly unbusinesslike approach for a community dedicated to the business man. Not only is the purveyor, by hypothesis, peculiarly ingenious in obtaining corrupt protection; not only, even when that fails, is he equipped with the most competent talent for legal defense and largely impervious, at least to fine, if he should lose. The very publicity of legal proceedings against him becomes a business asset to him, whereas the customer shrinks even from the publicity of an arrest. And while the purveyor gambles cheerfully, and in money terms, his present profits against his possible losses, and writes off a contingent reserve against his fines, the customer must put his reputation on the table as an additional stake.

It seems to me that the reason we have not thus far done much about the customer is that we have seen him in the light of the old assumptions about lust. He is a respectable citizen whose temporary lapses are brought on by forces he can control only with difficulty. To destroy his reputation would be gratuitously cruel.

But if this is not what the customer is really like; if the customer is really a workaholic who is too busy to go courting, or an emotionally deprived person hiding from life behind his Diners Club card, then we do him no wrong by dealing with him severely. He is the mainspring of the nefarious enterprise. It is his alienation that has made all the latent vendibilities coalesce into a major commercial undertaking. Where the prostitute is dehumanized by her economic condition, the customer has already been dehumanized, and is producing the economic condition as a result. He is a primary instance of the liberationist doctrine that dismantling the oppressive institution will liberate the oppressor as well as the oppressed. The laws punishing customers are on the books in many states. Even without such laws, the customer should be punishable as an accessory to whatever offense the prostitute commits. What is needed for strict enforcement is a new attitude.

As for the prostitute herself (or in many cases himself) there is nothing wrong with the statutory punishments now in effect, but they are applied so infrequently and so mindlessly as to be a mere cost of doing business. The legal penalties should be encouraging the prostitute to adopt some other way of making a living. How severe they have to be to accomplish that depends on what alternatives there are. Obviously, if a girl is abused at home, and is too young to get a job anywhere else, a fine will probably not make her stop being a prostitute. The situation is complicated by a process of acculturation that gives prostitutes a fairly hermetic world to live in, and cuts them off effectively from the outside. To liberate the prostitute from this combination of economic and cultural motivations requires job opportunities and social supports in addition to penalties consistent and serious enough to take the edge off the financial attractions.

Finally, there are the entrepreneurs in this business, the procurers and organizers. Like other white-collar criminals, they generally get off with fines that they can write off as a cost of doing business. They should be given jail sentences. Also, their profits from the business should be directly expropriated. There is federal legislation, the Racketeer Influenced and Corrupt Organizations Act (RICO), which with slight modification, could be effectively used for that purpose. In general, setting out to crush a business enterprise qua enterprise is a new idea in our legal system. But we have good reason to do it, and we have the legal tools. We should begin.

Besides prostitution, the chief contributor to the commercialization of sex is pornography. The laws on this subject are presently in considerable disarray because of the court cases applying the First Amendment. The problem with the prevailing doctrines is not so much that they are theoretically unsatisfactory (though I find them so) as that they are too subtle. Prosecution under them requires more time and effort, more public resources, than a typical prosecutor's office can afford to spend on anything but the most sensational murder.

I am not sure, though, that a better set of doctrines would be significantly easier to apply. The line between exploitive pornography and honest artistic or scientific treatment of sexual matters is evidently harder to draw than it looks. I persist in thinking that a way can be found to close down the bookstores and movie houses that have turned "adult" into a pejorative term without depriving the public of all access to *Ulysses* or *Lady Chatterley's Lover*, but neither the free speech people nor the anti-pornography people give me much encouragement.

For the purposes proposed here, there are more important measures than the total suppression of material deserving of so drastic a treatment. Stores that do not specialize in erotica will generally keep such material under the counter rather than exclude minors from the premises. And material kept under the counter does not sell as well as displayed material because people who are willing to buy it are still embarrassed to ask for it. Thus, restricting display of erotic material in places accessible to minors will considerably reduce its sales.

Zoning to prevent the adult bookstores, topless dancers, and peepshows from all being concentrated in one place also reduces the economic base of such enterprises. If most of the people on a particular stretch of sidewalk have the same thing in mind, they lend one another support and encouragement that they would other-wise lack. There are possibilities also in using the power of the state over alcoholic beverages to control the kind of entertainment that can be offered in bars. It is very hard to formulate a ban on topless dancing that would not interfere with, say, the lovely performance given on tour a few years ago by the National Dance Troupe of Senegal. But the National Dance Troupe does not perform in bars.

Some particularly objectionable movies and photographs re-quire violations of law in the making—sodomy, fornication, sex-ual abuse of minors, or statutory rape. This does not automatically make it illegal to show them. But it might mean that the profit from showing them could be expropriated under a statute like RICO. Here again, then, the economic base can be attacked at points where suppression would be impractical.

D. Preventing Victimization

Not all the victims of the sexual revolution are brought into commercial channels. The most numerous and the most final class of such victims is the unborn. It is hard to know what to say about abortion that has not already been said, but it needs to be men-tioned in the context of the other destructive and solipsistic uses of sex of which it is a paradigm. Any liberating legal agenda deal-ing with sex must involve restoring this practice to the status it oc-cupied before the decade just past.

Parents' sexual choices victimize children in other ways after they are born. The problems of child custody become more and more convoluted as parents move about in search of a more perfect union. In dealing with these problems, most courts follow pretty conscientiously their legal duty to investigate the existential situa-tion and award custody in accordance with the best interest of the particular child. The tendency to favor mindlessly one parent over the other (mother in case of young children, parent of same sex in case of older ones) is beginning to give way under the prodding of equal rights advocates. There is still some tendency to favor the parent with the mainstream lifestyle over the less conventional par-ent. This has been criticized, but the cases I have seen appear to reach just results. Some of them involve unmarried cohabitation or avowed homosexuality on the part of the rejected parent; the criticism of the denial of custody is basically a claim to validation of the living arrangement. In the most famous of the cases not involving sexual immorality, the ability of the rejected parent to provide the child with financial stability or a stable living arrangement was in doubt.

Divorce can victimize the divorcing spouses as well as their children. In most jurisdictions, the courts have a broad power to award support from one party to the other, and to distribute the property accumulated during the marriage in accordance with their respective contributions, needs, and deserts. There is, however, a tendency to settle these cases, and the settlements are generally given effect without regard to the considerations that would have affected a decision if there had been no settlement. Parties to a divorce often come from a traumatic experience of rejection, a life-long habit of dependence, or both. Often, too, they lack independent legal advice. They are often therefore in no position to negotiate proper settlements. The court should review the fairness of settlements before approving them, as it does in other cases where there is danger of overreaching.

The possibilities for victimization in divorce and child custody cases are enhanced by the high mobility of our people. Courts are usually perfunctory in their investigation of the facts in uncontested matrimonial cases, and states have a tendency to vie with one another in making divorce litigation painless for outsiders. Theoretically, they can deal only with the marriages of instate residents, but residence is one of the facts that they seldom bother to investigate. It is possible for a spouse to go travelling and come up with a divorce judgment that does considerable harm to another spouse who lacks either the heart or the money to litigate far from home.

The dissolution of a non-marital cohabitation offers the same possibilities for victimization as a divorce, only more so. The measures discussed above for giving a modicum of legal recognition to the relationship might help somewhat, but in the last analysis there is not much that the law can do for people in this situation. By excluding the legal institution of marriage, they have made doubly vulnerable all the investments of time, emotion, and lost opportunity that the legal institution is intended to protect. These investments are part of the reason for considering marriage to be called for by natural law. A sexual relationship without strings is not in accordance with human nature.

E. PREVENTING COERCION

"Sexual harassment" of women in their employment—i.e., demanding sexual favors as a condition for promotion or sometimes even for continued employment—has become a common complaint with the increase in the numbers of women who work. Indeed, with an increasing number of women in supervisory positions, a few men are beginning to make the same complaint. Other situations involving sexual coercion or overreaching appear regularly, albeit less frequently, in the newspapers and in the legal literature. These include business relations such as choosing between competitive bids; professional relations such as doctor and patient (sex has been proposed and sometimes accepted as both physical and psychological therapy), lawyer and client, even priest and penitent; authoritative or custodial relations such as teacher and student, policeman and criminal, jailer and prisoner. It seems obvious that the legal protection in all these cases should be as broad as the opportunities for coercion or overreaching. Actually it is not.

In the case of sexual harassment on the job, if the victim is fired or otherwise discriminated against for rejecting the advances of an employer or supervisor, she probably has a claim under state or federal laws against sex discrimination. The employer in a column of Art Buchwald's who makes equal advances to employees of both sexes is theoretically possible in real life, but not very likely. In at least one state, New Hampshire, the offending employer or supervisor may be liable for damages under the common law as well. But if the victim submits to the threats and the threatened firing or discrimination does not come to pass, it is not at all clear that anyone will be liable for anything. There is also an intermediate case where the offender neither gets what he wants nor does what he threatens, but merely makes the work environment unpleasant for his victim. If she quits, she can treat the situation as tantamount to a firing, but it is not clear that she can do much if she stays. To remedy the situation, we need legislation that directly addresses sexual harassment on the job, rather than treating it as a form of discrimination.

For American lawyers, the consideration of sexual overreaching in a professional relationship begins with Don Moran, the mid-nineteenth-century Michigan physician who persuaded a sixteen-year-old patient to submit to sexual intercourse as treatment for a uterine complaint by telling her it was the only alternative to an extremely painful and often fatal operation. His conviction of rape was reversed for an erroneous jury instruction, but the way the court left the case he was probably convicted the next time. The theory was that the misrepresentation of the alternative had the same effect as a threat. This is fair enough, but it does not cover all the possibilities of overreaching in professional relationships. For instance, a psychiatrist who tells a patient that a sexual relationship with him is the best way of curing her neurosis is not guilty of rape, but he should certainly be stopped. In such cases, malpractice suits are effective if the patient gets worse. But most of the burden of dealing with cases like these (and miscellaneous cases like that of the optometrist who makes female patients undress to have their eyes examined) must fall on the professional organizations and the licensing authorities. They do bring disciplinary proceedings from time to time, but there should probably be many more.

The problem of sexual overreaching in confidential or dependent relationships will not really be adequately dealt with until sexual transactions within such relationships are generally outlawed, or at least scrutinized as suspiciously as financial transactions are. The Model Penal Code takes the step of outlawing all non-marital sex only within the relationship of guardian and ward and the relation of a person in custody with the person responsible for her. The general preoccupation with choice seems to stand in the way of taking such restrictions further. But real freedom would be more enhanced by laws that would make it possible for a woman to enter into a relation of trust and confidence without fearing that it will be abused.

IV. THE CLASS ENEMY

It would be far-fetched to characterize the unchaste, as such, as a social class. On the other hand, there are aspects of the sexual revolution that seem to respond to *rentier* sensibilities, to the desire to control things that characterizes the elite in our society, or to the antipathy to deferred gratification that characterizes their children. Also, the laws in which the revolution is embodied tend to be class selective in their impact. They favor people who are more concerned with organizational and technical achievement than with personal relations. They favor the self-sufficient and the self-reliant over the economically or psychically dependent. Even the revision of our obscenity laws has a class bias. The people who profit from reading unexpurgated versions of *Lady Chatterly's Lover, Couples,* or even *Fanny Hill* are far from covering the demographic range of the people who worry about their children hanging around the drugstore looking at pictures of naked women on motorcycles in *Easy Rider* magazine. Naturally enough, the ideology of free choice has special attractions for people with the social, cultural, and economic base to do a lot of choosing.

Furthermore, unchastity itself has a strong economic base these days. There are the abortion clinics, often proprietary operations, sometimes nationwide in scope, generally successful in claiming constitutional freedom from statutes that require abortions to be performed in hospitals. There are the pornographers, who do many different kinds of high profit, low overhead business. There are the legitimate media driven by various competitive pressures, and I sometimes think, by a kind of literary Gresham's Law, to reach further and further into the realms of the unchaste. There are the denizens of the literary demimonde, *Playboy, Penthouse,* and the like, whose status as pornographers or legitimate media can be debated, but whose witness to the profitability of unchastity is clear. There are prostitutes and their allies, some of whom are pretty abject, but many of whom are expensive, and rich.

To be sure, not all the ideologues of unchastity have an economic stake. Some have other kinds of personal stake—homosexuals who wish to come out of the closet, or others who wish to appropriate mainstream status for their personal lifestyles. Some have only a philosophical stake. They are hedonists who believe that the requirements of chastity interfere with personal fulfillment, or libertarians who believe that the behavior of consenting adults is no one's business but their own.

Whatever their stake, these proponents and supporters of unchastity should be seen by Christians as a class of oppressors. They are responsible for a social ambiance in which it is becoming more and more of a burden to live by Christian sexual standards, to bear effective witness to them, and to pass them on to another generation.

It is important to recognize these people as oppressors, because the measures proposed here would otherwise appear to be oppressing them. In support of this recognition, we must bring clearly to mind the teaching of our faith, and our experience of trying to live by it. People need to lead chaste lives if they are to be fully what God wants them to be. And they need a supportive social ambiance if they are to lead chaste lives.

Measures that contribute to such an ambiance will be liberating to all concerned. For those who advisedly choose unchaste lifestyles, there is not much we can do through law except to confront their claim to be part of the social and cultural mainstream. For people who are led into unchastity (or the literary and artistic ancillaries of unchastity) by economic pressures — the prostitute who lacks other marketable skills or thinks she does, the publisher who puts out licentious books because his competitors do, the druggist who stocks raunchy magazines because his distributor includes them in a package with *Time* and the *Reader's Digest* — the law can provide a real liberation. For those who have not yet made up their minds about sex, or who are wondering if the choices they have made are the right ones, the law can provide a strong encouragement, a liberation from what is often a lonely confrontation with powerful and ill-understood forces.

There remain the disinterested proponents of the libertarian ideology. A firm intellectual confrontation with these people should accompany the advancing of legal measures inconsistent with their doctrines. Often they are aware of the socially destructive tendency of their position. They continue to adhere to it because they find it intellectually compelling. It would be liberating to them to find it less compelling than they thought. The mere bringing together of proof texts and political muscle is less of an intellectual effort than the situation demands.

The libertarian position is philosophically vulnerable on two points. The first, its disregard for any human value besides free choice, is the less obvious of the two, although perhaps in the long run the more serious. The other is its disregard for the effect of society on individual choices. Here it is belied not only by philosophy but by experience. The experience, if we keep pointing it out, will be apparent to many people who would not accept the philosophy. It was not terribly long ago that comparable libertarian arguments were being made, with comparable destructive consequences, in the realm of economics. It was not the philosophy of the common good that brought those arguments into their present merited disrepute, it was the experience of proliferating misery. We may hope for a similar evolution here.

V. THE CHURCH AND THE VISION OF CHASTITY

The foundation of the church's role as a sign and celebration of chastity must be, it seems to me, the witness of those who voluntarily dedicate themselves to celibate lives. By this witness, they show the gratuitousness of sex, which to my mind is a major element in the joy of being married. Conversely, most of the power of the arguments for relaxing the prohibition of premarital sex and permitting divorce with remarriage derives from an unspoken assumption that sex is a necessity, that no one can be expected to do without it for any length of time. The refutation of this assumption is essential to any form of real sexual liberation. Given the vicissitudes of life, not everyone can expect to find a compatible marriage partner, and not everyone who marries can expect a lifetime without sickness, separation, too much company, or any of the other things that stand in the way of the sexual relation on one occasion or another. Life would be pretty sleazy for a lot of people if no one could do without sex.

I do not intend to make this insight the basis of a general critique of the canonical arrangements for relieving clergy and religious of their vows. Still less do I intend to make it the basis of an apology for the rule that all clergy must be celibate. I only want to suggest that it is neither bizarre nor unduly burdensome to invite some people to undertake a permanent condition of celibacy, to make such an undertaking a condition for some offices in the church, or to hold people to such an undertaking when they have made it. I suggested in an earlier chapter that the life of consecrated poverty should be revised to reflect solidarity with the involuntarily poor. Similarly, the life of consecrated celibacy should reflect solidarity with the involuntarily celibate—which is most people for part of their lives, some people for all their lives.

Besides the witness of consecrated celibacy, we need from the church a teaching witness. It is still Christian doctrine that marriage is a lifetime commitment and that sex outside marriage is sinful. The more the wisdom of the world rejects these doctrines, the more they need to be firmly and authoritatively proclaimed by the church.

The proclamation has been attenuated lately by concern for those who have not lived up to the doctrines as proclaimed. Ministries to the divorced and remarried and to homosexuals have developed a good deal of organizational force, and tend to play down or reject outright any moral teaching that stigmatizes their respective constituencies. Within the church as in the state, these constituencies claim institutional validation and mainstream status. Young people who engage in premarital sex are not as highly organized, but there is some tendency in youth ministries and college chaplaincies to avoid confronting them too forcefully.

The church has many of the same problems here as the state. Like the state, it has tended in recent years to concentrate on people who have already made up their minds about sexual standards rather than on people who are in the process of doing so. As with the state, the result has sometimes been to give insufficient support to the making of traditional choices. There is a real dilemma here. It will not do to give Christians the message that God has no further concern for them if they violate a moral teaching; on the other hand, it will not do to give them the message that God is indifferent to whether they violate moral teachings or not.

A more rigorous distinction between pastoral and moral theology may be part of the answer. Ideally, moral theology should answer only one question: What should I do? Any question about the consequences of doing otherwise belongs to some other branch of theology or to some other discipline. If this distinction is kept sharp, it may be seen that it is neither necessary nor appropriate to ground the pastoral treatment of the sinner on an insistence that he has not sinned.

This will certainly help with the person who is trying to make up his mind about sexual standards. It will prevent the teaching about what his decision should be from being obfuscated by pastoral solicitude for people who have decided differently. But the people who have decided differently will not go away. When a person violates the moral teachings of the church and professes an intention to go on doing so, when he reaffirms his lifestyle, his liaison, or his invalid marriage despite the institutional witness of the church, it is up to the church to weigh both moral and pastoral considerations and develop an effective response.

The traditional response has been to exclude such a person from participation in the sacraments — either as an unrepentant sinner or as a heretic. If this is done with enough fanfare, it gives a highly convincing witness to the church's commitment to its moral teaching. It may also occasionally jar someone's conscience and lead him to change his ways: this is what St. Paul hoped to accomplish in the church of Corinth. Generally, though, at least in today's social milieu, those most concerned with the pastoral treatment of the people excluded feel that the exclusion does more harm than good.

I wish I had a better solution to this dilemma than I have. I believe that there is great room for new pastoral initiatives in these matters, but in the end I will have to say that I believe the attenuation of the church's moral teaching is too high a price to pay for the pastoral care of those who advisedly reject that teaching. So I end up, reluctantly, favoring the continued exclusion from the sacraments at least of those who publicly embrace a manner of living inconsistent with chastity or with the indissolubility of marriage.

The problem of balancing moral witness and pastoral concern has been particularly felt in the shifting practice of Roman Catholic marriage tribunals. Until fairly recently, these tribunals were strict to the point of obscurantism in granting annulments, lest they weaken the church's witness to the indissolubility of marriage. The position in fact was somewhat anomalous. Ex hypothesi, a couple with a meritorious case for annulment has never been married. The legitimacy of trying to bring them back together is hard to see. The problem was that the church's law was overly affected by the situation in a few countries (notably Italy) where there was no civil divorce, so that people with no great concern for Christian marriage sought church annulments for their civil effect. These people elicited a skepticism from the church courts that was inappropriate in other countries, where civil divorce is freely available and people seek annulment only for religious reasons.

Today, these religious reasons are being more taken into account. The tribunals are developing less formal procedures, addressed to real questions about whether people at the time they were married had the intention to enter into a binding commitment and the capacity to live up to it. A few of them are perhaps becoming too exuberant in granting annulments. There is sometimes talk of ecclesiastical Renos, and there is some feeling that almost any divorced Catholic can get an annulment if he knows the right people. On the whole, though, a better balance is being struck than before.

Those Christian bodies that do not carry the disciplinary freight of the Roman Catholic still have the problem of the balance to contend with. A church may teach the indissolubility of marriage and yet leave to the consciences of individual members how they will implement that indissolubility in their own lives. But if members slip in and out of wedlock as easily as other people, what is to become of the teaching? A church may teach chastity without insisting that the unchaste are to be excluded from communion. But if communicants proposition one another after the services, how does the congregation support chastity? To some extent, churches have escaped these questions simply by not attracting people who rejected their teachings. But the pressure for validation is now being felt in the church as well as in the state, and more and more denominations are having to reexamine what they really stand for.

The point is that no Christian body has a perfect solution to the problem of institutionalizing or not institutionalizing its sexual standards. As a Roman Catholic, I have some predilection for the arrangements that prevail in my own church, though I realize that very different ones might be adopted without doing violence to the Gospel. But, whatever way we choose to institutionalize them, there are these points that need to be remembered and are in danger of being forgotten. It is the chaste life that is the loving life, the committed marriage that is the loving marriage. The people who need community support are the people who aspire to lives of chastity and commitment, rather than the people who do not. And it is hard to know where Christians should look for community support if not in their churches.

7

Violence

It is widely felt that we are more prone to violence than other affluent and politically stable societies are. Violence seems in various ways to be built into our history and our culture. Not only do we have our share (and some say more than our share) of robberies, muggings, rapes, murders, fire bombings, wife beatings, and barroom brawls. We also tend to mark the important phases in our political and economic evolution with riots, lynchings, police brutality, assassinations, and occasional pitched battles. I shall try here to examine these phenomena and see what the law can do about them.

In this discussion I shall limit myself to forms of violence that are both physical and illegal. I am aware of what social dissidents call institutional violence—I have dealt with some of it under other headings. I am also aware that there is a sense in which all injustice is a kind of violence. But liberation from the threat of physical aggression—maintenance of the peace—is the oldest function of law and still has a privileged place among such functions.

I. PATTERNS OF VIOLENCE

Violence in our society takes a number of different forms, public and private. On the private side, there is the ordinary violent crime—murder, robbery, rape, battery, mugging—perpetrated by private persons motivated by private quarrels, private neuroses, or private greed. There is also private response to crime in the form of vigilante justice or lynch law. This kind of thing seems at present to be at a low ebb, but it has a solid place in our history and it could re-emerge. Often also the police respond to crime with illegal violence. The law reports are full of complaints about illegal searches, arrests, and interrogations. In addition, there are complaints in the newspapers and by word of mouth concerning harassment of suspects or potential suspects, beating of prisoners, shooting of fleeing suspects, and occasionally even encouraging suspects to flee in order to shoot them.

Turning to the public sector, i.e., the pursuit of economic, social, or political goals, we find mass picketing, demonstrations that sometimes turn into riots or near-riots, occupation of buildings, and sometimes bombings, hijackings, kidnappings, or assassinations. In response to this kind of illegality — and sometimes also in response to peaceful and legal demonstrations or strikes — the authorities have various ways of overreacting, often involving clubs, firehoses, and dogs. Shooting into crowds is fortunately rare, but one Kent State goes a long way.

Violent response to strikes and demonstrations is not limited to the police and the National Guard. Ideological opponents sometimes take to the streets, as the Ku Klux Klan has done against civil rights demonstrators, and vice versa. Farmers, mine owners, and other employers have their strikebreakers, goon squads, company police, and occasional hit men.

Our perceptions of the problem of violence in society depend partly on our ideological presuppositions and partly on which of these different forms of violence we have in mind. It is unfortunate that the different perceptions tend to compete with one another for our attention and our political allegiance. They are probably all pretty sound, and will have to be taken into account in any general treatment of the problem.

A. BREAKDOWN OF LAW AND ORDER

One such perception puts the blame on changes in the legal and ideological structure of the criminal justice system. The indictment is far-reaching. It begins with *Mapp* v. *Ohio* and its rule that illegally obtained evidence cannot be used to convict a criminal. The baneful effects of this rule are not limited to the case where a guilty defendant successfully invokes it and goes free. The rule turns the whole criminal process into a scrutiny of police procedures instead of an examination of what if anything the accused has done. An innocent person wrongly accused is hard put to turn even the attention of his own lawyer from the investigative process to the accusation.

A further result is that the lawyers involved in the process, whether prosecutors or defenders, are so busy with the minutiae of police procedure that they cannot handle their caseloads. They are forced to dispose of many cases by plea bargaining—that is, by allowing the defendant, instead of going to trial, to plead guilty to an offense less serious than the one he is accused of committing. Plea bargaining is one of a number of reasons why serious offenders often get off with trivial punishments. It is also a reason why innocent people often get trivial punishments instead of no punishment at all. Our measures for assuring the rights of the accused exemplify the maxim *summum jus summa injuria*. If few emerge from the process with condign punishment, still fewer emerge from it with dignity.

This disorientation of the law is reinforced by a disorientation of the prevailing ideology. The traditional purposes of criminal justice, deterring offenses and avenging victims, have both had hard usage in modern thought.

In the case of deterrence, the problem is more sociological than philosophical. There are philosophical objections to punishing past crimes in order to deter future ones, but they are not so persuasive as to elicit any widespread sentiment for abandoning the practice. What undermines our interest in deterrence is the zeal of social theorists for observing the economic and social causes of crime. There is a tendency to believe that since economic and social conditions cause crimes, the crimes cannot be deterred as long as the economic and social conditions persist. Thus, people who are perfectly willing to believe that the threat of losing a five dollar an hour job will deter a typist from resisting the advances of her employer, or that the threat of not getting tenure will deter a scholar from publishing the results of his research cannot be persuaded that the threat of a year or two in prison will deter a high school dropout from snatching a purse.

As for avenging the victim, most humanitarian thought since the Enlightenment has insisted that the victim has no business wanting to be avenged. Here, it is sociology that gives way and philosophy that prevails. It is fairly clear that punishment plays a part in the social orientation of victims—that people feel one way about a world in which they can be robbed, raped, and murdered, and another way about a world in which they can be robbed, raped, and murdered with impunity. It is entirely clear that most victims want criminals punished and are outraged when they get off. But since the punishment of the criminal does not enhance for the victim any of the common philosophical indicia of well-being, the tendency is to ignore the social orientation and to write off the prevalent desire as primitive if not sadistic.

Putting these attitudes together, we find that we have no very good reason for punishing anyone. A community where such attitudes prevail can look with considerable complacency on a system under which many people vulgarly regarded as punishable do not get punished.

B. BREAKDOWN OF SOCIAL CONSENSUS

Another widespread perception is that the erosion of supportive communities, especially in the inner city, has made people more subject to violence and less ready to protect one another against it. This is by no means a general explanation. A substantial proportion of our crimes of violence are committed within the family, and another substantial proportion between friends or at least social companions. Still, it stands to reason that you are safer on the street or alone in your room in a neighborhood where you know everybody, and safer still in a neighborhood where people are willing to take responsibility for what goes on. It stands to reason also that you are less apt to commit acts of violence if you are a member of a community with strong social discipline that frowns on your doing so. A number of studies have found that certain cultural enclaves characterized by strong family and religious ties can be relatively free from crime even though all the economic indicators of a high crime area are present. It would seem to follow that the loss of comparable ties in mainstream neighborhoods and the isolation of individuals or individual families increase the threat of violence.

Other forms of social disintegration have been blamed for our political violence. We express our economic and social grievances by burning things, throwing things, tipping over each other's automobiles, and punching each other because we have lost confidence in the capacity of our political process to redress our grievances, and we have lost patience with a society in which our grievances remain unredressed. These losses, in turn, are attributable to the loss of our feeling of being fraternal participants in a country that is by and large just and well-governed. To speak of a "loss" of these attitudes and feelings perhaps betrays an overly sanguine view of our past. There have been for a long time important groups of our people disillusioned with the system, and willing to push their disillusionment to the point of violence. The opponents of the draft in the 1960s can hardly be compared to those of 1863, and a historian of the labor movement would laugh at the assertion that violence is on the increase in our political and economic life. Still, it cannot be denied that if people bestowed more confidence, or at least patience, on one another and on the system, there would be less violence.

C. ALIENATION OF THE POLICE

Those who worry about police brutality and those who worry about the ineffectiveness of the criminal justice system have in common a perception of the police as becoming more an army of occupation than a service to the community. The situation is partly the cause and partly the effect of a broad based community hostility to the whole enterprise of law enforcement. This hostility has some ideological bases, which we have already considered. It also feeds on police responses to the ideology and the accompanying frustration.

Because the community maintains a critical attitude toward the police, and because the courts will exclude evidence if it was improperly obtained, the police do their work under constant scrutiny. They often have to be as much concerned with defending what they do as they are with doing it. As a result, they are bogged down in paperwork. In many cases, they will refrain from making an arrest because the time they will have to spend processing the case will drastically reduce either their free time or their time protecting the public.

The situation is exacerbated by light punishments, a result

partly of ideology and partly of overcrowded caseloads that neces-
sitate plea bargaining. The sentences imposed often make the police
feel that the time and effort necessary to prepare a case are not worth
putting in. They may also have a more sinister effect. Not long ago
there was a police show on television in which the hero was constantly complaining about light sentences and suppression rules, and
in which he always ended up shooting the person he was after. The
lesson of the series seems to be that the criminal justice system is
so absurd that the only time just results are achieved is when the
police are able to find some excuse for killing criminals instead of
bringing them to trial. There is of course nothing new about shows
in which policemen shoot suspects, but the didacticism that this series
brought to the process is unusual. One wonders how many policemen took it seriously.

The frustrations and the concomitant indiscipline are both
enhanced by the lack of contact between the police and the community. The replacement of foot patrols by cars, although probably
conducive to a more efficient use of manpower and a more effective response to crises, tends to prevent police from identifying with
the neighborhoods in which they work. Also, in many neighborhoods, often those most in need of police intervention, relations
with the police tend to be poisoned by racial tensions. Recruitment
of minorities into the police is hampered by the same things that
hamper their recruitment into other jobs. And even if a force has
minority members, it cannot put them all into the ghetto all the
time. The ghetto is an undesirable assignment, and reserving it for
minorities would be discriminatory. Thus, the ghetto is often policed
by people of a different racial and cultural background from its
inhabitants.

Another problem is misunderstanding about what the police
are supposed to accomplish. The juxtaposition of "law and order"
in popular rhetoric has obscured the fact that the enforcement of
the law and the maintenance of order are two different functions,
and they may compete with one another for the time and effort of
the available personnel. The policeman who is busy investigating
last week's burglary is not out preventing this week's mugging. Then,
as regards the enforcement of law, the ideological question of how
far "victimless" crimes should be retained on the statute books tends
to absorb the practical question of whether police time is well spent

running in pot smokers and breaking up poker games. The resulting confusion leaves the police not knowing what to do, not doing what they do best, not doing what most needs to be done, or not doing what people want them to do.

Finally, there are problems of corruption and inefficiency that are endemic to police departments. Recruitment and promotion are dependent on local politics rather than merit. Initiative is discouraged in a number of ways. The system of promotion from the ranks inhibits the development of management skills in the upper echelons. Some assignments are excruciatingly dull, and they go to the people who step on the toes of politicians. Graft takers are often not found out, or not turned in, so that their presence saps the professional commitment of their honest colleagues. The available funds are more apt to be spent on equipment than on people. All these elements enter into the professional frustration of police officers, the gulf between them and the rest of society, and their inability to control the spread of violence.

D. COOPTATION OF PUBLIC FORCE BY ENEMIES OF REFORM

The use of police and troops to suppress labor unions is no longer a serious problem in our major industries. It is still encountered, though, in agriculture, and in a few small town textile mills and the like. The traditional legal support for coercion in these cases was the injunction, generally issued on the theory that the proposed union action was a violation of the antitrust laws, of a contract, or of the rights of a court-appointed receiver (a number of major railroads were in receivership during crucial periods in their labor relations). Most of the bases for injunctions have been done away with by now. Labor organizations are generally immune from the antitrust laws as long as they do the normal things labor organizations do. The infamous yellow-dog contract has been abolished. The right of workers to organize, bargain collectively, strike, and picket has been established both by statute and by constitutional decision. Also, the situation of our major unions is much different from what it was. A union aggrieved by a court order has plenty of resources both to negotiate and to appeal. There would be no point in violating the order. And if a union does violate a court order the court will be more apt to sequester the union's bank accounts than to send for the troops. There have been exceptions, generally in the public sector, where injunctions have been handed down and then defied, but even here the physical coercion of former times does not ensue. Rather, the situation is resolved politically.

There remain the criminal trespass laws, the immigration laws, and the opportunities for petty harassment any police force has. The criminal trespass laws generally provide that anyone who is on another person's land and refuses to leave when ordered to do so is guilty of an offense. These provisions have been invoked to keep labor organizers, civil rights workers, and legal services attorneys out of factories, migrant labor camps, fields and company towns. Most of these uses of the law are violations either of the National Labor Relations Act or of the constitutional right of free speech, but they continue to furnish rural sheriffs and small town police with pretexts for arresting people, intimidating them, and occasionally roughing them up.

Aliens illegally in the country are especial targets for intimidation and harassment because if they complain they can be deported. Also, they are apt not to know the language, and therefore apt not to understand what is going on. They are inclined (not always mistakenly, I suspect) to judge the local police by their experience of the police in their home countries. While they have theoretically the same right as citizens to be free from unreasonable searches and seizures, they have little way of enforcing their right because they have no right to be in the country. Their liability to deportation makes them vulnerable to arbitrary arrest and invasion of their homes. This vulnerability, in turn, supports the general atmosphere of potential violence and multiple victimization in which they live. Also, because many of the illegal aliens are Mexicans, their vulnerability is communicated to Mexican-American citizens, who often experience the same kinds of victimization and harassment as the aliens they resemble.

The point about both the immigration laws and the criminal trespass laws is not that there is something wrong with them as written (that may or may not be the case), but that the people who enforce them have particular economic, social, and cultural biases. They tend to be more committed to private property and to laissez faire economics than is the society at large. They are more committed to authority and less willing to give potential trouble-makers the benefit of the doubt. They are more provincial and less willing to give space to minorities and foreigners. When pressed, they will not only distort trespass or immigration laws, they will distort traffic laws or even arrest people for no reason at all. With this kind of mindset, it is easy for them to be turned into agents for oppressive persons or forces in society.

As regards the labor movement, the agencies of law enforcement operate in this oppressive capacity only at the margins. But the margins still yield a regular quota of nightstick concussions and false arrests. If other movements for social amelioration do not produce a similar quota of police and military violence, it is because they are relatively quiet at the moment. The civil rights and antiwar demonstrations of the 1960s were vigorously (and lawlessly) attacked in many places by police or troops or both. The resulting carnage did not match that of the labor battles earlier in the century, but Selma, Chicago, and Kent State will be remembered.

I suspect that when there are new demonstrations there will be new incidents of the same kind. These confrontations are ostensibly brought on by efforts to enforce such banal and unexceptionable laws as those requiring permits for parades, those requiring parks to be closed at a certain hour, or those against obstructing traffic. But the real purpose of the authorities in such situations is to vindicate their authority for the mere sake of vindicating it. The kind of demonstrations we are dealing with are mounted to show loss of confidence in the orderly political process. The process often reacts very much like a miffed parent.

E. Guns

Most of the different forms of violence in our society are exacerbated by the ready availability of firearms. The presence of a pistol in the desk drawer turns domestic spats and quarrels between neighbors into fatal tragedies where they would otherwise result in cuts, bruises, or fat lips. A small investment in a weapon turns a purse snatcher or a mugger into an armed robber, or a paranoid into an assassin. A policeman cannot tell people where to park at the fairgrounds or help old ladies cross the street unless he is wearing a gun. Police probably misuse their guns less often than they do their nightsticks or their dogs, but most of us recall press items

about petty thieves being shot while running away with the loot
or innocent people being threatened with police revolvers. Another
agency oversupplied with fire power is the National Guard. Armed
for warfare, and lacking adequate training in either fire discipline
or riot control, Guard units have been responsible for several of
the bloodiest episodes in our political history. Even with their other
problems of inadequate training and discipline, it is doubtful that
they would have done as much damage if their weapons had been
more discriminatingly chosen.

F. THE CLASS ENEMY

It is hard to assess the exact significance of the fact that the
laws and the ideology with which we meet the problem of violence
in our society are developed by judges, lawyers, legislators, administrators, and academics who are themselves relatively immune. They
live in neighborhoods or communities where suspicious characters
are noticed, where neighbors call the police, and where the police
come if called. If they live in the city, they have locks on their doors
and doormen in the lobbies of their apartment houses. Their work
and their social lives are organized around moving in fast cars from
one similarly protected area to another. If on occasion they are
robbed or mugged, they are able, as they fill out their insurance
claims, to feel that they were not careful enough, rather than that
there has been a breakdown of law and order.

By and large, they are even safer from the police than they are
from criminals. They do not belong to groups of people whom the
police arrest on suspicion or harass on general principles. If they
are arrested, they know how to get released, and how to sue. The
point was sharply illustrated recently by the experience of two of
my students, Mexican-Americans, who were stopped by the police
while visiting a poor district of Chicago. They were searched, they
were threatened with guns, and generally subjected to a line of treatment all of which was illegal, some of which was outrageous, and
much of which was frightening—until they were able to establish
their credentials as law students. At that point, the encounter
changed its character entirely. The police became friendly, cheer-
ful, and at least a little bit embarrassed. These students had become
members of a class of people who do not have to be afraid of the

police unless they commit serious crimes. Given their background, the students were not altogether pleased at the transformation. But there was not much they could do about it.

As I say, it is not clear exactly how this personal immunity affects people's attitudes toward violence and the laws dealing with it. It is reasonable to suppose that both our ideology and our laws would show more concern for victims if there were more victims involved in writing them. It is also reasonable to suppose that our measures to protect people against harassment by the police would take a different form if our community leaders were themselves subject to such harassment.

Victims who are not themselves members of the elite seem to be adequately protected against violence only at the point where they become visible to the elite. Our primary protection against mistreatment by the police is the rule that excludes illegally obtained evidence from a criminal trial. This rule of course does not protect anyone who is not being prosecuted. It is no help to the peaceful householder who is stopped and searched on his way home from work or the suspect who is worked over and then released. The person who is being prosecuted is in contact with lawyers and other members of the elite, whereas the person who is being harassed and let go usually is not.

The relation between class and visibility on the part of the victims of police harassment is borne out by the experience of James Ahern, police chief of New Haven, Connecticut from 1968 to 1971. In connection with an anticipated demonstration involving Yale students and black militants, he says

> a group called the Medical Committee on Human Rights came to request access to police detention facilities over the weekend to make sure that those arrested would not be beaten or mistreated. I welcomed them — but I was curious to know where they had been for years when ordinary prisoners had suffered inhuman conditions in obscurity. As I suspected, although the group was quite outspoken over May Day, once the crisis had passed, I saw no more of them.

This is not altogether fair to a group which, after all, was not based in New Haven, and which did good service to a number of causes (notably compelling the SEC to recognize economic and social concerns of stockholders), but it does point up the fact that the victims of violence seem to be visible only while members of the elite are looking at them.

The importance of this kind of visibility is further borne out by the impact of the women's movement on our perception of rape. When the wives and daughters of professional and management people began systematically examining the grievances of their sex, rape was an obvious, indeed paradigmatic, candidate for their attention. Police routines involved close and often insensitive questioning of the victim, with nothing much in the way of comfort and support. Investigation was perfunctory, often inept. The victim was subject to humiliating cross-examination at trial, and standards of proof were often so stringent as to preclude conviction. The women's movement has made significant gains in improving all these conditions.

What is interesting for present purposes is how completely those gains run counter to the prevailing ideology of criminal justice, and how little the discrepancy is noticed. In fact, many of the indignities suffered by rape victims are suffered by the victims of all crimes. But nobody notices because by the prevailing ideology the victim has no legitimate stake in the punishment of the criminal. It would seem, then, that at particular points where the makers of ideology can be made to identify with the victims of violence, the ideology will change. Perhaps that is what has to be done across the board.

Besides the class that is immune to violence, there is a class, more or less coextensive, that benefits from it, or from the economic and social conditions in which it thrives. There are the large growers and small businessmen in whose interest workers and union organizers are harassed and intimidated. There are the politicians and employers who make deals with gangsters. There are the children of corporate America, who bite the hand that feeds them in order to assuage their guilt feelings at being fed. There are the theorists and organizers who gain notoriety, clout, and lecture fees by making themselves spokesmen for the unfocused violence of ghetto or campus. And besides all of these, there are the people who, without meaning to hurt anybody, simply fail to notice the relation between their own prosperity and the conditions that drive others to the point of violence. I have tried in previous chapters to give some idea of who these people are.

II. A LEGAL AGENDA

In dealing with problems of violence, the law has always had the twofold role of mediating legitimate power and confronting illegitimate power. In the present condition of affairs, it has also a role of class mediation. Many of our difficulties come from confusing or misunderstanding these roles — confronting forms of power that do not seem illegitimate; mediating forms of power that do; confronting one class in the interest of another instead of mediating between classes. I will try here to sort out these difficulties and offer an agenda that assigns each role its proper place. I will not go into the specific items in much detail. Most of them are already familiar. We are in an area where we have not lacked for proposals, often good proposals, for solving our problems.

A. MEDIATING LEGITIMATE POWER

St. Paul teaches that the rulers of the state, in addition to being a terror to evildoers, are God's ministers to the law-abiding for their good. The laws dealing with police procedure need to be framed with that ministry in mind. The police are mediators of that ministry. They are present in a particular community or neighborhood not to confront the local inhabitants, but to protect them.

It is idle to try to implement this perception of the role of the police through legal procedures calculated to determine whether they have acquitted themselves well or badly in a confrontive situation. Civil suits for false arrest and the like, disciplinary proceedings — whether internal or before a civilian board — based on mistreatment of offenders or suspects, and motions for the suppression of illegally obtained evidence all presuppose that there has been a confrontation between citizens and police. The inquiry, therefore, is in every case whether the confrontation has been carried out according to the procedures laid down for it. Whether the police should have approached the situation in a confrontive mode in the first place is at best a peripheral question in any such proceeding; often it is entirely irrelevant.

The significant legal and administrative contribution to overcoming the confrontive mindset is in the internal definition of the police officer's task. It has been argued persuasively that it is hopeless to try to come at such a definition for each neighborhood or community based on what that particular neighborhood or community wants. Certainly, though, the local inhabitants should have a voice, and certainly there should be room for a professional discretion based on the perceived needs of a particular neighborhood. Certainly also, the ultimate authority in generating any such definition must be the political authority in the community. This authority should be exercised officially and publicly rather than under the counter as it often is today.

In short, the police should have a set of standing orders defining their tasks. These orders should emanate from elected officials with both professional and public inputs. They should be published and available to anyone who wants to look at them. Police should be accountable to their superiors, to their professional colleagues, and to the public for carrying them out.

Substantively, these orders should be framed to reflect the perceived need for protection. There are other values besides protection that enter into the criminal law, but this is not the place to implement them. I want to stress this point because separating the question of what behavior should be punishable from the question of how police time and effort should be allocated is essential if either question is to be intelligently answered.

Physical violence, of course, is not the only thing from which people need to be protected. People need to be protected against drugs as well as against muggings, against falling or drifting into prostitution as well as against being raped. And there are some transactions against which the social ambiance needs to be protected even if the participants do not. Corresponding to the different needs for protection, I see three levels of appropriate police effort:

1. Some crimes should be the subject of a major effort to keep them from happening. Crimes of personal violence are in this category. A person at home, at work, or in a frequented public place should be reasonably secure from personal attack. The movable property in his home or his place of business should also be reasonably safe. This kind of safety must be the first priority for the police or any other agency engaged in the mediation of governmental power.

2. Some crimes should be addressed by trying to break up the organizational structures on which they depend. Crimes in this

category include not only those such as prostitution and drugs
that involve corrupting individuals but those such as price-fixing
and bribery that involve corrupting the economy. Here it is more
important to dismantle the unjust structures than to liberate individuals from their grip.
3. Some crimes should be prosecuted only when they intrude forcefully upon public attention. Transactions involving sex, drugs,
pornography, gambling, and the like, if they are neither violent
nor organized, would fall into this category. The need is not
to prevent them from happening or to dismantle structures that
give rise to them, but to protect the social ambiance for the encouragement of people who are minded to avoid them.

It should be noted that in the second and third of these
categories the use of power is ancillary to other forms of social control through law, whereas in the first it is primary. Illegal structures will on the whole be successfully dismantled if they are successfully investigated. Laws for the protection of the social ambiance
accomplish their purpose more by their existence than by their enforcement. The enforcement is merely to make the existence credi-
ble. But when it comes to murder, rape, robbery, arson, or assault,
law as such has but little to do with anyone's motivation to commit or not to commit these crimes. If the laws against these crimes
do not call forth an exercise of power, they do nothing at all. This
is a further reason why these crimes must be given first priority in
focusing the available power.

Just as potential victims of violent crime have a special claim
on the protective power of the state, actual victims have a special
claim on the process of detection and punishment. Such persons
have been injured not only in their persons or property, but also in
their orientation toward the world in which they live. All of us in
one way or another live out our lives under the power of other people. What keeps us reasonably content is a conviction that on the
whole the power that is exercised over us is (at least in principle)
benevolent and just. If we are subjected to an exercise of unjust and
malevolent power, we suffer not merely in our bodies or the con-
tents of our purses, but in our whole understanding of what life
is about. It is through the careful mediation of the agencies of
legitimate power that such an encounter with illegitimate power can

be transformed from a profoundly disorienting experience into a common misfortune.

To effectuate this transformation, the process of investigation, trial, and sentencing must be characterized by power over the criminal and concern for the victim. The acquittal of the accused on the basis of improper conduct by the police seems an insult to the victim in such a case. The current move for compensating victims at public expense, while there is nothing wrong with it, is an irrelevancy in this context. The redress which the victim needs is to witness the overthrow of unjust by just power when the criminal is forced to submit to punishment. In a deeper sense, that is probably what the criminal needs also.

Much of this perception of the role of the criminal justice system in violent crime is in the process of being articulated on behalf of rape victims. It is needed with almost equal urgency by other victims. Because of the special place of sex in the orientation of the personality, rape is a particularly poignant example of a traumatizing encounter with unjust power. But it is not the only example.

Aside from reformulating our understanding of what the police are supposed to do, our most puzzling problem with them is probably finding some way to assure their ideological and racial neutrality. It is a philosophical as well as a practical problem. Much of our law reflects ideological positions. Much of it reflects aspects of our culture that are not uniform for all racial groups. How can the enforcement of the law be neutral where the law itself is not?

The answer probably lies in a shift of emphasis from enforcing the law to enforcing the peace. Granted, someone has to investigate stock frauds, bigamy, embezzlement, practicing medicine without a license, and selling liquor to minors. Someone has to bring the violators to book. Granted too that this work cannot be ideologically or culturally neutral. Wresting it out of its ideological and cultural context would make it intolerable to the community. I submit, though, that rank and file police work is not of this kind. Rank and file police work is, or should be, devoted to protecting people against other people's violence. Its ideological and racial neutrality therefore, rests on a commitment to a society where people of different ideologies and races can live at peace with one another.

This point is really the same one that I have been making

throughout this chapter. Peace is not an ideology or a cultural idiosyncrasy. It is man's first claim upon God and God's first commission to the state. Nor is "law and order" an ideology or a cultural idiosyncrasy, despite the uses to which it has been put in recent times. It is, in fact, two distinct and sometimes competing values. Law has necessarily an ideological and cultural dimension, and should be pursued advertently with that dimension in mind. Order corresponds to peace: it can and should be pursued in ideological and cultural neutrality. It is only by making this distinction that we can hope to have proposals such as minority recruitment and community relations programs for the police work out as they are meant to.

There are symbolic aspects of police organization and procedure that also need to be considered. It has been suggested, for instance, that the military structure and military dress of the police contribute to their picture of themselves as an occupation force surrounded by enemies, and also to the intimidating picture that the rest of the population have of them. Several departments have experimented with putting officers in blazers and striped ties instead of the familiar military-type uniforms. My own feelings about this approach are ambivalent. The police presence should be a protective rather than a threatening mediation, but it still has to be a mediation of power, not of bureaucratic amiability. Whether the power can be effectively symbolized without the uniform is a debatable point.

The French police, who have generally a more military style than ours, use an interesting symbol to show how they are mediating power and to whom. When they are approached by a citizen on the street, they salute. Their dress and bearing shows that they know they are using power. The salute shows that they know for whom they are using it.

B. CONFRONTING ILLEGITIMATE POWER

Where illegitimate power is legitimate power gone wrong, the law is vigorous but not always effective in confronting it. I have alluded more than once to our elaborate provisions for frustrating illegal police procedures by suppressing evidence and acquitting suspects. On paper, police officers can also be held civilly and criminally liable for abusing their power. In practice, of course, things do not always work out as they should. A policeman may escape criminal proceedings because there is no one but his own colleagues available to investigate and prepare the case. He may escape civil proceedings because judges and jurors believe him when he denies any wrongdoing. The suppression of evidence may not affect him because he may harass people without ever arresting them or bringing them to trial. It is likely that the judicial scrutiny of police procedures has more effect on the honest mistakes of good policemen than on the flagrant misconduct of bad ones.

Some of the proposals for accountability to which I have referred here may improve this situation. So may policies of recruitment and assignment that develop closer ties between police and community. If we can alter the perception of a generally hostile relation between the police and the populace, if we can escape the confrontive army of occupation model of the police presence in the community, the individual officer who roughs up citizens can be seen as a deviant rather than as an over-zealous pursuer of the common purpose. The ordinary course of civil and criminal law should then be just as effective as it is with other deviants.

The peacekeeping role of the military raises similar problems requiring similar solutions. In the extraordinary situation of a mass disruption of the peace, military intervention may be a necessary mediation of legitimate power and a riot may be a manifestation of illegitimate power that must be confronted. But that does not make the suppression of a riot into a war or the rioters into an enemy force. It is standard doctrine in military training that a rioter was a peaceful citizen before the riot started, and will become one again when the riot is over. The mission of troops in a riot is to hasten the return of the rioters to their former condition. They can only be hampered in their mission by seeing it instead as one of fighting a battle. The battlefield model also hampers the law in confronting abuses of military power. There are laws governing the way battles are fought, but they presuppose a transaction between enemies. They cannot be an effective guide to riot duty, which involves a transaction between fellow citizens. Like the policeman who beats up suspects, the soldier who misuses his power cannot be effectively confronted until he is perceived as a deviant rather than a person who is over-zealous in pursuing a common cause.

The problem is starkly exhibited in the protracted litigation over the Kent State shootings in 1970. The wounded students and the families of the dead students brought suit not long after the tragedy occurred. The case was finally settled in 1979 with a substantial payment by the state of Ohio to the plaintiffs. In the meanwhile, it gave rise to three opinions of the United States Court of Appeals for the Sixth Circuit, one of the United States Supreme Court, and innumerable proceedings at the trial court level. What I find striking about the way this litigation was carried on through this prolonged course is the way the plaintiffs' ideologically tainted and factually untenable contention that the troops should not have been on the Kent State campus at all, overshadowed their virtually incontestable contention that the troops once there had conducted themselves outrageously.

What this indicates to me is that the litigation was dominated by a confrontive or battlefield model of the role of troops in riot control. If you insist on this model, you must either side with the rioters or side with the troops. Then, giving judgment for the plaintiffs is siding with the rioters. It is not surprising that the case could not be settled until after the Court of Appeals definitively rejected the claim that the troops should not have been called out. With that claim removed, there was room for a mediative model of the role of the troops. They were there to mediate the public peace for rioter and non-rioter alike. Under this model, the soldier who shoots promiscuously and the officer responsible for his doing so are deviants and can be dealt with accordingly. If they are negligent, they can subject the state to tort liability. If they are worse than negligent, they can be court-martialed. This is the way the aftermath of the Kent State situation should have been seen. Kent State was for the Ohio National Guard what a combination of My Lai and Little Big Horn would be for the United States Army. It is the friends, not the enemies, of the Guard's mission on campus who should have been clamoring for the punishment of those responsible.

Of course, the most common encounter of ordinary citizens with illegitimate power involves neither mobs nor soldiers nor police, but criminals. The main way the law has of confronting criminals (aside from taking away their guns, a reform so obvious that it hardly seems worth discussing) is catching and punishing them. I have already taken up the role of the criminal justice system in mediating just power to the victims of crime, and so healing as far as possible the psychic wounds that go with being a victim. The system has also the role of confronting unjust power and so limiting its effect on society. These two roles correspond roughly to the roles of retribution and deterrence assigned to the system by legal theory.

But that is not the whole story. Just as the victim has a stake in the criminal justice system that is not reducible to a vulgar desire to get even, so the public has a stake that is not reducible to a desire to keep the crime from happening again. If unjust power is not effectively confronted, the ensuing disorientation affects not merely the victims but the whole society as well. A society in which crimes of violence are committed with impunity is not merely a society with a high crime rate. It is a radically unjust society, one that fails to give effective witness to the divine ordering of the world.

The goal of confronting unjust power offers a useful perspective on the usual criticisms that are levelled at the criminal justice system as it now operates. Consider first the suppression of illegally obtained evidence. What is wrong with this principle is that it responds to reciprocal instances of unjust power by confronting neither. The person whom the evidence would have convicted is not confronted because he gets off for lack of evidence. But the policeman who violated the Fourth Amendment is not confronted either. He may be frustrated of his immediate purpose, and, if he is of a utilitarian turn of mind, he may be deterred from like violations in the future because they do not accomplish what he has in mind. But the exclusion of evidence has no effect on his actual power or his ability to use it when he chooses to. If I am right in thinking that confronting unjust power serves purposes beyond mere deterrence, those purposes are not served by the exclusionary rule. Developing police disciplinary procedures capable of affording a serious alternative is an essential response both to police misconduct and to crime.

From the standpoint of confrontation, the vice in the system of plea bargaining is that it relies on compromises between just and unjust power. Compromise, of course, is the antithesis of confrontation. Again, deterrence is not all that is needed from the criminal proceeding. Even if the plea bargain results in a sentence sufficient to deter, the perception that the power of the criminal has not been effectively confronted remains with its disorienting effect. An optional summary trial proceeding with a reduced maximum sentence

might be developed to retain the confrontive model without losing
the advantages of efficiency and dispatch that are looked for in plea
bargaining.

Some of the sentences that people object to seem to stem from
a perception of the criminal law as confronting the person, rather
than the power, of the criminal. It is important in sentencing to
consider both the character of the criminal and the need to deter
future crime (though in many cases these two values may work
against each other). But a sentence could be effective from either
or both of these standpoints and still not leave the criminal or the
public with the feeling that unjust power has been effectively confronted. This concern would seem to support some of the recent
initiatives in favor of mandatory minimum sentences or restrictive
environments short of prison ("half-way houses") as an alternative
to probation.

C. CLASS MEDIATION

It is possible to discern many of the social roots of violent crime,
and perhaps strike out at a few of them. Nevertheless, it seems clear
that for the foreseeable future most crime, especially violent crime,
is going to be committed by the poor or the alienated, and punished
by the governing elite. It is likely also that most of the victims of
violent crime, and almost all the victims of police violence will be
drawn from among the poor and alienated, and will have to look
to the elite for redress. In this process, where so much depends on
them, the elite tend to fall into an oppressive role because a great
deal of what happens is invisible to them. For them, a liberating
legal mediation will be one that enhances visibility.

I have referred to the increased visibility of rape victims due
to the women's liberation movement. To some extent, the civil rights
movement has similarly increased the visibility of the victims of police
harassment, many of whom belong to minority races. The movement for old people's rights might well do the same thing for mugging victims, many of whom are old—although it has in fact been
more concerned with other things.

To some extent, political initiatives of this kind can be ad-
vanced in the courtroom. In recent years victims have taken to su-
ing local governments in tort for mistreatment of citizens by the

police, and even for failure to provide adequate protection against crime. The legal obstacles to such suits are formidable. A policeman who beats up suspects is exceeding his authority; therefore by conventional principles of master and servant law the city, as his employer, is not liable. Furthermore, in deploying police the city is performing a governmental function. Therefore, with respect to anything that happens as a result, it partakes of the general immunity of government agencies from suit. Where the complaint involves not something the police did wrong but the mere failure to have adequate police forces on hand, the city is all the more immune. And even if the city were not immune from suit, it might be immune from liability. Where to put the available police forces and how to keep them under control is a matter of judgment. The courts, it is argued, should not supersede the judgment of responsible officials by imposing liability.

It appears that the effectiveness of these arguments is being gradually eroded. Here a state legislature and there a court is abolishing or restricting the doctrine of governmental immunity or extending the liability of a master for the intentional torts of his servants. An occasional judge is even taking seriously the possibility that failure to have police officers on duty at the right time and place or failure to apprehend a known and dangerous offender can be negligence for which the city can be liable. In a somewhat analogous case, a landlord has been held liable to a tenant in an apartment house for failure to take reasonable steps to keep the hallways safe from intruders. The presence of a mugger or a rapist has been held to expose the landlord to the same kind of liability as the presence of a rusty nail or a broken stair.

Whether these attempts to impose liability are successful or not, they increase the visibility of the problems to which they are addressed. They provide a mediation through which the concerns of one class can be forcefully brought to the attention of another. That crimes be prevented, that criminals be punished, that innocent citizens not be harassed by the police, are all demands made by the class of victims upon the class of people responsible for affording them redress. Arguing before courts and legislatures for limiting the cross-examination of rape victims, for restructuring governmental immunities, or for holding municipalities accountable for the deployment of the police is putting these demands of class upon class into legal form. In their legal form, they can be weighed, discussed, negotiated, and, on occasion, met. At the very least, they will be noticed.

III. THE CHURCH AND THE VISION OF PEACE

From the time it introduced sanctuary and the Truce of God into the medieval scheme of private vengeance, the church has attempted in one way or another to institutionalize a vision of peace for secular society. The witness has been not so much a condemnation of violence as an expression of a better alternative. The tradition continues with the growing theology and practice of nonviolence in the church. A few small churches have always been officially pacifist. In other churches, the nonviolent movement was first institutionalized by unofficial organizations formed to apply its principles to particular problems. It has since gained a good deal more official acceptance, with the formation of peace and justice commissions and the like, as well as with the personal participation of bishops and other church leaders. At the moment, it is largely addressed to international issues and issues of institutional violence, but it has had its successes in confronting actual physical violence on the domestic scene. Organizing agricultural workers in California and integrating public facilities in the South are the major examples.

The nonviolent witness appears in a somewhat different form in the urban pastorates and community centers that characterize the presence of the institutional church in the inner city. Here, where violence is casual and endemic rather than organized and purposeful, the need is more to repudiate it than to confront it. As two people involved in running a community center put it:

> The "good news" about the freedom of the sons of God becomes perceptible and significant when its liberating message is specified as . . . the possibility of escape from the cycle of violence enthralling teenagers.

Medieval thinking about sanctuary was rather similar.

Institutions of nonviolent confrontation and institutions that witness to the possibility of escape from the cycle of violence have in common that their primary function is prophecy, not reform.

They may accomplish important reforms, but they do so indirectly, by moving people's consciences.

These forms should be contrasted with the form taken by the inner city pastorate in a situation like that depicted in the film *On the Waterfront*. That situation involved a group of gangsters who maintained control of a union by intimidating, and if need be, killing the opposition. What the local priest undertook to do was provide organizational framework and moral support for honest workers trying to vote out the gangsters, testify against them in a legislative investigation, or denounce them to the police. The aim, in other words, was to use the institutions of the church to reinforce those of secular society—to have both sets of institutions operate harmoniously to bring about a desirable result.

Forms of both kinds are needed both at the national level and at the local level. Steadily and personally confronting the violent and the would-be violent with the Christian vision of peace is a matter of vital importance, and it is something that only the church can do. At the same time, the church cannot maintain an effective witness to social justice without both supporting and holding accountable the institutions we set up to protect peaceful citizens and give them redress.

This suggests that alongside its witness to nonviolence the church should offer a stepped-up witness to law enforcement. It should provide the police with an effective and visible—though not at all uncritical—chaplaincy. It should include support for citizen watches and other neighborhood anti-crime initiatives among the functions of the inner city ministry. It should include effective law enforcement among the things church leaders expect of the political authorities and denounce them for not providing.

Such a combination of forms can introduce a good deal of tension into the life of the church. Nonviolence and law enforcement can clash as easily as they can complement one another. If the identification of Christianity with nonviolence should become strong enough in the public mind, people might come to believe that there is no Christian way to exercise the coercive power of the state. Such a belief would obviously interfere with the work of a police chaplaincy, or with any attempt to remind political authorities of their duty to enforce the law. That this danger is not entirely fanciful is borne out by the experience of the medieval church with sex: for centuries, the emphasis on celibacy interfered with the development of an adequate moral and spiritual understanding of the married state.

The interference is probably inevitable, but we can minimize it by recognizing that nonviolence, like celibacy, is an ascesis rather than a moral imperative. As an ascesis it has very deep roots in Christian tradition. It has always figured among the canonical obligations of priests and religious in the Catholic Church, and it is commended as a personal choice by the Second Vatican Council:

> We cannot fail to praise those who renounce the use of violence in the vindication of their rights and who resort to methods of defense which are otherwise available to weaker parties too, provided that this can be done without injury to the rights and duties of others or of the community itself.

The ascesis of nonviolence, like that of celibacy, is vitally important as a sign of liberation. Just as the life of voluntary celibacy can be lived in solidarity with the involuntarily celibate, so the life of voluntary nonviolence can be lived in solidarity with the involuntarily nonviolent. These are not far to seek in our society. The old lady who is knocked down by a purse snatcher would defend herself if she dared, and would probably retaliate if she could. The citizen who has been worked over by a policeman might well want to shoot the next policeman he meets, but there are both practical and moral obstacles to his doing so. The tenant unjustly evicted from his home or the worker unjustly fired from his job might well turn violent if the landlord and the employer did not have the public force on their side. A complete nonviolent ministry will find ways to share and to protest these multiple victimizations, at least by maintaining an official and unprotected presence in the places where they go on. I do not see any inconsistency in trying to accept and sanctify the status of victim while still calling on the state for protection and redress.

8

Conclusion

I return at the end of this study to the concern that led me to undertake it—probably the dominant concern of American legal scholarship in my time. That is the use of law to bring about social change. The decisive contribution of the theology of liberation to legal theory is to rescue that concern from historical reflections that indicate that what it proposes is impossible and probably undesirable as well.

I need not detail here the optimism with which lawyers, law students, judges, and legislators during the early and middle decades of this century set about accomplishing great and beneficent changes through the application of the skills and techniques of their profession, nor the discouragement that set in when some evils proved intractable, and others seemed to arise out of the very measures of reform. It is worth pointing out, though, that historiography—the historians' account of what they are doing—and the philosophy of history—the philosophers' account of social change—give good reason for the discouragement.

The historiographers tell us that it is impossible to isolate in history the causes of a single effect or the effects of a single cause. As Herbert Butterfield put it in his deservedly influential little book, *The Whig Interpretation of History* (1931):

> Perhaps the greatest of all the lessons of history is this demonstration of the complexity of human change and the unpredictable character of the ultimate consequences of any given act or decision of men. . . .

211

> It is nothing less than the whole of the past, with its complexity of
> movement, its entanglement of issues, and its intricate interactions,
> which produced the whole of the complex present.

It follows that the overall effect on society of a given legal intervention can be neither predicted nor controlled.

The philosophers of history, for their part, tell us that history
develops dialectically, with things emerging from their opposites,
and good often coming out of evil or evil out of good. Elements
of both are inextricably intermingled in any given state of affairs.
As Maritain puts it, history is ambivalent:

> At each moment human history offers us two faces. One of these
> faces gives grounds to the pessimist, who would like to condemn
> this period of history. And the other gives grounds to the optimist,
> who would like to see the same period as merely glorious.

It follows that the overall effect of any intervention in history,
legal or otherwise, will be ambivalent rather than unambiguously
good.

It is the pessimism inspired by these reflections that the theology
of liberation dissipates with its bedrock insistence that every liberating act or event has its eschatological significance transcending
the unpredictability or ambivalence of its immediate effects:

> Faith proclaims that the brotherhood which is sought through the
> abolition of the exploitation of man by man is something possible,
> that efforts to bring it about are not in vain, that God calls us to
> it and assures us of its complete fulfillment, and that the definitive
> reality is being built on what is transitory. Faith reveals to us the
> deep meaning of the history which we fashion with our own hands:
> it teaches us that every human act which is oriented toward the con-
> struction of a more just society has value in terms of communion
> with God. . . .

My effort in these chapters has been to find ways of doing
jurisprudence in the light of that faith. I have tried, as I said I would,
to develop the applicable principles as the occasion arose, and to
say what I had to say about them along the way. But there are a
few points among them that I would like to underline one more
time before I leave off.

I

The first is the danger of cost benefit analysis. The prevailing pragmatism urges us to make no change without ascertaining that the benefits of making it outweigh the costs. But because history is not subject to prediction or control, the costs and benefits projected for a given change are never all the ones there are. They generally balance out handily in favor of the status quo. If a problem is familiar, the cost benefit analysis that supports doing nothing about it will be equally so. The justifications and rationalizations will be long in place, and the stock criticisms long since brought forward and refuted. The pros and cons alike will come trippingly over the tongue, and proceed familiarly to the inevitable conclusion that we dare not brave the dangers of altering what we have. It is in this spirit that we have been assured at one time or another that universal suffrage will mean the end of property rights; that if we free the slaves they will all starve; that women's suffrage will mean the downfall of the family, the state, or both; that white workers cannot be made to work with blacks. It is in the same spirit that we are told today that we cannot have prosperity without air pollution, or that we cannot compete with Japan unless we adopt technologies that preclude full employment.

There is a legal maxim *fiat justitia ruat coelum*, let justice be done though the skies fall. The theology of liberation teaches us to apply that maxim in the realm of social justice. To do so is in accord with the way major changes in our society have always come about. Those who supported religious freedom, compulsory education, the abolition of slavery, wages and hours legislation, collective bargaining, or civil rights could not really have foreseen the results of their efforts. Some of the results, indeed, they would have regretted. But most of them would not have given over, whatever results they foresaw. They committed themselves to their various causes because they believed those causes were right.

The will to impose standards of justice and morality on society without counting the cost is itself one of the facts of history. Even if we do not always know what will come of it, we know that we would not care to be without it. Our faith is that it is not in vain.

II

Much of the analysis in these chapters indicates that it is ig-norance, rather than malice, that does most of the harm in inflict-ing class-bound measures on our society and introducing class biases into our laws. We of the legal profession are very apt to be prey to this ignorance. By occupation, lifestyle, and mindset, we belong to the dominant elite and share its perceptions. If we do not watch carefully what we are doing, our initiatives toward law reform will go astray for this reason. We will set out to serve society and end up serving only people like ourselves.

The theology of liberation offers as an antidote to class bias the "preferential option for the poor." This is a constant will not to embrace an illusory classlessness, but to recognize the special in-terests of the ruling class and to decide against them. It insists that those who lack the minimum conditions for a decent and contrib-uting life must be provided with those conditions regardless of the cost in social amenities for anyone else. Charles Kingsley, writing in 1851, put this principle of the primacy of the poor into the mouth of his spokesman Lancelot Smith, whom I mentioned in an earlier chapter:

> "I think honestly," said Lancelot, whose blood was up, "that we gentlemen all run into the same fallacy. We fancy ourselves the fixed and necessary element in society, to which all others are to accom-modate themselves. 'Given the rights of the few rich, to find the con-dition of the many poor.' It seems to me that other postulate is quite as fair: 'Given the rights of the many poor, to find the condition of the few rich."

This conversion of priorities is supported by the same faith that liberates us from cost benefit analysis. We cannot *know* as a matter of prediction or analysis that giving the poor their rights will not cost us more than we care to pay. But we can and must *believe* as a matter of faith that God calls us to it and will turn it to our good.

III

Recognizing and allowing for class interests, and even choos-ing against them, will not make them go away. The power of the elite in our society comes from the possession of organizational and professional skills that we cannot do without if we are to go on feeding our people and providing them with reasonable amenities. Even if we reduce the scale of elitism all we can, we will still have a powerful elite to deal with. It is important, therefore, to develop measures for calling them to account and channeling their skills into the service of the wider society.

The necessary measures are powerfully impeded by the prevailing intellectual climate. Accepted doctrine both legal and nonlegal privatizes values, extrudes religion from public life, and erects ideological neutrality into a moral imperative. I will not try to sort out here the philosophical currents that have gone into the development of this state of affairs. What is of immediate concern is that accepted doctrine systematically suppresses any basis that a layman can have for challenging an expert or an outsider for challenging an organization. By supporting it in the courts, the legislatures, the universities, and the media, the elite are supporting their own dominance. To subject this dominance to control in the interest of the wider society, we must establish a system of publicly accepted values against which the agendas and achievements of the elite can be measured.

To my mind, this is not as tall an order as is sometimes supposed. I do not believe we lack a national consensus as to what is a decent, honest, and humane way to live. The trouble is that we keep telling each other that it is somehow un-American to introduce that consensus into our public life—that respect for the dissident in our society requires us to keep insisting that there is no mainstream.

Much of what I have said calls for a reexamination of these beliefs. Without a mainstream consensus there can be no accepted understanding of the common good. And without an accepted understanding of the common good there can be no liberation of our people from the domination of an unaccountable and self-serving elite. It is important to protect dissenters, to be sure, but I believe we can do so without pretending that there is nothing to dissent from.

Here again, liberation depends on faith. Respect for the neighbor comes not from believing in nothing, but from believing in the neighbor. God calls us to this belief, and bids us found our laws and institutions upon it, and order our organizations and our experts as it requires.

IV

The church's role as sign and celebration of liberation, as developed in these chapters, corresponds to the teaching of the Second Vatican Council in *Gaudium et Spes* that the church is "at once a sign and a safeguard of the transcendence of the human person." The church is called to bear a prophetic witness to the indestructibility of that transcendence, and to its culmination in a liberation that no oppressor can impede. It is also called to demand a practical recognition of that transcendence in the institutions and practices of society. The juridical forms that the church deploys in response to this twofold calling are an important part of the overall structure of the law. They give legal content to claims and aspirations that could not practically or could not justly be implemented by the law of the state.

V

Much of what I have said about law in these chapters implies a critique of the common American tendency to define law by the distribution and application of power. Law—civil law as well as ecclesiastical—has a crucial role of moral positioning that operates in many circumstances where power cannot be effectively applied, and in some where power cannot be justly applied. Indeed, the moral positioning is often needed in circumstances where power can and should be justly applied, but is in fact being applied unjustly or not at all.

In other words, law is primarily for guidance, only secondarily for coercion. It is effective primarily because people are willing to be guided by it, only secondarily because in some cases those who are willing can coerce those who are not. It is primarily not a thing done but a thing said. If it controls power or affects society, it does so because there is someone who hears it and is moved by it. In the long run, how well the law is heard and by whom will depend on how well it articulates the transcendence of the human person—the same transcendence that is signified and safeguarded by the church.

This articulation is achieved not in a master plan but in efforts to change specific institutions when they betray that transcendence by operating unjustly. It is our faith that the intractability of history cannot make these efforts vain. Their presence within history, and the presence within history of the will that called them forth, imparts to history a particular character. They make of it a human chronicle, a passage through time not of dumb victims of blind fate, but of men and women who desire justice and hope to find it in the end. We of the legal profession, through our participation in these efforts, can make ourselves spokesmen for that desire and that hope, the advocates of all who experience it.

We should, after all, be content with the role of advocates. In presenting our case for social change, we are no more responsible for the whole sweep of history than we are for what a personal injury client does with his compensation money or what a criminal defendent does when he gets out of jail. Our concern is to claim justice at particular points. In doing so, though we are no strangers to bizarre tribunals and equivocal results, we have the word of the Lord of history that those who hunger and thirst after justice will be filled.

Notes

PREFACE

The books referred to are G. Gutierrez, *A Theology of Liberation* (Maryknoll, N.Y., Orbis, 1973) (hereafter, Gutierrez); M. Djilas, *The New Class* (New York, Prager, 1957); W. Whyte, *The Organization Man* (Garden City, N.Y., Doubleday, 1957). The quotation is from the opening passage of *Gaudium et Spes*, the Second Vatican Council's Pastoral Constitution on the Church in the Modern World.

1. TOWARD A JURISPRUDENCE OF LIBERATION

p. 2   The reference to a privatized faith in a secularized world is paraphrased from Gutierrez, 224.

pp. 2-3   The conception of freedom behind this understanding of liberation is articulated §§ 17 and 31 of *Gaudium et Spes*, the Second Vatican Council's Pastoral Constitution on the Church in the Modern World. Similar views are set forth by Rabbi Abraham Joshua Heschel, who says that freedom is "openness to transcendence," and that it is our responsibility to maintain "all these political, social, and intellectual conditions which will enable every man to bring about the concrete actualization of freedom, which is the essential prerequisite of creative achievement." "The Religious Message" in *Religion in America*, (Cogley ed., New York, Meridian Books, 1958), 244, 260-61.

pp. 3-4   On Christianity and class struggle, see Guiterrez, 275-76. The "recent strictures out of the Vatican" are contained in

Instruction on Certain Aspects of the "Theology of Liberation" (1984). See also *Instruction on Christian Freedom and Liberation* (1986).

p. 4   On the church, see Gutierrez, 255-79.

p. 5   On the concept of social justice, see my *The Legal Enterprise* (Port Washington, N.Y., Kennikat, 1976: distributed by University of Notre Dame Press), 154-57.

pp. 8-10   The argument of this section is developed at greater length in my "Law, Social Change, and the Ambivalence of History," *Proc. Am. Cath. Philos. Assn.*, xlix (1975), 164. My philosophy of history is primarily that of J. Maritain *On the Philosophy of History* (New York, Scribner, 1957), and my historiography that of H. Butterfield *The Whig Interpretation of History* (New York, Scribners, 1931). See pp. 211-12, *infra*.

p. 9   I am using the term utopia in a different way from Gutierrez, 232-39. Gutierrez argues that utopian literature is to be understood as a critique, by means of contrast, of the society in which it is written, not as a claim that the society it describes would provide a definitive solution to all social problems. Thus, he objects to the pejorative use of the term. I am glad to accept his interpretation of the literature. It enables me to appreciate More's *Utopia* despite my strong conviction that the system envisaged would be impossibly intrusive and the social controls envisaged would not work. But when it comes to terminology, I think we need the term in its pejorative sense of a detailed proposal for an ideal society more than we need it in the sense in which Gutierrez uses it.

Pound's technological metaphors appear in especial profusion in *An Introduction to the Philosophy of Law* (New Haven, Yale, 1925), 96-99.

p. 10   On law as symbol, see my "A Prospectus for a Symbolist Jurisprudence," *Nat. L. F.*, ii (1957), 88.

pp. 10-11   The quotation is from Gutierrez, 270.

p. 11   The *Brown* case is 347 U.S. 483 (1954) and 349 U.S. 294 (1955).

p. 11   On liberating symbols in the criminal law, see my *The Legal Enterprise* (Port Washington, N.Y., Kennikat, 1976: distributed by University of Notre Dame Press), 82-88.

p. 12   Johnson's letter to MacPherson appears in J. Boswell, *The Life of Samuel Johnson*, c. 25.

p. 13   On the use of constitutional freedoms to confront the forces of economic regulation, and the resulting check to such regulation, see my "Due Process and Social Legislation in the Supreme Court—a Post Mortem," *Notre Dame Lawyer*, xxxiii (1957), 5. Other historical forces that constitutional freedoms have been called on, with varying degrees of success, to confront have ranged from the displacement of the Indians (*United States* ex rel. *Standing Bear* v. *Crook*, 25 Fed. Cas. #14,891 (D. Neb., 1879), and see the bill of complaint in *Cherokee Nation* v. *Georgia*, 30 U.S. 1 (1831)) and the construction of railroads (see *Olcott* v. *Supervisors of Fond du Lac County*, 83 U.S. 678 (1872) and cases cited) to the civil rights movement (*Heart of Atlanta Motel, Inc.* v. *United States*, 379 U.S. 241 (1964)), the limitation of welfare entitlements (LaFrance, Schroeder, Bennett, and Boyd, *Law of the Poor* (St. Paul, West, 1973), 266-90), and the legalization of abortion (*Byrn* v. *New York City Health and Hospitals Corp.*, 31 N.Y.2d 194, 286 N.E.2d 887 (1972), appeal dismissed, 410 U.S. 940 (1973); Noonan, *A Private Choice* (New York, Free Press, 1979), 16-18). For the latest on the deleterious effect of constitutional freedoms on the religiously committed, see *Estate of Thornton* v. *Caldor, Inc.,* 105 Sup. Ct. 2914 (U.S. 1985) (violation of establishment clause of First Amendment to require employer to give employee day off for Sabbath observance).

On absolute monarchy versus the rule of law, see R. Pound, *The Spirit of the Common Law* (Boston, Marshall Jones, 1921), 60-84.

p. 14   For the People's Charter, see Dawson, "Chartism," *Ency. Soc. Sci.*, iii (1937), 352.

p. 17   Although officially promulgated excommunication is generally obsolete, it was used in the late fifties against a number of Southern Catholics, including a prominent Louisiana politician, for resisting integration of Catholic parochial schools.

p. 19   It is sometimes useful for a religious body to maintain a court or similar body for dealing with private disputes in the light of religious principles. The evangelical denunciation proceeding of the medieval church seems to be obsolete (see Lefebvre, "Évangélique (dénonciation)," *Dictionnaire de Droit Canonique*, v, 557). But there is a growing program for bringing the authority of the Christian commu-

nity to bear on the resolution of disputes—the Christian
Conciliation Service of the Christian Legal Society. It uses
lawyers as mediators or arbitrators, and relies on varying
combinations of Christian doctrine and positive law for substantive principles to apply. More information about it can
be had from the Christian Legal Society, P.O. Box 2069,
Oak Park, Illinois 60303. Jewish communities in the Old
World generally had rabbinical courts for their disputes. The
Jewish Conciliation Board, operating in New York since
1920, draws on that tradition, J. Yaffe, *So Sue Me!* (New
York, Saturday Review Press, 1972).

p. 21   See M. Djilas, *The New Class* (New York, Praeger, 1957).
See also my "Greatness Thrust Upon Them—Class Biases
in American Law," *Amer. Jour. of Juris.*, lxxxiii (1983), 1.

2. POVERTY

pp. 22-23   The history of the poor laws up to the time of the Great
Depression is nicely summarized in Pipkin, "Poor Laws,"
Ency. Soc. Sci., xii (1934) 230. For the American law as
it stood just before the New Deal, see "Paupers," *Corpus
Juris*, xlviii (1930), 422.

pp. 23-25   The history from Roosevelt's time to 1970 is covered,
with documentary excerpts, in *Statutory History of the United
States—Income Security* (R. Stevens, ed., New York, Chelsea House, 1970). See also, W. Trattner, *From Poor Law
to Welfare State* (2d ed., New York, Free Press, 1979); Gir-
vetz, "Welfare State" in *International Ency. of the Social
Sciences*, xvi (1968), 520, and for a statement of the laws
presently in place, "Social Security" in *Corpus Juris Secundum*, lxxxi (1977), 1.

The parallel but rather earlier development of workmen's
compensation laws is covered in *Larson on Workmen's Compensation* §§ 4.00-5.00.

p. 24   For the attribution of the sixty-five year retirement age
to Bismarck, see W. Graebner, *A History of Retirement*
(New Haven, Yale 1980), 249.

p. 25   On inadequate skills, see the description of the "hard-core
unemployed" in Indiana Code 22-1-4-2.

Material up to 1976 on negative income tax and the like
is gathered in the casebook *Poverty, Inequality, and the Law*
(B. Brudno ed., St. Paul, West Pub. Co., 1976), 784-818.

On experiments indicating disincentives, see *Time*, December 4, 1978, and the editorial "So Why Work?" in the *South Bend Tribune*, November 24, 1978.

p. 26   On the use of the anti-poverty program to politicize the poor, see D. Moynihan, *Maximum Feasible Misunderstanding* (New York, Free Press, 1969); R. Kramer, *Participation of the Poor* (Englewood Cliffs, N.J., Prentice Hall, 1969).

p. 27   On the exclusion of agricultural workers from legislation that protects other workers, see D. Uchtmann and L. Bertagnolli, "The Coverage of the Agricultural Worker in Labor Legislation: Deviations from the Norm," *Agricultural Law Journal, 1980-81*, 606. The political and legislative history of the exclusionary provisions of one act, the National Labor Relations Act, are developed in A. Morris, "Agricultural Labor and National Labor Legislation," *Calif. L. Rev.*, liv (1966), 1939. It appears that for a while the Michigan Supreme Court held all discrimination against agricultural workers to be unconstitutional. *Gallegos* v. *Glaser Crandell Co.*, 388 Mich. 654., 202 N.W. 2d 786 (1972), overruled, *Follmer, Rudzewicz & Co.* v. *Kosco*, 420 Mich. 394, 362 N.W. 2d 676 (1984).

In some places, the farmworkers' plight is exacerbated by the position of their employers, the growers, who sell all their crops to two or three major canners. It seems that the canners have so much power that the growers cannot raise prices to meet increased labor costs. At the same time, the canners refuse to negotiate with the workers, on the ground that there is no employment relation between them. FLOC (Farm Labor Organizing Committee), an organization representing workers in the Ohio Valley, after trying for some years to promote a boycott of Campbell's and Libby's, the two largest canners, finally succeeded in establishing three-way negotiations.

For most of my information about illegal immigrants, and some of my information about agricultural labor, I am indebted to various Notre Dame Law School students who have worked with the Michigan Migrants Legal Assistance Project, Inc., Berrien Springs and Grand Rapids, Michigan, and have shared their experiences with me.

p. 28   The "traditional literature" referred to here includes not only such writers as Dickens and Zola in the nineteenth century, but also such as Orwell and Steinbeck in the twentieth.

The states that had adopted AFDC-U as of August, 1980 are listed in *Welfare Background Paper: Description of Selected Major Programs*, Congressional Research Service Report #81-124 (1981), Table 21. Twenty-five states, Guam, and the District of Columbia are listed.

p. 29   Michigan is an example of a state that has meshed its general assistance program with its categorical assistance, and uses a common intake. See Mich. Comp. L. § 400.25. Indiana, by contrast, has a rigorously separated program I.C. 12-2, with many quaint survivals of the Elizabethan system, including both local administration and complete local financing. In Virginia, a 1977 amendment of the applicable statute put the whole subject of general assistance on a local option basis. Va. Code § 63.1-106.

Food Research and Action Center, Inc., 2011 Eye Street, N.W., Washington, D.C. 20006 puts out a good pamphlet on the main features of the food stamp program. On the inadequacies of the coupon allotment, see *Rodway* v. *Department of Agriculture*, 514 F.2d 809 (D.C. Cir. 1975). The statute was amended in 1977 to conform to the government position attacked in this litigation. See 7 U.S.C. §§ 2012(o) and 2017(a).

p. 30   Housing problems are well treated in the casebook I use for my Public Welfare course, *Social Welfare and the Individual* (Levy, Lewis, Martin eds., Mineola, N.Y., Foundation Press, 1971), 977-1322. See also D. Mandelker, *Housing Subsidies in the United States and England* (Indianapolis, Bobbs-Merrill, 1973); *Housing in America: Problems and Perspectives* (R. Montgomery and D. Mandelker eds., Indianapolis, Bobbs-Merrill, 1979). The more recent *Report of the President's Commission on Housing* (1982) is comprehensive and readable, but flawed to my mind by a tendentious attachment to free market ideology. The subsidy experiments referred to in text were conducted by the Rand Corporation for HUD. The results appear in *Price Effects of a Housing Allowance Program*, R-2720-HUD (1982); *Experimenting with Housing: The Final Report of the Housing Allowance Supply Experiment* (I. Lowry ed. 1983). As one of the experiments was conducted here in St. Joseph County, Indiana, I have some personal acquaintance with its operation.

pp. 30-32   R. Segalman, *Poverty in American* (Westport, Conn., Greenwood Press, 1981) has good summaries of both housing and medical programs. The Levy, Lewis, and Martin casebook, *supra*, deals with medical programs on pages 1323-1422. See also T. Kinney, "Medicaid Copayments: A Bitter Pill for the Poor," *Journal of Legislation*, x (1983), 213; R. Freedman et al., "Why Won't Medicaid Let me Keep my Nest Egg?" *Hastings Center Report*, xiii, No. 2 (1983), 23-25. Other statements in text are based on personal experience, experiences of students and colleagues, and newspaper accounts that I have unfortunately not preserved. *Fullington* v. *Shea*, 320 F.Supp. 500, *affirmed*, 404 U.S. 963 (1970) upheld the constitutionality of these distinctions against equal protection objections.

p. 32   For my critique of the Supreme Court's doctrine on public support for religious schools, see "From *Pierce* to *Nyquist* — Free Churches in an Expensive State" in *Freedom and Education* (D. Kommers and M. Wahoske eds., Notre Dame, Indiana, Center for Civil Rights, 1978), 47.

pp. 33-35   Of the extensive general literature on the subject of the indignities suffered by welfare recipients, my favorite piece is M. Walton, "Rats in the Crib, Roaches in the Food," *Village Voice*, May 11, 1967, reprinted in the casebook *Law and Poverty* (Cooper et als. eds., St. Paul, West Pub. Co., 2d ed. 1973) 39-44. I can add a few experiences of my own, plus extensive experiences of friends, colleagues, and students.

p. 33   On loss of AFDC benefits through paternal concern, see *Freeman* v. *Lukhard*, 465 F.Supp. 1269 (E.D. Va. 1979); *Shannon* v. *Department of Human Services*, 157 N.J. Super. 251, 384 A.2d 899 (1978); *Hughes* v. *Adult and Family Services Div.*, 50 Ore. App. 478, 648 P.2d 1324 (1982). In *Brewer* v. *Simmons*, 205 A.2d 60 (D.C. Ct. App. 1964), a wife in a separate maintenance action sought to have her husband's visitation rights curtailed lest she lose her AFDC benefits. The trial court instead enjoined the welfare department from cutting off benefits on account of the visitation provided for. The appellate court reversed because divorce courts have no jurisdiction over the welfare department.

pp. 33-34   On making welfare recipients work, see, e.g., *Bueno* v. *Juras*, 349 F.Supp. 91 (D. Ore. 1972); *Anderson* v. *Burson*, 300 F.Supp. 401 (D. Ga. 1968); *Ramos* v. *County of*

Madera, 4 Cal.3d 685, 484 P.2d 93 (1971); R. Polangin, "Conscripted Labor: Workfare and the Poor," *Clearinghouse Review*, xvi (1982), 544.

p. 35　　One of my students, going over the text in manuscript, queried my reference to the expansion of legal services organizations. She is of course thinking of the drastic cutbacks in federal funding for such organizations since 1981. I am thinking of the time before the Economic Opportunity Act of 1964. On the expansion in the mid-sixties—which the current cuts are far from nullifying—see Note, *Harv. L. Rev.*, lxxx (1967), 805.

p. 36　　The unemployment compensation laws are cited and summarized in J. Hood and B. Hardy, *Workers' Compensation and Employee Protection Laws in a Nutshell* (St. Paul, West, 1984), 134-44.

p. 38　　*Wilkie* v. *O'Connor* is 261 App. Div. 373, 25 N.Y.S.2d 617 (4th Dept. 1941).

p. 39　　The quote from *Yeast* is from Chapter XIII, "The Village Revel." This scene is one of the most interesting parts of an extremely interesting social document. *Yeast* is not much of a novel, but as social analysis it is well worth reading.

p. 40　　The Better Jobs and Incomes Act was H.R. 9030. See G. Weil, *The Welfare Debate of 1978* (1978); Congressional Budget Office, *Welfare Reform, Issues, Objectives, and Approaches* (1977).

pp. 40-47　　My debt to the teaching of E.F. Schumacher, *Small is Beautiful* (New York, Harper & Row, 1973) should be obvious.

p. 44　　The history of size restrictions in the incorporation laws is set forth in Justice Brandeis's dissenting opinion in *Liggett Co.* v. *Lee*, 288 U.S. 517, 541 (1933).

Western Union Telegraph Co. v. *Kansas*, 216 U.S. 1 (1910) held that a state basing a franchise tax on capital cannot take into account capital not used in local business. The modern cases, such as *Container Corp.* v. *Franchise Tax Board*, 463 U.S. 159 (1983), allow state taxing authorities to take into account the entire operation of an integrated business, although they must find some reasonable formula for taxing only the local share. I believe the criteria of *Container* could be met by computing a graduated tax on the whole enterprise, then imposing a pro rata share of the tax so computed.

p. 45   The tax credit for new jobs is in Internal Revenue Code §§ 51-3.

p. 46   On the Japanese commitment to employment, see R. Guillan, *The Japanese Challenge* (Philadelphia, Lippincott, 1970), 96-119.

p. 47   The case of the stockholder who took Ford to court is *Dodge* v. *Ford Motor Co.*, 204 Mich. 459, 170 N.W. 668 (1919). The results were ambiguous.

pp. 51-52   These pages were written before the Roman Catholic bishops issued their draft Pastoral Letter on the Economy in the fall of 1984. My views on church teaching should be compared with that document, as well as with *Ethical Reflections on the Economic Crisis*, the 1983 statement of the Canadian bishops' Social Affairs Commission, *Strangers and Guests*, the 1980 statement of the Midwest bishops on agricultural policy, and *This Land is Home to Me*, the 1975 statement of the bishops of Appalachia. The question of how specific a reform agenda is appropriate in a church teaching document has been raised in connection with all of these documents, especially the 1984 draft pastoral. The introduction of specific proposals open to political debate obviously blunts the prophetic edge of a teaching document. On the other hand, it does a good deal to assure the attention of a pragmatic people. It also assures the inclusion of Christian principles in the political debate. When a concrete proposal is put forward as required by Christian principles, the opponents of the proposal generally assume the burden of showing that the principles in question do not require the proposal. This means that both sides are relying on Christian principles instead of ignoring them.

p. 52   The idea that the poor are suffering vicariously for the rich is one of many that I owe to William Stringfellow.

Rawls defines his "difference principle" in *A Theory of Justice* (Cambridge, Mass., Harvard, 1971) 75-83.

p. 54   See M. Muskowitz, "Social Proxy Fights Spice up Annual Meetings," *Business and Society Review*, No. 45 (1983), 23. On the SEC proxy solicitation rules, see *Medical Committee for Human Rights* v. *SEC*, 432 F.2d 659 (D.C. Cir. 1970) (the Dow Chemical case mentioned in text), and compare the present SEC Rule 14a-8 with the rule as it existed before that case. The litigation inauspiciously begun in *Sisters of the Precious Blood* v. *Bristol-Myers Co.*, 431

F.Supp. 385 (S.D.N.Y. 1977) ended in a settlement favorable to the Sisters' position. Correspondence from INFACT (Infant Formula Action Coalition), St. Paul, Minnesota.

3. TRIVIALIZATION

p. 57   While it appears that serious protectionism came in only after the War of 1812, "encouragement and protection of manufacture" was among the objects stated in the preamble to the first tariff act, 1st Cong., 1st Sess. c. 2, 1 Stat. 24 (1789). The history of the Mill Acts is set forth in *Head* v. *Amoskeag Mfg. Co.*, 113 U.S. 9 (1885), which established their constitutionality under the Fourteenth Amendment. While they are basically a nineteenth-century phenomenon — entirely so in their application to factories rather than grist mills — the first one was a Massachusetts statute of 1713. These acts were justified as an exercise of the power of eminent domain. They permitted a mill owner to build a dam and flood his neighbors' land, paying suitable compensation for his neighbor's loss. They conferred a privilege, not a right. See *Strom* v. *Manchaug Co.*, 13 Allen (95 Mass.) 10 (1866) (upstream owner may dig canal to prevent flooding). On tort law, see L.M. Friedman, *A History of American Law* (New York, Simon and Schuster, 1973), 409-27.

pp. 57-58   On the place of law generally in early economic development, see *Id.*, 157-78.

pp. 60-61   The educational provision of the 1816 Indiana constitution is Art. 9, Section 2. Compare the more limited aspirations of Art. 8, Section 1 of the 1851 constitution. For another discussion of the purposes of the the early school system, see *Stuart* v. *Kalamazoo School District*, 30 Mich. 69 (1874).

p. 61   The leading case on inequality of bargaining position is *Henningsen* v. *Bloomfield Motors, Inc.*, 32 N.J. 358, 161 A.2d 69 (1959). The quote is from *Coppage* v. *Kansas*, 236 U.S. 1, 17 (1915). Justice Holmes, dissenting in that case, 236 U.S. at 26, referred to the "equality of bargaining position at which freedom of contract begins." His view was accepted as a constitutional doctrine before it was made part of the law of contracts. Its introduction into contract law was perhaps foreshadowed by *Restatement of Contracts* (1932), § 493(d), Illustration 15, an example of duress based on necessitous circumstances of one party for which the other party is not responsible.

p. 64 The Mayer book was published by Harper, New York, in 1958. The waitress who spoke Lithuanian and Spanish was a visiting relative of the owners of the hotel. She had migrated to Uruguay when they had migrated to the United States.

p. 67 See Eccles. 9:11.

p. 69 The much publicized change in the formula of Coca Cola in the spring of 1985 is a notable example of the process described in text.

p. 70 The latest Christmas crib case, *Lynch* v. *Donnelly*, 465 U.S. 668 (1984), provoked a number of comments back and forth about what does and what does not trivialize Christmas.

p. 71 See the chapter "Job Redesign" in U.S. Dept. of Health, Educ. and Welfare, *Work in America* (1973), 93-120.

pp. 71-72 The treatment of quantified test scores under the civil rights laws is taken up in "Civil Rights" § 122, *Am. Jur. 2d*, xv (1976).

p. 72 On real estate taxes, see J. Juergensmeyer and S. Wadley, *Agricultural Law* (Boston, Little, Brown, 1982), i, 125-30; "An Analysis of Differential Taxation as a Method of Maintaining Agricultural and Open Space Land Uses," *U. of Fla. L. Rev.* xxx (1978) 821. The estate tax provision is *Int. Rev. Code* § 2032A.

On zoning out the poor, see *Southern Burlington County NAACP* v. *Township of Mount Laurel*, 67 N.J. 151, 336 A.2d 713, *appeal dismissed and cert. denied*, 423 U.S. 808 (1975).

pp. 72-73 See *Pierce* v. *Society of Sisters*, 268 U.S. 510 (1924) (right to send children to private schools); *Wisconsin* v. *Yoder*, 406 U.S. 205 (1972) (right to forego schooling); *Meyer* v. *Nebraska*, 262 U.S. 390 (1923) (right to maintain private school with foreign language of instruction); *Lau* v. *Nichols*, 414 U.S. 563 (1974) (Federal Civil Rights Act requires public school system to make some provision for students who speak no English).

p. 75 The British Town and Country Planning Act of 1947, 10 & 11 Geo. 6 c. 51, did not expressly nationalize development rights, but it forbade further development without permission, and provided for compensating landowners for the loss of their right to develop, and for charging them for the increased value if permission to develop was later given. See D. Hagman, *Urban Planning and Land Development Control Law* (St. Paul, West, 1975), 597-98; D. Kmiec, "Deregulating Land Use," *Univ. of Pa. L. Rev.* cxxx (1981), 28, 115-27. Kmiec also refers to a few modest moves in some American states to recapture at least part of the unearned increment in land values.

pp. 75-76   On family farms, see U.S. Catholic Conference, *The Family Farm* (1979); H. Breimyer, *Farm Policy: 13 Essays* (Ames, Iowa U. Press, 1977). Most of the protection we give now is through zoning and the like, J. Juergensmeyer and J. Wadley, *Agricultural Law* (Boston, Little, Brown, 1982), i, 75-77, 118-19, 131-64, or laws restricting corporate ownership of farms, *Id.*, ii, 148, 154-69. On conservation easements, see *Id.*, i, 114-15; D. Sutte and R. Cunningham, *Scenic Easements* (Washington, Nat. Research Council, 1968). The latter work deals with easements to preserve the view along highways. There is more experience with them for this than for other purposes.

pp. 77-78   On the effect of dull work on health, see the chapter "Work and Health" in U.S. Dept. of Health, Educ. and Welfare, *Work in America* (1973). Compensation for gradually developing mental disorders is covered in A. Larson, *Workmen's Compensation Law* § 42.23 (b). On the collective bargaining process, see Oldham, "Organized Labor, the Environment, and the Taft-Hartly Act," *Mich. L. Rev.*, lxxi (1973), 935.

p. 78   E.F. Schumacher, *Small is Beautiful* (paperback ed. 1975), 241-71 deals with various ways of reducing the scale of large enterprises and encouraging smaller ones.

pp. 79-80   The American Law Institute's draft, *The Principles of Corporate Governance: Restatement and Recommendations* (Tentative Draft No. 1, 1982), § 2.01 allows corporate management, "even if corporate profit and shareholder gain are not thereby enhanced," to "take into account ethical principles that are generally recognized as relevant to the conduct of business," and to "devote resources, within reasonable limits, to public welfare, humanitarian, educational, and philanthropic purposes." C. Stone, *Where the Law Ends* (New York, Harper & Row, 1975) contains some proposals for changing management goals within the corporation.

My experience as an in-house lawyer for an insurance company indicates a number of examples of corporate personnel following assigned goals with little regard for overall corporate interests. The underwriters, whose job it was to see that the company took risks only on an actuarially sound basis, were at odds with the salesmen, whose job it was to sell as many policies as they could. Claim investigators, who were generally commended for prompt payment, paid claims that the lawyers, who were praised for winning cases, would have resisted. People in charge of subrogation—that is, collecting from third parties who had caused damage to the property of an insured—pursued remedies even to litigation against third parties who had liability policies with the company.

I have heard one or two academic engineers question the professional ethics of designing for planned obsolescence. It would be interesting to explore this ethical issue further.

p. 81   On broadcasting, see Note, "A Regulatory Approach to Diversifying Commercial Television Entertainment," *Yale L. J.*, lxxxix (1980), 694. A new FCC move in the direction of leaving program content to market forces was upheld in *FCC* v. *WNCN Listeners Guild*, 450 U.S. 582 (1981). On the fairness doctrine, see H. Nelson and D. Teeter, *Law of Mass Communications* (Mineola, N.Y., Foundation Press, 1978), 472-87, and *Brandywine-Main Line Radio, Inc.* v. *FCC*, 473 F.2d 16 (D.C. Cir. 1972), especially Judge Bazelon's dissent, *Id.*, at 63. Religious broadcasting and the restrictions on it are discussed more at large in A. Hardy and L. Secrest, "Religious Freedom and the Federal Communications Commission," *Valparaiso U. L. Rev.* xvi (1981), 57.

pp. 83-84   On Mill and Millianism, see J. Feinberg, "Autonomy, Sovereignty, and Privacy: Moral Ideals in the Constitution?", *Notre Dame Law Review*, lviii (1983), 445. Feinberg appears to be a more uncompromising Millian than Mill himself. Mill recognizes that many people would not be able to handle the liberty he advocates. *On Liberty*, c. 1. That concession is broader than he seems to suppose. It is inconsistent with a general philosophical objection to coercing people for their own good.

p. 86   On accommodation of minority religions as a violation of the establishment clause, see Note, *Notre Dame Lawyer*, li (1976), 481; *Isaac* v. *Butler's Shoe Corp.*, 511 F.Supp.

108 (N.D. Ga. 1980). The prevailing view, however, accepts such accommodations, provided they are not so expensive as to confer a significant benefit on members of the accommodated group. *Tooley* v. *Martin-Marietta Corp.*, 648 F.2d 1239 (9th Cir. 1981). Compare *Estate of Thornton* v. *Caldor*, 105 Sup. Ct. 2914 (U.S. 1985). The argument that an agenda promoted by a religious group cannot be adopted without violating the establishment clause was made — and rejected — in *Harris* v. *McRae*, 448 U.S. 297, 318-20 (1980). The leading case on gay rights organizations is *Gay Lib* v. *University of Missouri*, 558 F.2d 848 (8th Cir. 1977). On religious organizations, compare *Lubbock Civil Liberties Union* v. *Lubbock Indep. School Dist.*, 669 F.2d 1038 (5th Cir. 1982) 198 *reh. den.* 680 F.2d 424, *cert. den.* 103 Sup. Ct. 800 (1983) with *Widmar* v. *Vincent*, 454 U.S. 263 (1981). See J. Smart, "*Widmar* v. *Vincent* and the Purpose of the Establishment Clause," *Journal of Coll. and Univ. Law*, ix (1983) 469.

p. 87   Tocqueville is quoted from *Democracy in America*, pt. ii, c. 5 (Reeve Trans., 1900).

4. POWERLESSNESS

p. 91   The story of the squire and the cricket player comes from *The Collected Essays, Journalism and Letters of George Orwell*, iii (1968), 121. The Agricultural Holdings Act of 1948, 11 & 12 Geo. 6, c. 63, protected agricultural tenants from being put out without good cause. Protection against the squire was completed by the Rent (Agriculture) Act 1976, c. 80, dealing with the "tied cottages" of agricultural workers who are not tenants.

pp. 91-93   The instances not specifically documented are ones I have read about in the newspapers without recording citations. The case of the farmer in trouble for growing grain for his own use is *Wickard* v. *Filburn*, 317 U.S. 111 (1942). The question of state regulation of private schools comes up in a number of cases. See the Annotation, 18 A.L.R.4 649. The fullest discussion is found in *State* v. *Whisner*, 47 Ohio St. 181, 351 N.E.2d 750 (1976) — one in which the state authorities lost. The cases of Knauff, Black, and Solow are, respectively, *United States* ex rel. *Knauff* v. *Shaughnessy*, 338 U.S. 537 (1950); *Ewing* v. *Black*, 172 F.2d 331 (6th

Cir. 1949); *Solow* v. *General Motors Truck Co.*, 64 F.2d 105 (2d Cir. 1933). The background and belated happy ending of the Knauff case are described in E. Knauff, *The Ellen Knauff Story* (New York, Norton, 1952).

p. 98   During the spacious early days of the anti-poverty program, I served as legal advisor to an organization that performed a useful, if peripheral, educational service. One of my tasks was to revamp the structure of the organization so it would be eligible for federal funding. I not only experienced the impatience attributed in text to the professionals, I am afraid I shared it.

p. 100   The reference to the law's delay is from the "To be or not to be . . ." soliloquy in *Hamlet*, Act. 3, Scene 1.

p. 102   On shareholder democracy, see pp. 104-5, *infra*. Note also *Sisters of the Precious Blood* v. *Bristol-Meyers Co.*, 431 F.Supp. 385 (S.D.N.Y. 1977), which seems to hold that a stockholder whose concern is to bring up moral objections to management policy has no standing to complain of false statements in a management proxy solicitation.

p. 103   The constitutional right of lawyers to advertise was established in *Bates* v. *State Bar of Arizona*, 433 U.S. 350 (1977). On the role of juries as fact finders, see the remarks of the judges on the special verdict in *Skidmore* v. *B. & O. R.R.*, 167 F.2d 54 (2nd Cir. 1948). The general idea is that if juries had to answer specific questions about the facts of a case instead of giving a general verdict for one side or the other, they would be less apt to give effect to concerns not officially reflected in the law.

p. 104   The federal Freedom of Information Act is 5 U.S.C. § 552b. The Indiana state act is I.C. 5-14-3. Indiana's sunshine law is I.C. 5-14-1.5. There is no corresponding federal law. On freedom of information laws generally, see B. Schwartz, *Administrative Law* (2d ed. Boston, Little, Brown, 1984), 129-32. On sunshine laws, B. Schwartz, *Administrative Law: A Casebook*, (2d ed. Boston, Little, Brown, 1982), 247-51.

On lobbying, see "Lobbying," *Am. Jur.2d*, li (1970), 991. The reference to "reason and understanding" refers to Can. 26 of the former Canons of Ethics of the American Bar Association: "It is unprofessional . . . to use means other than those addressed to the reason and understanding to influence action." Ethical Consideration 7-16 of the present Code of Professional Responsibility is much vaguer.

pp. 104-5   On shareholder democracy, see D. Schwartz, "The Public Interest Proxy Contest: Reflections on Campaign GM," *Mich. L. Rev.*, lxix (1971), 419. On Rule 14a-8, see *Medical Committee for Human Rights* v. *SEC*, 432 F.2d 659 (D.C. Cir. 1970). The SEC amended 14a-8 to conform to the doctrine of that case. The case on stockholder lists referred to in text is *State* ex rel. *Pillsbury* v. *Honeywell, Inc.*, 291 Minn. 322, 191 N.W.2d 406, 50 A.L.R.3 1046 (1971).

p. 105   The right of privacy was launched in the famous article, Warren and Brandeis, "The Right to Privacy," *Harv. L. Rev.*, iv (1890), 193. For its current situation, see L. Tribe, *American Constitutional Law* (Mineola, N.Y., Foundation Press, 1978), 886-990.

p. 106   Cost benefit analysis is discussed in B. Schwartz, *Administrative Law* (2d ed. Boston, Little, Brown, 1984), 155-57. The case referred to in text is *American Textile Mfrs. Inst.* v. *Donovan*, 452 U.S. 490 (1981).

p. 107   See B. Schwartz, *Administrative Law* (2d ed. Boston, Little, Brown, 1984), 235-54 on the expansion of the concept of due process in administrative law, and, in particular, *Goldberg* v. *Kelly*, 397 U.S. 254 (1970) (welfare); *Goss* v. *Lopez*, 419 U.S. 565 (1975) (school discipline); "Associations," *Corpus Juris Secundum*, vii (1980), §§ 20-26; 63 Pa. Stat. §§ 118.1-118.28 (automobile dealerships).

p. 109   The difference between being subject to law and being subject to administrative intervention is illustrated by *Kentucky State Board* v. *Rudasill*, 589 S.W.2d 877, 18 A.L.R.4 637 (Ky. 1979), holding that a private school cannot be subjected to certification requirements, but can be required to maintain a certain standard of achievement for its students.

Proposition 13 appears as Article 13A of the California constitution.

pp. 109-10   For what constitutes a "public use," see "Eminent Domain," *Corpus Juris Secundum*, xxixA (1965) §§ 29-86. The Florida case referred to in text is *Baycol, Inc.* v. *Downtown Development Authy.*, 315 So.2d 451 (Fla. 1975).

pp. 110-11   The commerce clause analysis referred to in text is elaborated in L. Tribe, *American Constitutional Law* (Mineola, N.Y., Foundation Press, 1978), 232-44, 300-18.

p. 111   Indiana's sunset law is I.C. 4-26-3. On such laws generally, see B. Schwartz, *Administrative Law: A Casebook* (2d ed. 1982), 75-88.

pp. 111-12   On administrative inspections and the requirement of warrants, see B. Schwartz, *Administrative Law* (2d ed. Boston, Little, Brown, 1984), 96-104. The OSHA case referred to in text is *Marshall* v. *Barlow's Inc.*, 436 U.S. 307 (1978).

p. 112   The principle of subsidiarity is developed in the papal encyclical *Quadrigesimo Anno* (1931) ¶ 79-80, and reaffirmed in *Mater et Magistra* 1961 ¶ 53, 117, and *Pacem in Terris* (1963) ¶ 140-41. For a discussion, see my *The Legal Enterprise* (Port Washington, N.Y., Kennikat, 1976: distributed by University of Notre Dame Press), 157-59.

p. 113   It appears that the Russians do a good deal of judicial business at the neighborhood level. See G. Feifer, *Justice in Moscow* (New York, Simon & Schuster, 1964). On central funding for local government in England, see "Local Government," *Halsbury's Laws of England* (4th ed.), xxviii (1979) ¶ 1262-76. On decentralization in London, see "London Government," *id.*, xxix (1979) ¶ 74-200.

pp. 113-14   On the low level of participation in neighborhood antipoverty elections, see D. Moynihan, *Maximum Feasible Misunderstanding* (New York, Free Press, 1969), 137; R. Levy, T. Lewis and P. Martin, *Social Welfare and the Individual: Cases and Materials* (Mineola, N.Y., Foundation Press, 1971), 1537n.

p. 114   On the Campbell's and Libby's boycott, see note to page 27 supra.

pp. 114-15   The proposal that outside constituencies be represented on corporate governing boards is taken up in M. Eisenberg, *The Structure of the Corporation* (Boston, Little, Brown, 1976), 19-24. The elaborate German provisions for such representation are described in Federal Ministry of Labour and Social Affairs, *Codetermination in the Federal Republic of Germany* (1978).

p. 115   The New Deal cases referred to in text are *Ashwander* v. *TVA*, 297 U.S. 288 (1936) and *Helvering* v. *Davis*, 301 U.S. 619 (1937). The earlier case of *Hill* v. *Wallace*, 259 U.S. 44 (1922) is to the same effect. For Brandeis's views on this subject, see 297 U.S. at 341, and 259 U.S. at 72. The subject of stockholders preventing illegal corporate action is taken up generally in N. Lattin, *Lattin on Corporations* (2d ed., Mineola, N.Y., Foundation Press, 1971), 417-21. For a statement of the prevailing business judgment rule, see American Law Institute, *Principles of Corporate Governance: Restatement and Recommendations* (Tentative Draft No. 1, 1982) § 4.01 (d), and accompanying Comment. On accountability to stockholders, see pp. 104-5 and accompanying notes, *supra*.

pp. 116-17   See M. Eisenberg, *The Structure of the Corporation* (Boston, Little, Brown, 1976), 70-84 on the uses of the stockholder's right to be bought out. Note that the buyout is the only form of disinvestment that actually reduces the capital embarked in the objectionable enterprise.

A further problem in the way of stockholders imposing moral standards on management is that prevailing doctrine seems to allow management to follow moral standards only if it pays to do so, or if the standards are "generally recognized." American Law Institute, *Principles of Corporate Governance and Structure: Restatement and Recommendations,* (Tentative Draft No. 1, 1982), § 2.01(b). Ilustration 13 accompanying says that management may not turn a chain of restaurants vegetarian to accommodate the moral principles of a 40% stockholder. The illustration is too easy. Harder questions would be presented by closing a profitable chain of abortion clinics, stopping production on a profitable line of war materials, or giving up trying to sell milk substitutes to illiterate mothers who do not know how to use them properly. In giving up the last of these practices, companies have responded to public agitation; it is fairly arguable that they can appeal to the general principle of maintaining profit instead of the particular one of following generally recognized ethical principles. Thus, it is not clear that they would have been free to take the same step in the absence of any public agitation.

pp. 117-18   On union security, see R. Gorman, *Basic Text on Labor Law* (St. Paul, West, 1976), 639-76; *The Developing Labor Law* (C. Morris, ed., 2d ed. Washington, Bur. of Nat. Affairs, 1983), ii, 1359-1419. Right to work laws are listed and cited in Morris, 1392n. On fair representation, see Gorman, 695-728; Morris, 1285-1378.

pp. 118-19   On when a plaintiff does and does not need expert testimony in a medical malpractice case, see D. Harney, *Medical Malpractice* (Indianapolis, Smith, 1973 and Supp.) § 3.2; Anno., 81 A.L.R.2 598. The Hodgkin's disease case referred to in text is *ZeBarth* v. *Swedish Hosp. Med. Center*, 81

Wash. 2d 12, 499 P.2d 1 (1972). There were expert witnesses in the case, but the jury was not required to rely on them in determining the standard of care.

p. 121   The *Natonabah* case is 355 F.Supp. 716 (D. N.M. 1973). See M. Gross, "Legal Assistance in Indian Education," *Notre Dame Lawyer*, xlix (1973), 78 for a general discussion of problems of accountability in legal representation of Indians, with this case as only one example.

p. 124   The quote is from T. Shaffer, *Legal Interviewing and Counseling in a Nutshell* (St. Paul, West, 1976), 33-35.

p. 125   On resistance to establishing an Anglican bishop in America, see A. Stokes, *Church and State in the United States* (New York, Harper, 1950), i, 231-40.

p. 126   *Watch Tower Bible & Tract Soc.* v. *Dougherty*, 337 Pa. 286, 11 A.2d 147 (1940) stems from an egregious, and fortunately obsolete, use of clerical power along the lines described in text.

p. 127   Comparison of Canons 289-329 of the new code of Canon Law with Canons 685-90 of the former Code indicates that the law of the Roman Catholic Church is moving gradually in the direction suggested in text. The corporate recognition of non-Catholic "ecclesial communities" throughout the new code is probably of even greater significance in this regard.

5. ROOTLESSNESS

p. 129   This section owes much to R. Gabriel, *The Course of American Democratic Thought* (New York, Ronald Press, 1940). The place of law is treated especially on pp. 101-4.

p. 132   On the forces militating against residual identification, see W. Whyte, *The Organization Man* (New York, Simon and Schuster, 1956), 299-301. On the intellectual domination of the mainstream, see Tocqueville, *Democracy in America*, Pt. II, Bk. I, c.9. On religious identification, see W. Herberg, *Protestant, Catholic, Jew* (Garden City, N.Y., Doubleday, 1955).

p. 133   The leading cases on the revision of landlord-tenant law referred to in text are *Javins* v. *First Nat. Realty Corp.*, 428 F.2d 1071 (D.C. Cir. 1970) and *Marini* v. *Ireland*, 56 N.J. 130, 265 A.2d 526 (1970).

p. 135   On the responsibilities of a lawyer, see Ethical Consideration 7-8 of the Code of Professional Responsibility: "In the final analysis, . . . the lawyer should always remember that the decision whether to forego legally available objectives or methods because of nonlegal factors is ultimately for the client and not for himself." Compare this language, adopted by the American Bar Association in 1970, with Canon 15 of the Canons of Professional Ethics, adopted in 1908: "The office of attorney does not permit, much less does it demand of him for any client, violation of law or any manner of fraud or chicane. He must obey his own conscience and not that of his client." The most sophisticated proponent of the modern view is Professor Monroe Freedman. See his "Personal Responsibility in a Professional System," *Cath. U. L. Rev.*, xxvii (1978), 91.

pp. 136-37 On destruction of neighborhoods, see C. Hartman, D. Keating and R. LeGates, *Displacement: How to Fight It* (Berkeley, Nat. Housing Law Project, 1982) (hereafter, *Displacement*). On restrictive zoning, see *NAACP* v. *Mt. Laurel*, 67 N.J. 151, 336 A.2d 713 (1975). On busing, see L. Tribe, *American Constitutional Law* (Mineola, N.Y., Foundation Press, 1978), 1032-42. Siting of public housing is discussed further at pp. 144-45 and accompanying notes, *infra*.

p. 137 The discussion in E. O'Connor, *The Last Hurrah* (Boston, Little, Brown, 1956), explaining why Frank Skeffington lost his bid for reelection is an excellent description of the downfall of neighborhood politics.

p. 140 The adoption and abandonment of the policy of "terminating" Indian tribes is treated in F. Cohen, *Handbook of Federal Indian Law* (1982 ed. Charlottesville, Va., Michie), 152-206.

p. 143 The process described here has been given the name "gentrification." See *Displacement*, 149-68. See particularly the Gentrification Blues, words and music on p. 159. On the receivership program and its effect on the poor, see *Social Welfare and the Individual* (Levy, Lewis, and Martin eds., Mineola, N.Y., Foundation Press, 1971), 1041-42, 1127-29. The case referred to in text is *Community Renewal Foundation* v. *Chicago Title and Trust Co.*, 44 Ill.2d 284, 255 N.E.2d 908 (1970).

p. 144 On urban homesteading, see *Displacement*, 68-71. On condominiums, see Note, "Tenant Protection in Condominium Conversions: the New York Experience," *St. John's U.*

L. Rev. xlviii (1974), 978; *Displacement*, 45-50. The British laws protecting tenants are described in "Landlord and Tenant," *Halsbury's Laws of England* (4th ed.), xxvii (1981), Par. 657-88.

pp. 144-45 On siting of public housing, see *James v. Valtierra*, 402 U.S. 137 (1971); *Gautreaux v. Chicago Housing Authority*, 296 F.Supp. 907 (N.D. Ill. 1969), *affirmed*, 480 F.2d 210 (7th Cir.), *cert. denied*, 414 U.S. 1144 (1974); *Shannon v. HUD*, 436 F.2d 809 (3d Cir. 1970); "The Battle of Forest Hills, Who's Ahead," *N.Y. Times Magazine*, Feb. 20, 1972, p. 8, reprinted in *Law and Poverty* (Cooper et als. eds., St. Paul, West Pub. Co., 2d ed., 1973), 801-4. Rent subsidies are dealt with in Levy, Lewis, and Martin, *supra*, 1149-51, and in *Report of the President's Commission on Housing* (1982), 18-26. The Rand Corporation experiment is described in *Report*, pp. 18-19, and in material cited in the note to page 30, *supra*.

pp. 145-46 There is need also for measures to stop inner city building owners from burning down their buildings and using the insurance money to build somewhere else. *Displacement*, 42-45.

p. 146 Whyte's point, referred to in text, is on pp. 320-27 of *The Organization Man* (New York, Simon and Schuster, 1956).

p. 149 Herberg's book is *Protestant, Catholic, Jew* (Garden City, N.Y., Doubleday, 1955). Whyte's chapter on the church is on pp. 405-22 of *The Organization Man*.

6. SEX

Most of this chapter appeared as "Sex, Law, and Liberation," *Thought*, lviii (1983), 43.

pp. 153-54 Examples of the legislation referred to include Offences Against the Person Act, 24-5 Vic. c. 100, §§ 58-9, 61-3 (1861); Criminal Law Amendment Act 1885 — Protection of Women and Girls, 48-9 Vic. c. 69; Indecent Advertisements Act 1889, 52-3 Vic. c. 18; 17 U.S. Stat. at Large 598 (1873); 24 *id.* 635 (1887); N.Y. Penal Code 1881, §§ 282, 284, 294-97, 316-18. The *Hicklin* case is L.R. 3 Q.B. 360 (1868). On divorce laws, see "Divorce" in *American and English Encyclopedia of Law*, v. (1885), 745, 777-809. On seduction, see "Seduction and Criminal Conversation" in *id.*, xxi (1893), 1009.

p. 154   On feminist agendas, see Elizabeth Cady Stanton, "The Natural Rights of Civilized Women" (1860) in *The Annals of America* (Ency. Brit. ed.) ix (1968), 151-56. Examples of laws abolishing disabilities of married women include Married Women's Property Act 1870, 33-4 Vic. c. 93; Married Women's Property Act 1882, 45-6 Vic. c. 75; N.Y. Laws 1848 c. 200, 1860 c. 90, 1884 c. 381; Ind. Statutes 1879 c. 67, 1881 c. 60. On infliction of mental distress as a ground for divorce, compare "Divorce" in *American and English Encyclopedia of Law*, v (1885), 745, 793-94 with "Divorce" in *Cyclopedia of Law and Procedure*, xiv (1904), 556, 603-9.

pp. 154-55   The New York legislation referred to in text is N.Y. Laws 1906 c. 413; cf. N.Y. Laws 1902 c. 83 regarding girls under eighteen. The White Slave Traffic Act is 36 U.S. Stat. at Large 825 (1910), the Paris treaty 35 *id.* 1979 (1908). The quote is from G. May, "Prostitution" in *Encyclopedia of the Social Sciences*, xii (1937), 553, 558. The developments in the law of seduction are taken up in "Seduction" in *Cyclopedia of Law and Procedure*, xxxv (1910), 1289, 1294-97.

p. 155   The concept of redeeming social importance was launched in *Roth* v. *United States*, 354, U.S. 476 (1957). Compare the classic opinion in *United States* v. *One Book Entitled "Ulysses,"* 5 F.Supp. 182 (S.D.N.Y. 1933), *affirmed*, 72 F.2d 705 (2d Cir. 1934).

pp. 155-56   See the discussion of incompatibility in *Poteet* v. *Poteet*, 45 N.M. 214, 114 P.2d 91 (1941). The possibilities of conciliation are explored in *Cases and Materials on Family Law* (C. Foote, R. Levy, F. Sander eds., Boston, Little, Brown, 1976), 1090-98, and L. Burke, *With This Ring* (New York, McGraw Hill, 1958). For an example of compulsory conciliation legislation, see Wis. Stat. §§ 767.081-83, 767.112.

pp. 156-57   The contraception cases referred to in text are: *People* v. *Sanger*, 222 N.Y. 192, 118 N.E. 637 (1917); *United States* v. *One Package*, 86 F.2d 737 (2d Cir. 1936); *Commonwealth* v. *Corbett*, 307 Mass. 7, 29 N.E.2d 151 (1940); *Griswold* v. *Connecticut*, 381 U.S. 479 (1965). It was *Griswold* that declared laws against contraception unconstitutional. The quote is from pp. 485-86 of 381 U.S.

p. 157   The nineteenth century abortion legislation is cited in a note to pp. 153-54, *supra*. *R.* v. *Bourne* is reported in [1939] 1 K.B. 687. The section of the Model Penal Code referred to is § 230.3. See Note, *Notre Dame Lawyer*, xxxvii (1962), 649, 702-4. The Supreme Court's decision on the subject is *Roe* v. *Wade*, 410 U.S. 113 (1973). It has been suggested to me that abortion should be taken up in my chapter on Violence rather than here. Philosophically, I take the point. But historically and politically, the subject can be better understood in the present context.

pp. 157-58   The Wolfenden Report is Home Office and Scottish Home Department, *Report of the Committee on Homosexual Offences and Prostitution*, Cmnd. 247 (1957). The Street Offences Act 1959, 7-8 Eliz. II c. 57 and the Sexual Offences Act 1967, c. 60 were evidently framed with the doctrine of this report in mind. The Sexual Offences Act 1956, 4-5 Eliz. II c. 69, based on older attitudes, is still partly in force. The position of the Model Penal Code appears in Articles 213 and 251. See L. Schwartz, "Morals Offenses and the Model Penal Code," *Columbia L. Rev.*, lxiii (1963), 669. The New York Legislature retained an offense of "consensual sodomy" in the midst of what was otherwise pretty much the Model Penal Code. N.Y. Penal Law § 130.38. Note the slightly miffed tone of the comment in the standard edition of the New York statutes. *McKinney's Consolidated Laws of New York Annotated*, xxxix (1975), 481. Section 130.38 was declared unconstitutional in *People* v. *Onofre*, 51 N.Y.2d 476, 415 N.E.2d 936, 20 A.L.R.4th 987 (1980), *cert. denied*, 451 U.S. 987. *Eisenstadt* v. *Baird* is reported at 405 U.S. 438 (1972). On interpretation of the health criterion for abortion, see J. Noonan, *A Private Choice* (New York, Free Press, 1979), 115-116.

p. 158   On rape in general, see Mills, "One Hundred Years of Fear" in *Judge, Lawyer, Victim, Thief* (N. Rafter and E. Stanko eds., Boston, Northeastern U. Press, 1982). On the immunity of the husband, see *State* v. *Smith*, 85 N.J. 193, 426 A.2d 38 (1981), holding that the immunity was never absolute in New Jersey, and should not be made so. Sir Mathew Hale, *Pleas of the Crown*, i, 629, has considerably obfuscated this subject by justifying the immunity of the husband on the ground that the wife's consent, given at the time of the marriage, is irrevocable. In my opinion, the true ground is that marital intercourse is qualitatively different from sexual intercourse outside of marriage. There are, oddly enough, very few cases on the subject. My theory is supported by the fact that a husband who has intercourse with his wife against her will can be guilty of assault and battery even though in most jurisdictions he cannot be guilty of rape. *R. v. Miller*, [1954] 2 Q.B. 1953. If consent were irrevocable, it would be a defense to assault and battery as well. Note also that Merriam-Webster's *Third International Dictionary* defines rape as "*illicit* sexual intercourse without the consent of the woman. . . ." (my italics). Compare the *American Heritage Dictionary* definition, which includes any intercourse without consent.

pp. 158-59   Judge Frank's opinion is *United States* v. *Roth*, 237 F.2d 796, 801 (2d Cir., 1956) (concurring opinion). The 1973 Supreme Court decisions are *Miller v. California*, 413 U.S. 15 (1973), *Paris Adult Theatre I* v. *Slaton*, 413 U.S. 49 (1973), and three other cases decided at the same time. For the 1970 commission report, see *Political and Civil Rights in the United States* (Emerson, Haber, and Dorsen eds., 4th ed. Boston, Little, Brown, 1976), i. 537-47.

p. 159   The move toward no-fault divorce is described in *Cases and Materials on Family Law* (C. Foote, R. Levy, F. Sander eds., Boston, Little, Brown, 1976), 1101-08. On the proof required to establish breakdown, see *McKim* v. *McKim*, 6 Cal.3d 673, 493 P.2d 868 (1972); *Bromley's Family Law* (6th ed., London, Butterworth, 1981), 240.

p. 161   The restrictions on brothels' advertising are in Nev. Rev. Stat.§§ 201.380, 201.390, 201.420, 201.430, 201.440. *Bigelow* v. *Virginia*, 421 U.S. 890 (1975) holds that at a time when abortion was legal in New York and illegal in Virginia, Virginia could not prevent New York abortion services from advertising in Virginia papers.

p. 162   Professor Karst's article is "The Freedom of Intimate Association," *Yale Law Journal*, lxxxix (1980), 624. The quoted language is from pages 633 and 637.

pp. 165-66   For employers or school administrators to penalize sexual immorality may violate sex discrimination laws if pregnancy is their only way of discovering that such immorality has taken place. See "Civil Rights" § 183, *Am. Jur.2d*, xv.

pp. 167-68   For a compilation of the latest material on the validity of legal restraints on sexual acts, see *Political and Civil Rights, supra*, i, 1008-13. The Canadian Criminal Code, §§ 146-68 embodies a good deal of the approach I am advocating here. Note particularly § 157, which penalizes acts of "gross indecency," but is followed by § 158, which exempts acts between consenting adults in private—with a fairly strict definition of what is private. The cases referred to in text are *State v. Saunders*, 75 N.J. 200, 381 A.2d 333 (1977) and *Lovisi v. Slayton*, 363 F.Supp. 620 (E.D. Va. 1973), *affirmed*, 539 F.2d 349 (4th Cir. 1976). Other cases illustrating points made in text include *Pederson* v. *Richmond*, 219 Va. 1061, 254 S.E.2d 95 (1979) (solicitation); *Byrd* v. *State*, 65 Wis.2d 415, 222 N.W.2d 696 (1974) (rape charge, lack of consent not proved, accused convicted of fornication); *Gaunt* v. *State*, 50 N.J.L. 490, 14 Atl. 600 (1898) (fornication conviction; bastard involved); *Bass* v. *State*, 103 Ga. 571, 29 S.E. 966 (1898) (fornication conviction; relationship publicly flaunted); *State* v. *Johnson*, 69 Ind. 85 (1879) (notoriety required for cohabitation conviction); *Richey* v. *State*, 172 Ind. 134, 87 N.E. 1032 (1909) (ditto). For the First Amendment argument referred to at the bottom of p. 168, see G. Fletcher, *Rethinking Criminal Law* (Boston, Little, Brown, 1979), 383-84.

pp. 170-71 Examples of current statutes forbidding cohabitation are Mass. Anno. Laws c. 372, §§ 16, 18; Mich. Comp. Laws § 750.335. On common law marriage, see *Cases and Materials on Family Law, supra*, 685-86. *Marvin* v. *Marvin* is reported at 18 Cal.3d 660, 557 P.2d 106 (1976). The Oregon case referred to is *Latham* v. *Latham*, 274 Ore. 421, 547 P.2d 144 (1976). For material on proposed alternatives to traditional marriage arrangements, see *Cases and Materials on Family Law, supra*, 712-48.

pp. 171-72 For the proposed adoption of de facto marriage in Quebec, see Quebec Civil Code Revision Office, Draft Civil Code 1977, Bk. 2, art. 49, 266, 338; Bk. 3, art. 42. Some of the reactions are reported in the *Commentaries* accompanying the draft, pp. 112-14. See also the two articles by F. Héleine, "Les conflits entre mariage et concubinage ou le rencontre du fait et du droit," *Revue du Barreau du Quebec*, xxxviii (1978), 679, and "Le concubinage, institution à la merci des politiques législatives des différents départements ministériels," *id.*, xl (1980), 624. The case of In re *Marriage of Cary*, 34 Cal. App.3d 345, 109 Cal. Rptr. 862 (1973) would have established something very like de facto marriage for California, but it was rejected in *Marvin* v. *Marvin, supra*, in favor of the contractual approach.

pp. 172-74   See Gagnon, "Prostitution" in *International Encyclopedia of the Social Sciences*, xii (1968), 592. The quote is from K. Llewellyn, "Law Observance versus Law Enforcement" in *Jurisprudence* (Chicago, U. of Chicago Press, 1962), 399, 409. Examples of laws punishing prostitutes' customers include Ind. Code 35-45-5-3, and Model Penal Code § 251.2(5).

pp. 174-75   RICO is 18 U.S.C. §§ 1961 et seq. See R. Rhode, "The Massage Parlor and RICO" in *Materials on RICO* (G. Blakey, ed., Ithaca, N.Y., Cornell Inst. on Organized Crime), iii (1980), 1562. RICO proceedings are set in motion by a series of what are called predicate offenses. Prostitution is not now such an offense, and should be made one.

pp. 175-76   Ind. Code 35-30-11.1 is an example of legislation against displaying erotic material in places accessible to minors. Zoning of the kind proposed in text was upheld in *Young v. American Mini Theatres, Inc.* 427 U.S. 50 (1976). *California v. LaRue*, 409 U.S. 109 (1972) upheld the power of the state to control the type of entertainment offered in bars. *People v. Parker*, 33 Cal. App.3d 842, 109 Cal. Rptr. 354 (1973) upheld the punishment of an act of sodomy involved in the making of a motion picture.

pp. 176-77   A parent cohabitating with a person to whom she was not married was denied custody for that reason in *Jarrett v. Jarrett*, 78 Ill.2d 337, 400 N.E.2d (1979). Other cases go the other way on this. See *Political and Civil Rights in the United States* (Emerson, Haber, and Dorsen eds., Supp. 1981), ii, 242-43. A parent in an avowedly homosexual relationship was denied custody in In re *Jane B.*, 85 Misc.2d 515, 380 N.Y.S.2d 848 (Sup. 1976). What I refer to as "the most famous of the cases not involving sexual immorality" is *Painter v. Bannister*, 258 Iowa 1390, 140 N.W.2d 152 (1966).

p. 177   The Uniform Child Custody Jurisdiction Act, adopted by the Commissioners on Uniform State Laws in 1968, and now in force in all states, is mitigating one of the most serious aspects of interstate divorce, the interstate child custody battle.

p. 178   On sexual harassment as sex discrimination, see *Political and Civil Rights, supra*, ii, 195; *Miller v. Bank of America*, 600 F.2d 211 (9th Cir. 1979); *Barnes v. Costle*, 561 F.2d 983 (D.C. Cir. 1977) 29 C.F.R. § 1604 (1980). The New Hampshire rule is established in *Monge v. Beebe Rubber*

Co., 114 N.H. 130, 316 A.2d 549 (1974), creating a tort of wrongful discharge.

p. 179   Don Moran's case is *Don Moran* v. *People*, 25 Mich. 356 (1872). Sex as malpractice is taken up in B. Schutz, *Legal Liability in Psychotherapy* (San Francisco, Jossey-Bass, 1982), 34-38. The optometrist case is *Cardamon* v. *State Board of Optometric Examiners*, 165 Colo. 520, 441 P. 2d 25 (1968). For similar cases, see "Physicians and Surgeons" § 83, *Am. Jur. 2d*, lxi, 226. The Model Penal Code provision referred to is § 213.3. The Canadian Criminal Code § 153 goes a little bit farther. It punishes all illicit sex between an employer or supervisor and a woman in his employ or under his direction—but only if she is under twenty-one and of previous chaste character.

p. 181   The Canadian Criminal Code § 161 forbids a distributor to refuse to sell a retailer a publication because the retailer refuses to take a different publication that he is afraid may be obscene.

p. 185   For a careful and sophisticated statement of contemporary practice in Roman Catholic marriage tribunals in this country, see L. Wrenn, *Annulments* (Washington, Canon Law Soc. of America, 4th ed. 1983); L. Wrenn, *Decisions* (Washington, Canon Law Soc. of America, 2d ed. 1983).

7. VIOLENCE

p. 186   The social sciences have produced an immense literature on crime in general and violent crime in particular. The best synthesis of their work is still President's Commission on Law Enforcement, *The Challenge of Crime in a Free Society* (Washington, 1967) (hereafter, *Challenge*). There is also an extensive literature on police problems. The work I have used most is J. Ahern, *Police in Trouble* (New York, Hawthorn Books, 1973) (hereafter, Ahern). I owe to this work a good deal of my perception both of the problems and of the solutions. In addition to consulting these and other works, I have read newspapers, watched television, and listened to people involved in the criminal justice process, all during the course of many years. Much of what I say here comes from such sources as these.

p. 187   *Mapp* v. *Ohio* is reported at 367 U.S. 643 (1961). As the Court points out, many states had already adopted the same rule.

p. 188   The plea bargaining process was upheld against constitutional objections in *Bordenkircher* v. *Hayes*, 434 U.S. 357 (1978). The argument was that by imposing a substantially heavier liability on a person who elects to defend himself, the process denies his constitutional right to do so. In this case, the accused was alleged to have forged an eighty dollar check. The prosecutor offered, in exchange for a guilty plea, to forego a habitual offender charge with a mandatory life sentence. The accused elected to plead not guilty, and ended up with a life sentence. I would have decided the case in his favor.

p. 189   *Challenge*, 36 alludes to slum neighborhoods where the "inhabitants are bound together by an intense social and cultural solidarity that provides a collective defense against the pressures of slum living."

p. 190   The 1863 draft riots are dealt with in most histories of the Civil War, as well as many histories of race problems or urban problems. See, e.g., *Report of the National Advisory Commission on Civil Disorders* (New York, 1968), 212-13. There are also a number of books out on the subject, of which the most recent in our library is A. Cook, *The Armies of the Streets* (Lexington, Ky., Univ. Press of Ky., 1974). There is a good history of labor violence in the United States, incident by incident, in P. Taft and P. Ross, "American Labor Violence: its Causes, Character, and Outcome," in *Violence in America* (H. Graham and T. Gurr, eds., New York, Bantam, 1969), 270-376.

p. 191   I have forgotten the name of the television series. It did not last very long. Perhaps its view of the criminal justice system contributed to its early demise, but I doubt it.

pp. 192-94   See Taft and Ross, *supra*. See also *Statutory History of the United States: Labor Organization* (R. Koretz, ed., New York, Chelsea House, 1970).

p. 194   On the process reacting like a miffed parent, see T. Shaffer, "The Law and Order Game," *Transactional Analysis Bulletin*, April, 1970, p. 41.

p. 195   On the National Guard, see *Report of the National Advisory Commission on Civil Disorders* (New York, 1968), 497-506, and the parallel treatment of the army in *id.*, 506-9.

pp. 196-97   The quote is from Ahern, 222. *Medical Committee for Human Rights* v. *SEC*, 432 F.2d 659 (D.C. Cir. 1970) is discussed in a note to pp. 104-5, *supra*.

p. 198   The Pauline teaching referred to is Rom. 13:3-4.

pp. 198-99   See Ahern, 167-89.

pp. 200-1   See Attorney General's Task Force on Violent Crime, *Final Report* (Washington, 1981), 88-89 on the fair treatment of victims.

p. 203   See *Report of the National Advisory Commission on Civil Disorders* (New York, 1968), 503: "Controlling a civil disorder is not warfare. The fundamental objective of National Guard forces in a civil disorder is to control the rioters, not to destroy them or any innocent bystanders who may be present."

pp. 203-4   On the Kent State incident, see P. Davies, *The Truth about Kent State* (New York, Farrar, Straus, Giroux, 1973). The last reported decision in the ensuing litigation is *Krause* v. *Rhodes*, 671 F.2d 212 (6th Cir. 1982), concerning the disposition of the discovery materials accumulated in the course of the proceedings. The other ten reported opinions are cited in a note on page 213 of the report.

pp. 206-7   Drunk driving is not exactly the kind of crime we are considering in this chapter, but it is worth noting that a determined campaign to increase the visibility of the victims has had a profound effect on both legislatures and courts in this area.

              On municipal tort liability for failure of the police to protect against violent crime, see "Municipal, School, and State Tort Liability," §§ 243-56 in *Am. Jur. 2d*, lvii (1971); Annotation, 46 A.L.R.4th 1084 (1972). A landlord was held liable for inadequate security in *Kline* v. *1500 Mass. Ave. Apt. Corp.*, 439 F.2d 477 (D.C. Cir. 1970).

p. 208   The quote is from M. Groden and M. Clasby, "Church as Counter-sign: Process and Promise," in *The Underground Church* (M. Boyd, ed., New York, Sheed and Ward, 1968), 102, 113-14. On medieval analogies, see my *Ecclesiastical Administration in Medieval England* (Notre Dame, Ind., U. of Notre Dame Press, 1977), 52-56.

p. 210   The quote is from *Gaudium et Spes*, par. 78.

8. CONCLUSION

pp. 211-12   See my "Law, Social Change and the Ambivalence of History," *Proceedings of the American Catholic Philosophical Association*, xlix (1975), 164. The quotes are from H. Butterfield, *The Whig Interpretation of History* (New York, Scribner, 1931), 21; *Id.*, 19; J. Maritain, *On the Philosophy of History* (New York, Scribner, 1957), 52; Gutierrez, 237-38.

p. 214 See my "Law, History, and the Option for the Poor," *Logos,* vi (1985), 61. The term comes out of documents adopted by the Latin American Catholic hierarchy at Puebla in 1979, and was picked up by the American bishops in their draft pastoral letter on the economy, par. 52-54, and by the Vatican Congregation for the Doctrine of the Faith in its *Instruction on Christian Freedom and Liberation*, par. 66. The *Yeast* quote is from chapter 6.

pp. 215-16 Gutierrez, 194-203, speaks of a conversion to the neighbor. The *Gaudium et Spes* quote is from par. 76.

Index

Abortion, 153, 157, 166, 180
Abundance, as American goal,
    57-58, 82
Accountability, 98-105
    of business organizations, 114-17
    of clergy and theologians, 127
    of experts, 97-98, 118-22, 123-24
    of government agencies, 111-12
    of labor unions, 117-18
    of lawyers, 121-22
Administrative agencies and admini-
    strative law, 98-99, 107-8
    and inspections, 111-112
    see also particular agencies
Advertising, 63-64, 66
    of professional services 103,
    119-20
AFDC, 24, 28-29, 33-35, 55
Agriculture
    department of, 29, 91-92, 94
    protection of workers in, 27, 91,
    114
Ahern, James, quoted, 196
Aliens, problems of, 27, 193-94
Arts and crafts, 69-70, 78, 80-81
Aspirations, jurisprudence of, 10,
    141-43

Better Jobs and incomes Act (pro-
    posed in 1978), 40
Bismark, Otto von, 24

Black Muslims, 52
Boycotts, 17, 54, 114, 126
Bracton, Henry de, 12
Brandeis, Louis D., 115
Britain
    abortion in, 157
    divorce law of, 159
    ideology and politics in, 13, 14,
    25-26, 39
    land use and development laws
    in, 75
    laws of, concerning sex, 157
    local government in, 113
    poor laws in, 22-23
    protection of tenants in, 91, 144
Broadcasting
    effect of market on, 68-69
    regulation of, 81
Brown v. *Board of Education*, 11
Buchwald, Art, 178
Building permit requirement, 92, 94
Butterfield, Herbert, *The Whig Inter-
    pretation of History*, quoted,
    211-12

Capital intensive production, 27-28,
    43-47, 65-66
Charity and justice, 55
Chartism, 14
Chastity, support for, 166-72, 182-85
Child custody, 176-77

Chile, overthrow of Allende government in, 14
Church, the
and annulment of marriage, 184-85
and chastity, 182-85
and culture, 87-89
discipline within, 17, 183-85
elitism in, 127, 150
and history, 151-52
law of, as liberating force, 16-18, 216
liberationist doctrine concerning, 4, 16
and nonviolence, 208-11
and organizations for social reform, 54
and poverty, 51-55
and power, 124-27
and roots, 149-52
and social services, 18
and stock ownership, 54
Civil Rights Laws, 14, 59
quantified measures as violating, 71
as requiring "reasonable accommodation" of religious beliefs, 73
Class, 214-5
corporate managers as 47-48
Djilas's doctrine concerning, x, 21
liberationist doctrine concerning, ix, 3-4, 20-21
Marxist doctrine concerning, ix, 3, 21
mediation, 14
natural law and, 8
poverty and, 47-49
and powerlessness, 122-24
and rootlessness, 137-41
and sex, 179-82
and violence, 195-97, 206-8
Cohabitation, unmarried, 135-36, 169-72, 177-78
laws against, 153
Common good as end of law, 6, 214-15

Community life
in American history, 130
dismantling of, 136-37
law and, 134-35
and prevention of violence, 189-90
restoration of, 143-49
Condominiums, 144
Confrontation
with history, 12-13, 51
with the Industrial Revolution, 40-47
with power, 12, 108-22, 202-6
with the Sexual Revolution, 164-79
with trivializing ideologies, 82
with violence, 208
"Consciousness raising," 10-11
Conservation easements, 76
Consumers and consumption
and boycotts, 114
incentives to, 65-67
liberation of, 79-80
and religious life, 88-89
Contraception, 153, 156-58, 165, 169
Coppage v. Kansas, quoted, 61
Corporations
expansion of, 43-45
legislative encouragement of, 57
representation of outside constituencies in management of, 114-15
social responsibility of, 47-48, 54-55
stockholders' power over, 54, 99-100, 102, 104-5, 115-17
Cost benefit analysis, 50, 115, 213
and administrative regulation, 106
and community, 148
and environment, 76-77
Courts and litigation, 99, 100, 120-22
class actions, 121-22
Credit, effect of, on consumption, 66
Criminal law
ideology of, 188-89, 197, 204-6

role of, 198-202
    symbolic function of, 11
    system of, 187-88
    and witness of church, 209-10
Culture, 80-81, 138-39, 147
    see also Arts and crafts; Quality
        of goods and services; Workers

Demonstrations, 16-17, 54, 187,
    194
Diversity, 62, 80-81
    see also Pluralism
Divorce, 154, 155-56, 159-60, 166,
    176-77
Djilas, Milovan, The New Class,
    x, 21
Dow Chemical Company, 54
Due process, 106-7

Education
    control of, 98
    and culture, 138-39
    and employment, 28
    and equality, 60-61, 72-73, 80
    government support of, 58, 81
    language and, 73, 80
    and neighborhoods, 136, 137,
        146
    and poverty, 32
    quality of, 70
    religion and, 70-71, 73
Eminent domain, 72, 75, 76,
    105-6, 109-10
Environment, protection of, 71,
    74-77
Equal Rights Amendment, proposed,
    11
Equality, ideologies of, 60-63,
    84-85
Evidence, illegally obtained,
    187-88, 196, 203, 205
Expertise, 96-98
    and accountability, 118-22,
        123-24

Feminism, 154
Food and Drug Administration, 92,
    94
Food stamps, 24-25, 29, 37
Ford, Henry, 47, 62
Franchise and chain operations, 63
Frank, Jerome, 158-59
Freedom, 10
    alternative ideologies of, 59-60,
        83-84, 129-30, 134, 168-69,
        181-82
    constitutional, 13
    and sex, 157-60, 181-82
Freedom of Information Laws, 104
Freud, Sigmund, 20, 155, 157

Gaudium et Spes, quoted, x, 210,
    216
Gentrification, 143
Griswold v. Connecticut, 156-57,
    158, 167
General assistance, 22-23, 29, 31
Government, role of,
    in economic infrastructure, 57-58
    in education, 58
Grey, Thomas, Elegy in a Country
        Churchyard, 51
Guns, 194-95, 204
Gutierrez, Gustavio, ix, 10
    quoted, 212

Harris, Sydney, 69
Handicapped persons, rights of,
    92
Health insurance, 36-37
Herberg, Will, Protestant, Catholic,
        Jew, 149
History
    and American goals, 73-74, 129-
        30, 141-42
    Herbert Butterfield on, 211-12
    and church, 151-52
    and disillusionment, 131
    Gustavo Gutierrez on, 212

historical school of jurisprudence, 142-43
law as confrontation with, 12-13, 51
liberation and, 8-10, 49-51
Jacques Maritain on, 212
and sex, 153-60
and social change, 211-12
Homosexuality, 153, 160, 169
Housing, 30, 143-46

Indiana
  constitutional provision for education in, 61
  sunset law, 111
Indians
  legal representation of, 121
  tribal institutions of, 140
Industrial development
  effects of, 40-47
  government encouragement of, 57-58
Initiative, referendum, and recall, 103-4
Interdependence, 94-95, 105-6
  limitation of, 108-9
Interstate commerce, federal power over, 110-11

Jobs
  creation of, 24, 45-46
  marginal, problems of, 27
  satisfaction with, 71, 77-79
  training for, 25, 28, 41
Johnson, Samuel, 12
Juries, 103
Justice
  as end of law, 5-6, 9
  pursuit of, 213, 216-17

Karst, Kenneth, quoted, 162
Kent State University, shootings at, 187, 194, 203-4

Keynesian economics, 24, 54, 82
Kingsley, Charles, Yeast (novel), quoted, 39, 214

Labor unions and collective bargaining, 27, 78, 99, 117-18, 126, 192-94
Land, use and development of, 68, 72, 74-77
  see also Housing
Law
  as aspiration, 141-43, 216-17
  and civic virtue, 134-35
  as controlling institutions, 99, 100
  and ideology, 100, 134-35, 201-2
  and liberation, 4-8, 10-16 and passim
  pragmatic approach to, 133-34, 216
  as protecting against political process, 101
Lawyers and legal services, 35, 102-3, 120-22, 216-17
  attitudes, 124
  Code of Professional Responsibility, 122
  and criminal justice system, 188
  duty to clients, 122, 135
  fees, 122
Liberation, theology of, ix, 2-4, 20-21, 212, 214 and passim
Libertarianism, see Freedom, alternative ideologies of; Mill, John Stuart
Licensing laws, 96-97, 119-20
Llewellyn, Karl, quoted, 173
Lobbying, 93, 104
Local government, 112-14
  and control of police, 198-99, 206-8
Lovisi v. Slayton, 168

Malpractice litigation, 118-19
Mapp v. Ohio, 187-88

Maritain, Jacques, *On the Philosophy of History*, quoted, 212
Market
    control of business through operation of, 100, 101-2
    effect of, on arts and crafts, 69-70
    pursuit of shares of, 68-69
Marriage, 162, 166
    and church law, 18, 184-85
    see also Cohabitation, unmarried; Divorce
Marvin v. *Marvin*, 170-71
Marxism
    and class struggle, ix, 3, 6, 21
    and law, 1
Mass production, 62-63, 77-78
Mayer, Martin, *Madison Avenue, U.S.A.*, 64
Mediation
    between classes, 14, 206-8
    of elite agendas, 137-41
    of industrial development, 41-42
    of interdependence, 105-6
    law and, 14-15
    of legitimate power, 198-202
    of organization and expertise, 106-8
Medical expenses and Medical Assistance, 24, 30-32, 33, 36-37, 158
Medieval society and thought, 11, 13, 17, 22-23, 84-85
Metrication, 93-94
Mill Acts, 57
Mill, John Stuart, on freedom, 19, 20, 83-84, 105, 157
Model Penal Code, 157-58, 179
Monarchy, 13
Morality
    and law, 5, 142-43; *see also* Freedom; Sex
    and pastoral concern, 183

National Guard, 195, 203-4
Natural law, 7-8

and American ideology, 129, 131, 133
and sex, 164-65
Need, determination of, under welfare programs, 33
Negative Income Tax, 25
Neighborhoods
    associations, 54, 146-57
    dismantling of, 136-37, 140
    restoration of, 143-47
    role of, in local government, 112-14
    and violence, 189
Nevada, legalized prostitution in, 160, 161
New Deal, ideology and legislation of, 23-24, 45
Nonviolence, 208-10

Obscenity, 154, 155, 158-59, 161, 166, 174-76, 180, 181
On the Waterfront (film), 209
Opportunity
    American belief in, 58-59
    value of, 83
Organization, 95-96, 122-23
    confrontive approaches to, 111-12
    ecclesiastical, 124-27
Orwell, George, 91
OSHA, 77, 92, 111-12

Peace
    as end of law, 4-5, 202
    as witness of church, 208-10
Personal injury law, 57, 115
Pluralism, 73, 80-81
    and ideological neutrality, 134
    and race identification, 140
Police
    accountability of, 203, 205
    church's ministry to, 209
    function, organization and deployment of, 195-96, 198-202, 206-8

misconduct of, 194
problems of, 190-92
Political process
    access to, 93
    and community life, 137
    empowerment through, 99, 101
    involvement in 113-14
    and protection against violence,
        206-8
Poor, the,
    attitudes toward, 32-35, 37-40
    condition of, see Poverty
    housing of, 144-45
    preferential option for, 214
    relief of, see Welfare legislation
    representation of, in anti-poverty
        programs, 26, 98
Pound, Roscoe, 9
Poverty, 22-55
    burdens of, 26-38
    relief of, see Welfare legislation
Power, 216
    confrontation with, 12, 108-22,
        202-6
    mediation of, 198-202
Powerlessness, 90-127
    feudal, defined, 90-91
    structural, defined, 91-92
Pragmatism
    and law, 133-34
    and organizational elite, 137-41
    see also Cost benefit analysis
Privacy, right of, 105, 167-69
Professions
    attitude of persons in, 120, 124
    entry into, 96-97, 119-20
    ethics of, 119-20, 122
    liability of, 118-19
    peer review in, 119
    and sexual harassment, 178-79
    see also Accountability; Expertise;
        Lawyers and legal services;
        Medical expenses and Medical
        Assistance
Proposition 13 (California initiative

measure limiting property tax),
    104, 109
Prostitution, 153, 154-55, 160, 161,
    172-75, 181

Quality of goods and services,
    extrusion of, 69-70
    restoration of, 77-80
Quantification, 67-68, 71-72
Quebec Civil Code, proposed, and
    de facto marriage, 171-72

Race and sex discrimination, 11, 14,
    59, 71, 73, 80, 92
    and integration, 147-49
    and police assignments, 191, 201
Rape, 158, 167, 179, 197, 201
    liability of husband for, 158
Rawls, John, A Theory of Justice,
    52-53, 61
Receivership of substandard dwelling
    units, 143
Religion
    freedom of, and school attendance,
        73
    and identification of Americans,
        132, 149
    public attitudes toward, 70-71,
        86-87
    "reasonable accommodation" of,
        under civil rights laws, 73, 86
Religious life, 55, 88-89, 182-83
Rent subsidies, 143, 145
Retirement, 24
    benefits under Social Security, 93
RICO, 175, 176
Ritter, Bruce, 160, 173
Roosevelt, Franklin D., 15-16, 23
    see also, New Deal
Rootlessness, 128-52
    meaning of, 128-29
    sources of, in American life,
        129-37
Routinization, 64-65, 95-96

Securities laws and SEC, 41-42
  and stockholder proposals, 54,
    104-5, 115-16, 196-97
Service occupations, protection of,
    78
Sex, 153-85
  and abuse of confidential rela-
    tions, 179
  Christian principles concerning,
    160-66, 180-85
  education, 169
  illicit, laws against, 153-54,
    166-72, 176
  history of legal attitudes toward,
    153-60
Shaffer, Thomas L., quoted, 124
Sisters of the Precious Blood, and
    accountability of corporate
    management, 54
Small claims procedures, 102
Social casework, 33-35, 40, 48
Social change
  as end of law, 8-10
  history and, 211-17
Social Security, see Retirement
Social services, church and, 18
SSI, 24, 29, 39, 40
Standard of living, 46-47
Standardization, 62-64
Subsidiarity, principle of, 112-13
Sunshine laws, 104
Supreme Court, United States
  and abortion, 59, 157-58
  and administrative regulation, 106
  and advertising by lawyers, 103,
    119
  and contraception, 156-57
  and corporate management, 115
  on equality of bargaining posi-
    tion, 61
  and foreign language education,
    73
  and government inspection of
    private property, 111-12
  and obscenity, 158-59
  and private schools, 32, 73

and professions, 103, 119-20
and school segregation, 11
see also names of cases
Symbolism in law, 10-11, 38-40

Taxation
  as affecting capital expansion,
    43-45
  as affecting education, 32
  as affecting land use and develop-
    ment, 68, 72, 75
  constitutional limits on, 109
Technological metaphors in law, 9,
    15, 133
Tocqueville, Alexis de, Democracy in
    America, 87

Unemployment, effects of, 35-38
  causes of, 27-28, 41-44, 65-66
Unemployment compensation, 36
"Urban homesteading," 144
Utilitarianism, 21
Utopia, 9

"Values," 140
Vatican, instructions concerning lib-
    eration theology, 3
  see also Gaudium et Spes
Vendibility, 68-69, 72
Vietnam war, 99, 131
Violence, 187-210
Virtue
  as end of law, 5
  law as substitute for, 134-36

Welfare legislation, 14-15
  administration of, 33-35, 38-40, 48
  attitude toward welfare recipients,
    33-35, 38-40
  eligibility conditions under, 33-34
  history and ideology of, before
    1933, 22-23, 39

history and ideology of, since
1933, 23-26
welfare rights organizations, 54
see also particular programs
Whyte, William H., *The Organization Man*, x, 122-23, 137-38, 149
Wolfenden Report, 157
Work
as cultural value, 42
and eligibility for welfare, 25, 33-34, 39
routinization of, 65, 71

Workers
legal protection for, 16, 23, 37
and poverty, 48-49
rights of, 3, 23
and sexual harassment, 178
wages and working conditions of, 26-28, 65, 71, 77-79, 115
Workmen's Compensation, 36, 77-78, 115

Zoning, 72, 74, 76, 137, 175-76